Volume 1 of *Thunderstorms: A Social, Scientific, and Technological Documentary*

**The Thunderstorm in Human Affairs**

Thunderstorms distribute heat received at ground level from the sun, water the earth, fix a little of the nitrogen used by plants, and may, through their violent manifestations, suddenly alter lives and the landscape. (Photo by Gordon Gerber, 18 August 1968, 70 miles southwest of Omaha, Nebr.)

Volume 1 of *Thunderstorms: A Social, Scientific, and Technological Documentary*

# The Thunderstorm in Human Affairs

*Second Edition, Revised and Enlarged*

**Edited by
Edwin Kessler**

**University of Oklahoma Press**
Norman and London

By Edwin Kessler

*On the Distribution and Continuity of Water Substance in Atmospheric Circulations* (Boston, 1969)

(Editor) *Thunderstorms: A Social, Scientific, and Technological Documentary,* 3 vols. (Washington, D.C., 1981–82)

(Editor) *The Thunderstorm in Human Affairs,* 2d ed. (Vol. 1 of *Thunderstorms: A Social, Scientific, and Technological Documentary*), (Norman, 1983)

(Editor) *Thunderstorm Morphology and Dynamics,* 2d ed. (Vol. 2 of *Thunderstorms: A Social, Scientific, and Technological Documentary*) (Norman, 1986)

(Editor) *Instruments and Techniques for Thunderstorm Observation and Analysis,* 2d ed. (Vol. 3 of *Thunderstorms: A Social, Scientific, and Technological Documentary*) (Norman, 1988)

Library of Congress Cataloging in Publication Data

Main entry under title:

The Thunderstorm in human affairs.

(Thunderstorms—a social, scientific, and technological documentary; v. 1)
Includes bibliographical references and index.
1. Thunderstorms—United States. 2. Thunderstorms—Social aspects—United States. I. Kessler, Edwin.
II. Series: Thunderstorms—a social, scientific, and technological documentary (2d ed., rev. and enl.); v. 1.
QC968.T48   1983 vol. 1     363.3'492s     83-47836
                   [363.3'492]
ISBN: 0-8061-2153-X

# Contents

## Preface to the Second Edition

The preparation and first appearance of this book were a project of the National Severe Storms Laboratory and its parent organization, the Environmental Research Laboratories, in the National Oceanic and Atmospheric Administration, U.S. Department of Commerce.

For this edition, in addition to correcting a few typographical errors in the first edition, we have revised the content to provide the latest available data and statistics and have added a new chapter, "Lightning Damage and Lightning Protection," and an index. The costs of typesetting and color plates for this edition were supported by the College of Geosciences of the University of Oklahoma through its Cooperative Institute for Mesoscale Meteorological Studies and Department of Meteorology.

I particularly thank Lindsay Murdock and Patricia Peterson for their remarkable editorial services in the first edition and am grateful for the support of friends and colleagues along the sometimes tortuous path to publication of this work.

EDWIN KESSLER

*National Severe Storms Laboratory*
*Norman, Oklahoma*
*June, 1983*

# Preface to the First Edition

In 1976, I sought participation by my colleagues to produce comprehensive documentation of the thunderstorm phenomenon in all its aspects. This result of the effort presents some social dimensions of thunderstorm phenomena as recently perceived, with emphasis on experience in the United States. We have not strived to provide last-minute updates on all details, since that function lies with the professional periodical literature. The morphology and dynamics of thunderstorms and means for observing them and analyzing their data are topics of subsequent volumes.

Our readers need bring only a little specialized scientific background to their study of this volume. The first chapter is an introduction to the others; to facilitate continuity in reading, we have not provided cross references, but readers will find considerable elaboration of chapter 1 materials in other chapters.

As presented here, our materials should be widely available at low cost, and we hope that the perspective afforded by our work will contribute a little to development of decent relationships between human society and its enfolding environment. With its numerous references, this collection should also be an effective introduction to further study.

I thank the authors for their cooperation in submitting their works and participating in the editorial processes, which took somewhat longer than I had planned. I also thank reviewers Ron Alberty, Karl Bergey, Robert Davies-Jones, L. L. McDowell, L. D. Meyer, H. B. Osborn, Ann Patton, E. H. Seely, and Fred Sanders. I particularly thank the staff of the Environmental Research Laboratories, Publications Division, Boulder, Colorado, without whose critiques laced with encouragement the effort would have faltered. Finally, the work benefited immeasurably from the unflagging support and assistance of my secretary, Barbara Franklin.

EDWIN KESSLER

*Norman, Oklahoma*
*April, 1981*

# Abbreviations Used in This Book

| | | | | |
|---|---|---|---|---|
| A | ampere | | L | electrical inductance |
| AC | alternating current | | l | liter |
| atm | atmosphere (unit of pressure) | | lb | pound |
| bu | bushel | | m | meter |
| C | coulomb | | mb | millibar |
| cfs | cubic feet per second | | mg | milligram |
| cm | centimeter | | mi | mile |
| cos | cosine | | min | minute |
| d | day | | mm | millimeter |
| dBZ | decibel measure of reflectivity factor Z | | ms | millisecond |
| DC | direct current | | $\mu$s | microsecond |
| ft | foot | | mo | month |
| g | gram (also force of gravity) | | N | newton (also nitrogen) |
| h | hour | | NA | not available |
| ha | hectare | | nmi | nautical mile |
| i | electrical current | | ppm | parts per million |
| in | inch | | Q | electrical charge |
| J | joule | | R | electrical resistance |
| J-m | joule-meter | | $R_g$ | ground resistance |
| K | kelvin | | s | second |
| kA | kilo ampere | | $\int i^2 R dt$ | action integral |
| kg | kilogram | | t | tonne (metric ton) |
| km | kilometer | | v | voltage, volt |
| kN | kilo Newton | | W | watt |
| kn | knot | | yr | year |

# The Thunderstorm in Human Affairs

# 1. Thunderstorms in a Social Context

*Edwin Kessler and Gilbert F. White*

## Introduction

Free oxygen in the Earth's atmosphere today is essential to most of the Earth's plant and animal life. Yet, according to several lines of evidence, almost all the oxygen in the Earth's atmosphere more than three billion years ago was combined with other elements. If we accept the conclusion of Urey (1952) and others, there were then probably significant amounts of water vapor, hydrogen, nitrogen, methane, ammonia, and probably carbon dioxide and some other gases. Our Sun with its planets had long since condensed from clouds that included small proportions of the heavy elements dispersed during explosions of predecessor massive stars. Our Sun was shining much as it does today, and the oceans were already well established, though still devoid of life. In this setting, primeval thunderstorms may have helped produce the seeds of life that would modify the atmosphere through liberation of oxygen and would flourish in the oceans, on the land, and in the air.

In the absence of an ozone layer, ultraviolet radiation from the Sun penetrated the atmosphere all the way to the Earth's surface; otherwise, the atmosphere was about as transparent as today's. If people had been there, they might have found skies rather cloudy but marvelously blue and clear between the clouds, and sometimes reddened by volcanic eruptions. Often the rising air currents that carry heat of solar origin upward from surface layers must have shown puffy clouds of water drops, white or dark, depending on the position of the Sun, sometimes, as today, ascending to great heights and producing showers of rain with lightning and thunder (Frontispiece). And with the lightning flashes, these primeval thunderstorms were, along with the ultraviolet light and cosmic rays, creating some complex organic compounds, including amino acids, the building blocks of proteins, which formed part of the brew in which life itself is supposed to have developed—life that through oxygen production was to transform radically the very atmosphere and ultimately to resculpture the surface of the Earth (Oparin, 1953).

Today, eons later, rain showers heralded by lightning and thunder continue to nurture the life they may have helped create (Frontispiece and Figs. 1.1a and b). Although irregular, our showers are almost as inevitable as sunrise. Rapid overturning of air warmed by sunlight absorbed near the Earth's surface, and moistened by evaporation over our vast oceans, produces first a towering cloud and then irregular rain with electric discharges and sometimes with hail, strong straight-line winds, and tornadoes.

Thunderstorms occur on a scale of one to tens of miles, both in isolation and as parts of larger weather systems. As detailed in studies of storm climatology and dynamics, thunder cells assume rather different forms depending on the type of associated weather. Latitude and distributions of land and water masses have their influence, so that diurnal and seasonal storm patterns over a tropical ocean, for example, are different from storm patterns in and adjoining a mountain chain. Thus, in some places and seasons thundershowers recur almost daily at about the same time; in others they occur rarely or irregularly. Some last but a few minutes, and on other occasions a succession of related events may last most of a day. Only a small number of thunderstorms are perceived as damag-

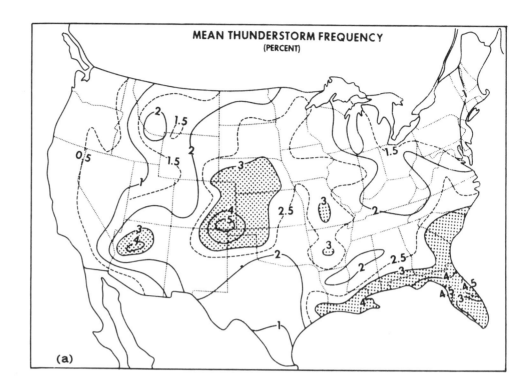

**Figure 1.1a.** Mean frequency of thunder reported on hourly observations during June–August, the period of greatest occurrence over most of the United States (Rasmussen, 1971).

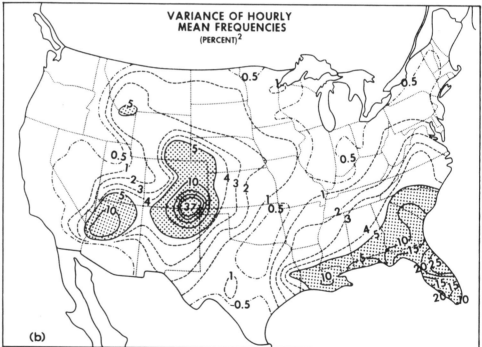

**Figure 1.1b.** Variance of the 24 values of mean hourly frequency of thunderstorm occurrence. Maxima in the southeastern United States and Rocky Mountains associate with a strong tendency for thunderstorm occurrence in afternoon. In the Plains States of the central United States, there is a tendency for most thunderstorms to occur at night (Rasmussen, 1971).

ing; most are welcome and markedly beneficial.

## Social Dimensions of Thunderstorms: Benefits and Costs

The social dimensions of thunderstorms are summarized here to provide a perspective for view of subsequent analyses on the effects of different storm phenomena. From a social standpoint the significant features of thunderstorms are high wind velocity, lightning, intense precipitation, and hail. All these are variable features that appear in many combinations. Some additional characteristics important for meteorological explanation, such as temperature differentials within a storm, do not usually have readily measured effects on human activities.

Every thunderstorm carries possible benefits and costs for people. Benefits may embrace increase in plant growth, nitrogen fixation, certain aspects of grass and forest fires, scouring of stream channels, and accumulation of surface water. Costs may include loss of property and lives from lightning and lightning-caused fires, strong winds, and flash floods; crop and property damage from hail; and the investment made to cope with the extreme event, including warnings, insurance systems, control measures, and readjustments in land use and structures.

Every society in a climate that spawns thunderstorms makes some adaptations to those events. Building design, cropping pattern, and commercial practices are among the adjustments that take the probability of a thunderstorm into account. In addition, special social adjustments to thunderstorms are made in the form of research projects, forecasting systems, insurance programs, disaster relief actions, building codes, and information programs. But we have great difficulty assessing situations and adapting appropriately where the benefits and costs flow differently in time, as is often the case. People have not yet come to terms with nature in flood plains where early benefits of economic activity in vulnerable areas may dim their willingness to forgo some of those benefits in order to avoid heavy losses to the community when the intense storm strikes. Urban residential and commercial developments may be permitted to hasten storm runoff without compensating storage, though the ultimate cost accrues to the downstream community through the effects of larger and more frequent flood peaks. Mobile-home residents face up reluctantly to the desirability of trailer tie-downs representing an immediate and definite cost, with the benefit perceived as uncertain in amount and time of return, and possibly available only to a later occupant (Jackson, 1977; Langston, 1977).

The social costs of thunderstorms range from loss of human life to small increments in the expense of operating public services. Damages and deaths directly attributable to storms accompanied by lightning and thunder in the United States are listed in Table 1.1. Note that aggregate thunderstorm-related losses exceed $1 billion annually, and deaths approach 500. The principal categories of social costs are as follows:

Direct costs:

    Loss of life, human and animal
    Injuries
    Property damage
    Interruption of economic activity

Measures to alleviate direct costs:

    Administration of insurance
    Administration of public relief and rehabilitation
    Preventive measures: weather modification, lightning
      protection
    Measures to reduce vulnerability

**Table 1.1.** Storm-related Deaths and Damage in the United States

| Type of event | Approximate average annual deaths (1970-76) | Approximate average annual property damage (1970-76) ($ million) |
|---|---|---|
| Tornado | 125 | 300 |
| Lightning | 110 | 200* |
| Hail | Fewer than 5 | 750† |
| Thunderstorm flood | 165 | ~100‡ |

*Includes livestock.
†Includes damage to crops, about $680 million at 1973 price levels or about 1.6% of farmers' cash receipts received that year for all crops.
‡Damage from all floods was about $1 billion annually. The loss from thunderstorm floods has since risen sharply, reflecting both inflation and increased development in floodplains.

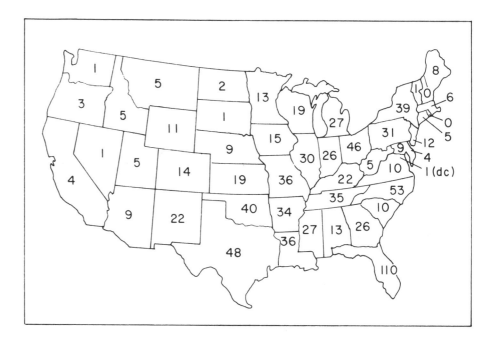

**Figure 1.2.** Lightning deaths by states for the period 1968-76 (Mogil et al., 1977).

The more obvious and better-publicized class of costs comprises the fatalities, injuries, and property loss that appear in newspaper headlines and that serve frequently to justify public expenditures for relief and rehabilitation. The quality of the statistics on even these consequences is low for the most part, and no accurate set of information is available that permits rigorous comparisons of events or of different dimensions of thunderstorms. There is scattered information on costs of forecasts, insurance, and building modification. Property-damage data are incomplete. The only relatively comparable data over a long time are for reported lives lost. Thus, the estimates given here and in the following essays cannot give a comprehensive picture.

The beneficial effects of thunderstorms are less likely to command direct public attention, and they are even more difficult to quantify than costs. Their major forms are water supply from torrential downpour, improved health of forest stands, and additions to the fixation of nitrogen. Thus forest ecology now recognizes the gains to tree growth from relatively frequent lightning-caused low-temperature burning of the ground cover in forest stands. It also values the reduction, thereby, of fuel accumulation on the forest floor so that the danger of catastrophic, high-temperature fires reaching the tree crowns is reduced.

A clearly beneficial effect of lightning is the nitrogen it causes to be oxidized and made available for removal from the atmosphere and addition to the soil as a nutrient. A significant fraction of the nitrogen oxides present in rainfall each year is derived from lightning-produced NO. Although large uncertainties remain in our understanding of the global nitrogen cycle, recent calculations indicating that about 6 million metric tons of fixed nitrogen are produced globally by lightning each year imply that lightning is responsible for about 2% of the total input of fixed nitrogen to the biosphere (see chapter 4, "Nitrogen Fixation").

### Phenomenology

We here outline the principal effects of each major manifestation of thunderstorms: lightning, high winds, tornado, hail, and intense precipitation, giving emphasis to the United States experience.

#### Lightning

Lightning is usually distinct in its effects, and storms with lightning occur in all 50 states of the United States. Lightning strikes are not accurately documented, but the record of fatal accidents and forest

**Table 1.2.** Deaths from Lightning and Tornadoes, 1890-1982

| Year | Lightning | | Tornadoes |
|---|---|---|---|
| | Weather Bureau | | Weather Bureau or successor agency |
| 1890 | 120* | | N/A* |
| 1891 | 204 | | 55 |
| 1892 | 251 | | 662 |
| 1893 | 209 | | 166 |
| 1894 | 336 | | 236 |
| 1895 | 426 | | 399 |
| 1896 | 341 | | 276 |
| 1897 | 362 | | 108 |
| 1898 | 367 | | 273 |
| | National Center for Health Statistics | Zegel† | |
| 1959 | 183 | 157 | 58‡ |
| 1960 | 129 | 105 | 47 |
| 1961 | 149 | 121 | 51 |
| 1962 | 153 | 126 | 28 |
| 1963 | 165 | 216 | 31 |
| 1964 | 129 | 109 | 73 |
| 1965 | 149 | 126 | 296 |
| 1966 | 110 | | 99 |
| 1967 | 88 | | 114 |
| 1968 | 129 | | 131 |
| 1969 | 131 | | 66 |
| 1970 | 122 | | 72 |
| 1971 | 122 | | 156 |
| 1972 | 94 | | 27 |
| 1973 | 124 | | 87 |
| 1974 | 112 | | 366 |
| 1975 | 124 | | 60 |
| 1976 | 81 | | 44 |
| 1977 | 116 | | 43 |
| 1978 | 98 | | 53 |
| 1979 | 63 (tentative) | | 84 |
| 1980 | 78 (tentative) | | 28 |
| 1981 | NA | | 24 |
| 1982 | NA | | 64 |

*Data source in annual summaries in *Monthly Weather Review*.
†From Zegel (1967).
‡National Oceanic and Atmospheric Administration (NOAA), Environmental Data and Information Service.

protection from lightning strikes, but persons on beaches and golf courses and in rural areas are relatively vulnerable. Figures on lightning deaths from the turn of the century (Table 1.2) suggest the high vulnerability of our then-large farm population, unprotected by the closed metal cabs of modern farm machines.

Deaths of persons and animals by lightning are produced by direct strokes, but it seems not widely known that death is often caused by sidestrokes and even by nearby strokes to trees or ground. Thus, death to persons and animals under trees struck by lightning may result from a spark from the tree or from voltage differences induced in the ground (Fig. 1.3). A momentary difference of several thousand volts between feet on the ground can induce a fatal surge of current through a body. In severe-lightning situations, the safer locations

**Figure 1.3.** Elk killed by lightning in a Montana wilderness area. (Photo courtesy of R. W. Mutch, U.S. Forest Service.)

fires attributed to lightning is clear indication of its wide distribution.

Human deaths caused by lightning in the United States are identified by states in Fig. 1.2. Vigansky (1979) estimates fatalities for the period 1959-79 to be 2,210 and injuries to be 5,142. In urban areas, large structures and vehicles provide substantial

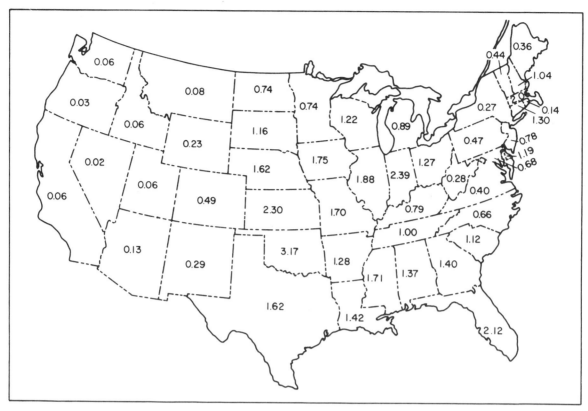

**Figure 1.4a.** The average number of tornadoes per $10^4$ km$^2$ per year for 1953-74 (multiply by 2.59 to obtain units of $10^4$ mi$^2$).

are indoors away from metal and electrical connections, or wholly inside a metal structure such as an automobile.

Lightning has significant effects on plants, including immediate and obvious physical damage, delayed effects in vulnerability of trees to insects and disease, and damage by fire (Taylor, 1969). More than 10,000 reported lightning-caused fires are started each summer in United States forests and grasslands (Barrows, 1966). Before dense settlement of interior North America, lightning-, volcano-, and human-caused fires ranged more widely. Plant communities often are highly inflammable, and thousands of years of their evolutionary development in the presence of fire have produced plant species well adapted to recurrent fires. The routine suppression of fires in recent times has caused organic fuels to accumulate, contributing to some fires of unnatural size and intensity. In many National Parks and Wildernesses, from Florida's Everglades to California's High Sierras, some lightning fires are now allowed to burn under observation to perpetuate these fire-adapted ecosystems. Lightning-set fires are estimated to burn more than 35% of the total forest and brushland consumed by fire in the United States and are a significant factor in forest management.

### Strong Straight-Line Winds and Tornadoes

Strong straight-line winds accompany thunderstorms more often than tornadoes and may be as damaging to persons and property as small tornadoes. In addition to damage to homes and other buildings, strong and shifting winds along thunderstorm gust fronts have been associated with tragic accidents to commercial aircraft.

Practically every United States resident of school age or older knows that tornadoes are fearsome storms; usually they move from the southwest, the

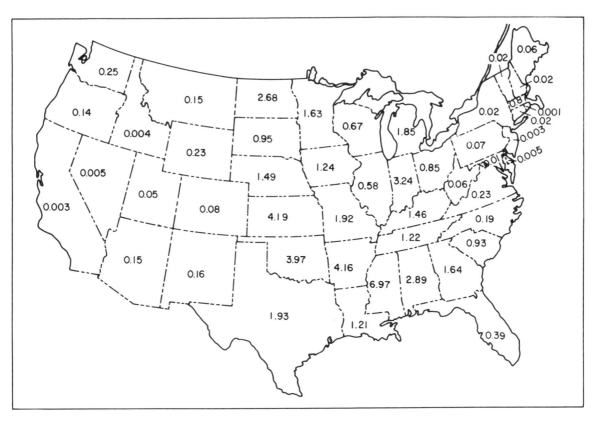

**Figure 1.4b.** Relative tornado threat, by state, from a combination of death and damage statistics multiplied by tornado frequencies.

more severe at forward speeds around 100 km/h, accompanied by winds of 350 km/h (220 mi/h), perhaps even faster. Kessler and Lee (1978) discussed frequency of tornadoes in the United States for the period 1953-74 (Fig. 1.4a) and assessed the distribution of tornado threat in terms of combined data on tornado casualties and damage, normalized to state population densities and property valuation indices (Fig. 1.4b). Although the small area covered by individual tornadoes, their ephemeral character, and vagaries in tornado reports make it difficult to gather accurate data, it seems definite that the center of tornado threat in the United States is somewhat east of the center of tornado frequency. A large fraction of the many tornadoes reported from Oklahoma and Kansas is represented by relatively small and less intense systems. Kessler and Lee found that national patterns of death and damage are similar to each other and do not suggest a link between the distribution of tornado deaths and cultural features of populations in various areas; this, however, is somewhat controversial and worthy of further study (Sims and Baumann, 1972).

Since the tornado core is rarely larger than 1 km in diameter, destructive winds generally last at one place for less than a minute, but practically all human construction (short of reinforced concrete and steel), and much else in nature, can be broken by severe tornadoes in just a few seconds (Figs. 1.5a and 1.5b). More intense than the worst hurricanes, the severe tornado commands much attention because of its sudden and violent onslaught and occasional sharp alterations in path. A tornado can destroy a substantial part of a medium-sized city almost instantly, with casualties that severely tax local facilities and require mobilization of the entire community. In smaller towns, disruption is characteristically more severe (Francaviglia, 1978). The sudden onslaught, casualties,

**Figure 1.5a.** Tornado at Union City, 24 May 1973. (NOAA photo by Joseph Golden.)

**Figure 1.5b.** Tornado damage at Union City, Okla., 24 May 1973. This bus was hurled 75 yd. (Photo by John McGinley.)

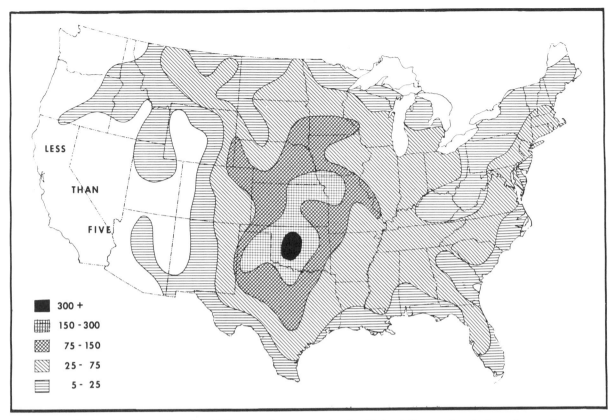

**Figure 1.6.** Distribution of major-hailstorm frequency in the United States. Isopleths refer to the number of reports of hail ¾ in in diameter or larger, 1955-67, in areas 2° latitude by 2° longitude (Pautz, 1969). The distribution of tornado frequency is very similar.

and damage together compare with effects of tidal waves, earthquakes, volcanic eruptions, and even intense bombardment in small areas. The long-term effects, measured over a period of a decade, may be barely perceptible in the standard economic indices, but effects at the time may be traumatic.

## Hail

The strongest effect of hail is in agriculture. In the United States the annual harvest of small grains in the plains states lies under omnipresent threat of loss to hail by lodging of stalks and shattering of seed. Annual losses in the 1970s were between $0.5 and $1 billion, or about 1.5% of cash receipts for all crops. World agricultural losses from hail are estimated to approach $2 billion annually (Zalikhanov and Davitaya, 1980). In the United States, maximum incidence of damaging hail (Fig. 1.6)

does not coincide with the highest per acre value of cropland, but this is not so everywhere. For example, the high incidence of hail characteristic of Italy's Po Valley, northwest Argentina, and the Soviet Caucasus is associated with much damage to cultivated vineyards and vegetables.

Nowhere does hail appear to be so frequent and damaging that it prohibits human activities. Rather, there is acceptance of occasional loss (Fig. 1.7) or adjustment by insurance. For example, more than $300 million was paid by United States farmers in 1975 to insure crops valued at more than $8 billion; just under 60% of the premiums were paid back in loss payments. Farmers in hazardous areas may also cope with the extreme storm by choosing hail-resistant crops and by scattering the location of cultivated fields to reduce the danger of losing a large proportion of the harvest to one storm (Farhar et al., 1977).

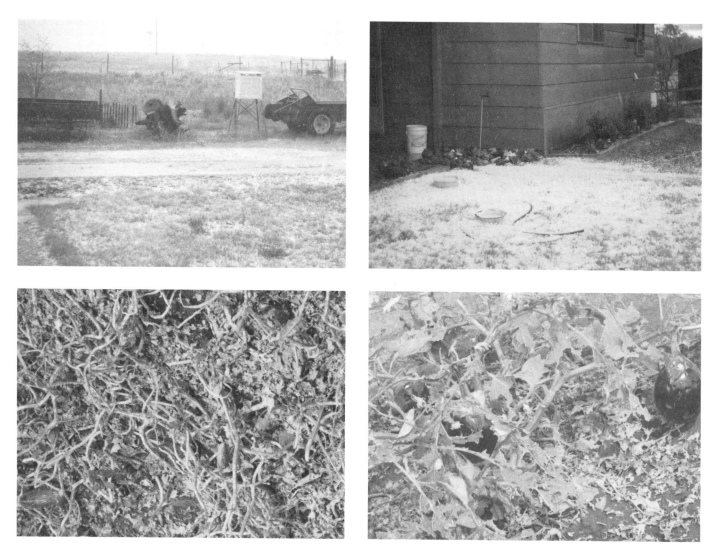

**Figure 1.7.** (Upper left) Severe hailstorm in progress near Criner, Okla., 6 October 1978; falling hailstones appear as streaks. (Upper right) After the storm hailstones covered the ground and in some places remained more than 12 h before melting completely. (Lower photos) Cucumbers (left) and eggplants damaged by the storm. Lightning with this storm started at least four prairie fires within a 2-mi-diameter circle, three of which were doused by subsequent precipitation. The fourth fire was outside the area receiving rain and hail and destroyed baled hay valued at more than $1,000 before being extinguished by a rural fire department.

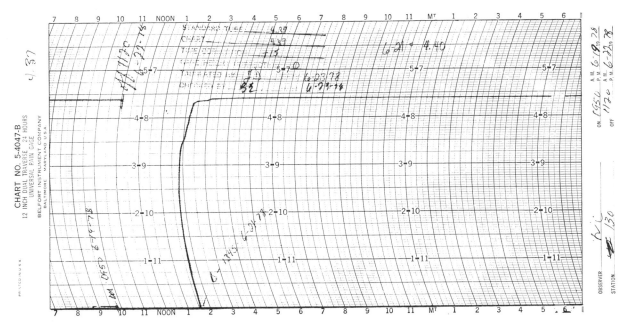

**Figure 1.8.** Record of an Oklahoma cloudburst 8 mi south-southwest of Anadarko, Okla., in the watershed of Tonkawa Creek on 21 June 1978. Three inches of rain fell in 15 min, 4.4 inches in 1½ h. Average rainfall was approximately 3 inches over 25 mi². The resulting flood in this sparsely populated area washed out a V-notched weir established to gage the streamflow and washed out a bridge 8 mi south of the rain gage.

## Heavy Rain

Some rain falling on land is absorbed and held in surface layers, some infiltrates to the water table, and some runs off the surface. During and immediately following prolonged or intense rains, the surface runoff and contributions from subsurface flow cause streams and rivers to swell. Overbank flow occasionally causes damage to crops, structures, and soil, but the larger soil losses probably come from sheet, rill, and gully erosion (Meinzer, 1939).

Some sources estimate that about a third of United States flood damage is produced by flash floods, for which excessive rains produced by intense and often slow-moving thunderstorms are the immediate cause (Fig. 1.8). Flood-damage data are inconsistent, and it is difficult to determine the total or the proportion caused by severe storms. Occasional major events produce dramatic landscape changes in which the human role is only incidental, but human modification of the land is intrinsic to many floods.

Fertile alluvial plains are produced through the dynamics of river flow and maintained by sediments deposited during floods at irregular intervals. Often these areas are sites of extensive development, so that rivers and river beds are restricted by dikes and thus gradually raised. Dikes, channel improvement, and detention dams may lower the flow line of minor floods, but they have sometimes tended to worsen major floods, through both occasional catastrophic dam failures and the encouragement, by the presence of improvements, of the use of areas subject to less frequent but more damaging overflow. Cultivation may increase runoff and reduce infiltration; the effects are seriously compounded when headwater areas are subjected to heavy grazing and practices that reduce soils' organic content and cause closer packing of soil particles (Fig. 1.9). It should be noted, however, that occasional flood peaks help maintain the capacity of channels that tend to build up silt from smaller discharges.

It is widely recognized that the paving and building associated with urbanization reduces infiltra-

tion to nearly zero and may maximize runoff unless offset by storage. Then peak flows following heavy rains are roughly comparable with those from undeveloped areas as much as a hundred times larger.

The social cost of flash-flood runoff is leading to adjustments in the form of insurance coupled with floodplain regulation (White, 1975). The national program for flood loss reduction and floodplain management is placing the several tools of flood warning, flood control, building design, land-use management, and Federal Insurance Administration insurance in a unified framework (Weekly Compilation . . . , 1978). Inclusion of flash floods in the program brings special demands that local communities develop flood warning systems.

### The Choice Process

The particular combination of adjustments adopted in each place experiencing thunderstorms is a product of individual choice, influenced by public policy that imposes incentives and constraints on what people or corporations may be inclined to do. Thus the action taken by a farmer who perceives the approach of a black cloud reflects his own interpretation of the possible danger, but also is guided by what he has learned from earlier information and from radio warnings and by the extent to which his home was designed to withstand severe winds.

Much action is taken independently of public agencies, some is wholly dependent on public measures, and in many cases there is lively interaction of individual and government decisions.

Individual Decisions

Individual action is bound to incorporate what

**Figure 1.9.** Cultivation or intensive grazing of sloping lands in areas subject to high rainfall leads to deterioration of agricultural values and damage to downstream facilities. Repair effort such as that shown here does not wholly restore fertility that existed before abuse. (Top) Gullies near Criner, Okla., before treatment for soil conservation. (Center) During April 1976, the gullies were filled with adjacent soil, then fertilized and planted to prevent further losses. (Bottom) Fall 1978: Pasturage values are slowly restored under a conservation plan that emphasizes sharply reduced grazing. Eighty percent of the direct cost of the treatment illustrated here was borne by the federal government through the Soil Conservation Service.

# 2. Disaster by Flood

*Lee R. Hoxit, Herbert S. Lieb, Charles F. Chappell, and H. Michael Mogil*

## Introduction

Flash floods are a fact of life—and death—along the rivers and streambeds and arroyos of the United States. They can result when rains overfill natural and constructed drainage systems. They can be caused by dam failures, ice jams, and heavy rain following rapidly melting snow. Most, however, result from localized heavy rain and usually occur within a few hours after precipitation.

During the 1970s flash floods were the leading cause of death and destruction from weather-related storms; they have devastated parts of nearly every state. The flash flood is now the major natural-disaster-warning problem in the United States (AMS, 1978), and the Federal Disaster Assistance Administration has reported that 85% of all presidential declarations of major disaster are related to floods.

The flash-flood death toll averaged about 200 during each year in the 1970s, twice the yearly rate of the 1960s and triple the yearly rate of the 1940s. Most fatalities occurred in a few catastrophic events. Annual property damage during the late 1970s was about $1 billion, and according to the U.S. Water Resources Council, annual damage from floods and flash floods will reach $3.5 billion by the year 2000 unless floodplain management is improved.

More than 15,000 United States communities and recreational areas have been identified by the Flood Insurance Administration as vulnerable to flash floods. Increased use of mountainous areas for recreation and canyons for home building has greatly increased the potential for disaster. Mobile-home parks and campsites in scenic hilly areas bring thousands of visitors to fish and camp, usu-

ally in the summer, when the probability of flash flooding is highest. The design of bridges, culverts, and buildings sometimes obstructs the normal flow of water. Continued urban development increases the peak flow rates in small streams.

The most significant flash-flood disasters of the 1970s have been documented and are summarized below in chronological order. One of these—the Big Thompson Canyon flash flood—is discussed at length to represent the meteorological processes involved in a storm, the problems of warning and preparedness, and the human response to floods.

Arizona, September 1970: Twenty-three died in a flash flood caused by the remnants of a tropical storm (NOAA, 1971).

Black Hills, South Dakota, June 1972: A series of thunderstorms dropped extremely heavy rains on the eastern slopes of the Black Hills. Catastrophic flash flooding developed along the two-block-wide, 12-mile-long stretch of Rapid Creek that flows through Rapid City. A total of 237 people perished, and more than $100 million in damage was recorded (Dennis et al., 1973).

Mid-Atlantic states, June 1972: As the remnants of Hurricane Agnes moved up the mid-Atlantic seaboard and then curved westward into New York and Pennsylvania, torrential rains caused both floods and flash floods and extraordinary destruction. Entire communities were ravaged, and 118 people died (NOAA, 1973; Baily et al., 1975).

Big Thompson Canyon, Colo., July 1976: Intense thunderstorms produced up to 12 in of localized rainfall within a few hours over the rugged Big Thompson River drainage in north-central Colo-

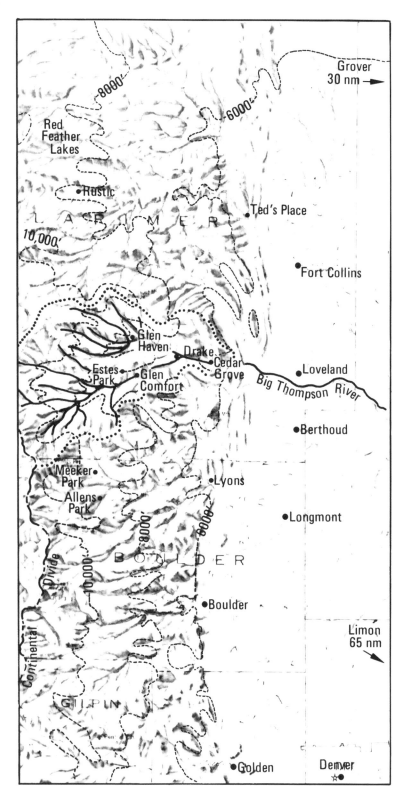

**Figure 2.1a.** The region surrounding the Big Thompson Canyon with locations of many of the cities and towns referred to in the text (Maddox et al., 1977).

rado. The flash flood that swept through the canyon and onto the plains resulted in 139 casualties and property damage estimated at $35 million (NOAA, 1976; Maddox et al., 1977).

Appalachia, April 1977: Heavy rains caused flooding and flash flooding, claimed 22 lives, and caused more than $500 million worth of property damage (NOAA, 1978a).

Johnstown, Pa., July 1977: Between 9 P.M. on 19 July and 4 A.M. on 20 July, up to 12 in of rain fell near Johnstown. The resulting flood killed 77 persons and caused property damage worth more than $200 million (Hoxit et al., 1978).

Kansas City, Mo., September 1977: The "calm, gentle, peaceful, serene" Brush Creek flowing through the heart of Kansas City, Mo., became a torrent, killing 25 and causing property damage worth $90 million (Hales, 1978).

Toccoa, Ga., November 1977: Heavy rainfall contributed to the failure of an earthen dam. Nearly 40 people, half of them children, were swept to their death. Most had lived in mobile homes less than 1 mi below the dam (Land, 1978; Sowers, 1978).

Southern California, February-March 1978: In February 1978, southern California was hit by one of its worst rainstorms ever. Twenty lives were lost in floods in the Los Angeles area (NOAA, 1978b). A repetition of rain and mud slides a month later brought the death toll to nearly 40, with damage totaling more than $80 million.

**The Big Thompson Canyon Flood**

Centennial weekend, 31 July-1 August 1976, marked the one hundredth anniversary of Colorado statehood. By Sunday morning, 1 August, the news was dominated not by celebration but by the unfolding tragedy of the Big Thompson Canyon flash flood.

East of Estes Park (the most popular entrance to the Rocky Mountain National Park) lies the Big Thompson Canyon, the rugged, scenic, and the most developed of Colorado's eastern-slope canyons (Fig. 2.1a). Canyon elevations range from 5,200 ft at the mouth a few miles west of Loveland, Colorado, to more than 9,000 ft along ridge tops east of Estes Park. The sides of the canyon are steep and in many places very rocky (see Fig.

**Figure 2.1b.** Typical terrain along the sides of Big Thompson Canyon. (Photo courtesy of U.S. Geological Survey.)

2.1b). U.S. Highway 34 parallels the Big Thompson River the entire length of the canyon. Tourist attractions, including novelty shops, motels, campgrounds, and summer cabins, were strung out along the highway.

In an average July the canyon area receives 1½ to 2 in of rain. Scarcity of water is much more common than flooding. After spring runoff from melting snow the Big Thompson River's flow decreases dramatically. By late July, the stream is typically 15 to 20 ft wide and only 1 to 3 ft deep. But at least 12 significant floods occurred there between 1864 and 1951.

### Saturday, 31 July 1976

The morning of 31 July began as a normal summer Saturday in Colorado. National Weather Service forecasts indicated a 30%–40% chance of afternoon and evening showers and thundershowers, typical for midsummer. Several hundred thousand residents and tourists ventured into the mountains, many choosing the Big Thompson Canyon.

Unusually moist air was already present over much of Colorado. A cold front had moved into the eastern half of the state, bringing an air mass having 60°F dew points into northeast Colorado.

A second front was located across southwest Nebraska and was advancing southward and westward (Fig. 2.2). In the middle troposphere (Fig. 2.3) the flow was weak and very moist over the central Rocky Mountain area. An upper-level ridge was located just east of Colorado, and a weak short wave was moving into the state from the south and southwest. During the early afternoon, the first cold front remained roughly stationary along the eastern foothills of the Rockies. The cooler moist air behind this front was fairly shallow. Meanwhile, the second front pushed into northeast Colorado. The air mass just behind this front was deeper and more moist, and conditionally very unstable. This meant that condensation accompanying moderate ascent of the air could trigger rapid overturning within the air mass.

The midafternoon regional surface analysis in Fig. 2.4 and the sequence of 2-hour satellite photos in Fig. 2.5 show the meteorological changes during the afternoon. Thunderstorms formed in eastern Wyoming, eastern Colorado, and central Kansas along the second front. At the same time strong and widespread mountain thunderstorms developed in southwestern Colorado, northern New Mexico, and southern Utah as the upper-level short wave advanced northward. The Big Thompson

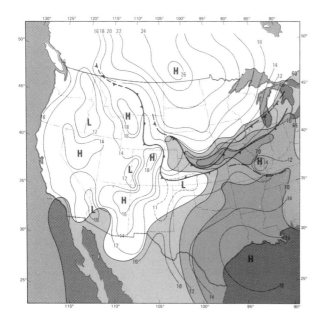

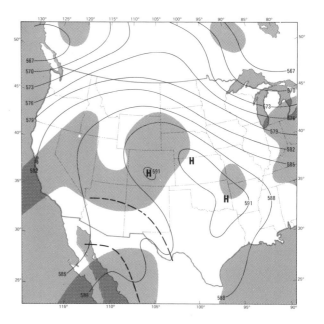

**Figure 2.2.** Synoptic-scale surface analysis for 1200 GMT (0600 MDT), 31 July 1976. Surface pressures are analyzed at 2-mb intervals (12 = 1012 mb). Regions with dew points temperature >60°F are shaded (Maddox et al., 1977).

**Figure 2.3.** Analysis of the height of the 500-mb pressure surface at 1200 GMT (0600 MDT), 31 July 1976. Height contours are drawn at 30-m intervals (e.g., 570 = 5700 m). Trough lines are dashed, and the regions where the dew point is less than 6°C below the dry-bulb temperature are shaded (Maddox et al., 1977).

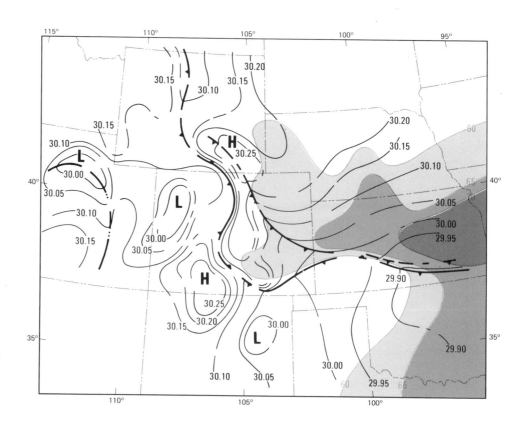

**Figure 2.4.** Regional surface analysis for 2200 GMT (1400 MDT), 31 July 1976. Pressure analysis is based on altimeter settings at intervals of 0.05 in. Regions with dew-point temperature ≥ 60°F are shaded (Maddox et al., 1977).

**Figure 2.5a-c.** A series of geostationary operational environmental satellite (GOES-1) photographs showing afternoon distribution of clouds at 2-h intervals. a. 2000 GMT (1400 MDT), 31 July 1976.

**Figure 2.5b.** GOES-1 photograph for 2200 GMT (1600 MDT), 31 July 1976.

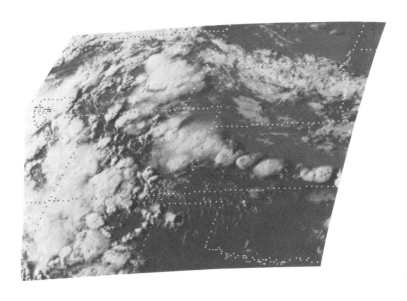

**Figure 2.5c.** GOES-1 photograph for 0000 GMT, 1 August 1976 (1800 MDT 31 July).

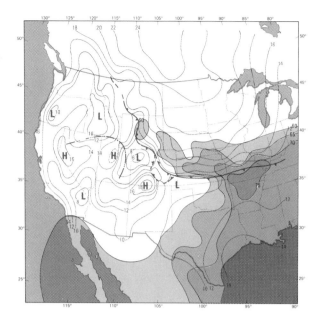

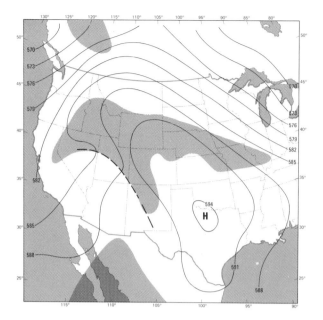

**Figure 2.6.** Synoptic-scale surface analysis for 0000 GMT, 1 August 1976 (1800 MDT 31 July) (Maddox et al., 1977).

**Figure 2.7.** 500-mb analysis for 0000 GMT, 1 August 1976 (1800 MDT, 31 July 1976) (Maddox et al., 1977).

Canyon region itself remained almost free of thunderstorm activity during this period.

Broader-scale meteorological conditions on the evening of July 31 are summarized in Figs. 2.6 and 2.7. Widespread convective activity was present along and north of the trough axis. The surface low over western Colorado had deepened in response to the short wave and afternoon heating, thereby increasing the east-to-west pressure gradient across Colorado. The second frontal surge had moved into the northeast Colorado foothills, and the first thunderstorms were developing in the foothills from Boulder, Colorado, north to the Wyoming border.

In the canyon the day was beautiful, and few of the 3,000 people there could have realized that these rapidly developing storms signaled the beginning of a major natural disaster.

### Saturday night, 31 July 1976

As the second frontal surge moved into the northeastern Colorado foothills, thunderstorms there developed very rapidly (Fig. 2.8), while thunderstorms over the plains decreased. By 6:45 P.M.

MDT the National Weather Service radar at Limon was indicating maximum storm tops just north of Drake, Colo. Several of the cells as seen with radar were associated with cloud tops above 50,000 ft. Figure 2.9 shows a portion of the storm system as seen from the ground.

The rainfall-producing potential of such a storm is indicated by the storm model in Fig. 2.10. Abundant low-level moisture and a conditionally unstable atmosphere (Fig. 2.11) triggered large storms as the air was lifted by the topography. Strong easterly winds at low levels and light southerly winds at middle and upper levels produced a slow northwesterly movement of the cells into the eastern-slope mountains. Continued uplift triggered new cells in roughly the same locations, thereby contributing to stationarity of the storm system as a whole (Fig. 2.12). Moreover, the relatively weak wind shear in the cloud layer, combined with very low cloud bases, produced storms with very high precipitation efficiencies.

The most intense rains fell in the middle and upper portions of the canyon as the storm system propagated very slowly northwestward. Total rainfall for the storm period 31 July–1 August is shown

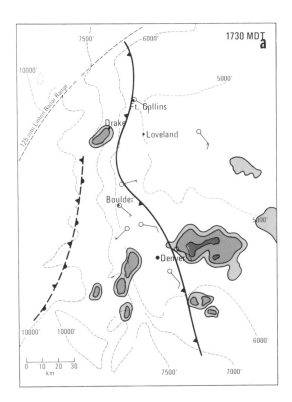

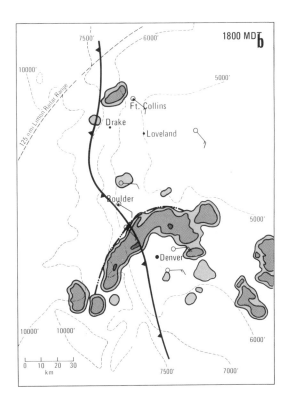

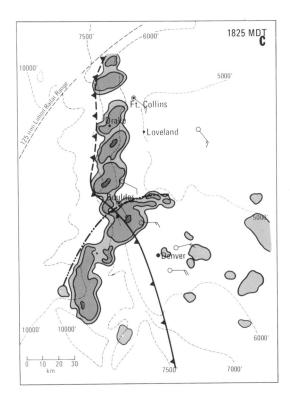

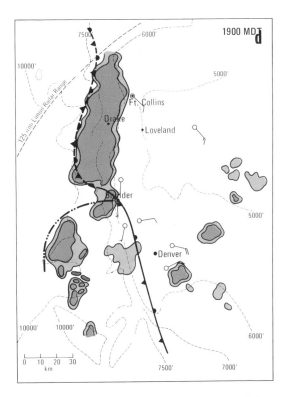

**Figure 2.8.** Local-scale surface analysis with Limon, Colorado, radar echoes, as represented by contour mapping device, the Video Integrating Processor (VIP). VIP Level-1 return is shaded light gray, VIP Level-2 medium gray, VIP Level-3 (heavy rain) dark gray. (a) 1730 MDT, (b) 1800 MDT, (c) 1825 MDT, and (d) 1900 MDT, 31 July 1976 (Maddox et al., 1977).

**Figure 2.9.** A large thunderstorm located approximately 10 miles south of the Big Thompson Canyon between 1830 and 1845 MDT. (Photo by John Asztalos.)

**Figure 2.10.** Physical model of the Big Thompson thunderstorms (Maddox et al., 1977). LCL = lifting condensation level; LFC = level of free convection. Airflow is indicated by heavy-line arrows. Reflectivities from a research radar at Grover, Colo. (approximately 70 nmi east of the Big Thompson Canyon) are shown at 10-dBZ intervals beginning with the 15-dBZ level.

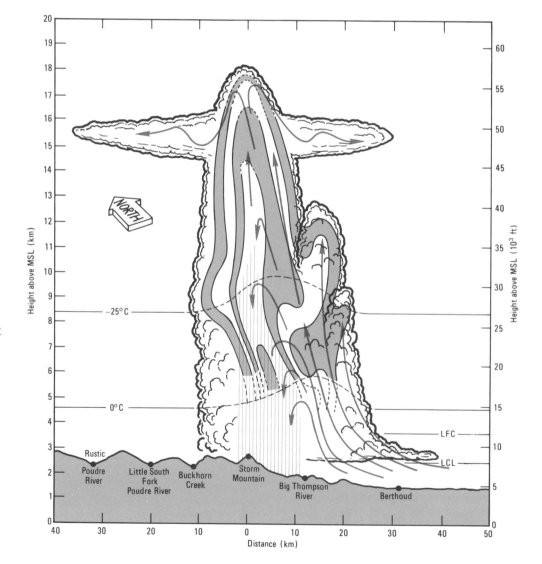

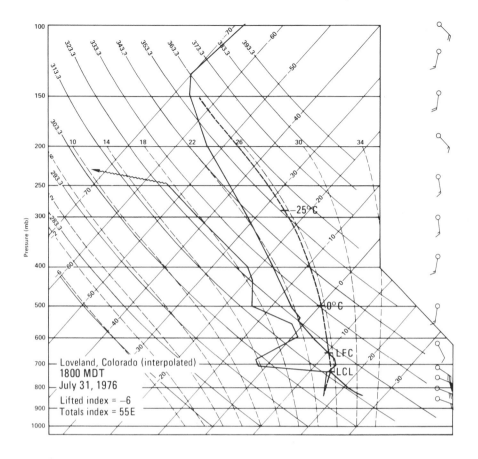

**Figure 2.11.** Plot of an upper-air sounding constructed for Loveland, Colo., using surrounding rawinsonde surface and boundary layer wind data. Time is 0000 GMT, 1 August 1976 (1800 MDT, 31 July). LCL, LFC, and moist adiabat are shown for a lifted parcel with mean thermodynamic characteristics of the lowest 100-mb layer.

in Fig. 2.13. Most fell in a 4-to-6-h period during the night of 31 July. Estimated rainfall rates in the maximum rainfall zone near Glen Haven and Glen Comfort are presented in Fig. 2.14. Probably 7 to 8 in of rain fell there in less than 2 h.

The normally placid Big Thompson River received great quantities of water from several small tributaries between Lake Estes (within the limits of Estes Park) and Drake. Near Drake, the flow on the river just before the rain began was only 137 cubic feet per second (cfs); the peak flow of 31,200 cfs occurred at 9:00 P.M., according to the U.S. Geological Survey. The estimated peak stages on the Big Thompson River occurred shortly after 8:00 P.M. at Glen Comfort, and at about 11:00 P.M. at the mouth of the canyon about 8 mi west of Loveland (Grozier et al., 1976). Only a few short hours separated the onset of heavy rain from the flood crest passing the canyon mouth and quickly subsiding on the plains below.

The first hint of trouble came when Colorado State Patrolman Bob Miller, on duty at Estes Park,

was asked to investigate rock and mud slides on the canyon road. At about 8:35 P.M., Miller issued the first warning of a serious flood problem: "Advise them we have a flood. The whole mountainside is gone. We have people trapped on the other side [of the river]. I'm going to have to move out. I'm up to my doors in water. Advise we can't get to them. I'm going to get out of here before I drown."

Patrolman Tim Littlejohn, coming from Fort Collins reached Drake and began warning campers and residents. Sgt. Hugh Purdy, of the Colorado State Patrol, coming from Loveland, never reached Drake, his destination. He was trying to find the headwaters of the flood; his last radio transmission was at approximately 9:15: "I'm right in the middle of it. I can't get out . . . about one-half mile east of Drake on the highway. [Tell the cars] to get out of the low area down below." Purdy's body was found about 8 miles downstream from the site of his last radio transmission. His car was ground up beyond recognition and was identified

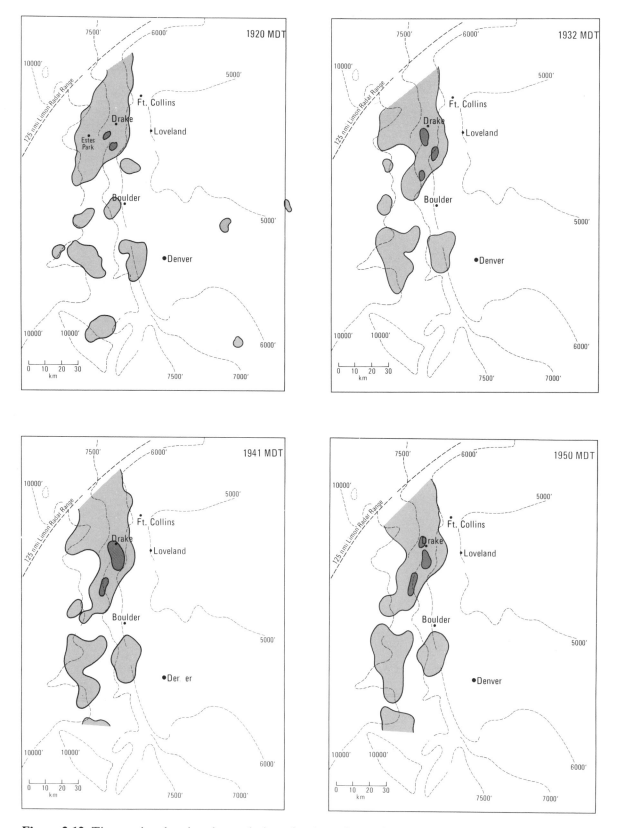

**Figure 2.12.** Time series showing the evolution of radar echoes observed by National Weather Service radar at Limon, Colo., approximately 205 km southeast of Big Thompson Canyon. VIP levels 1 and

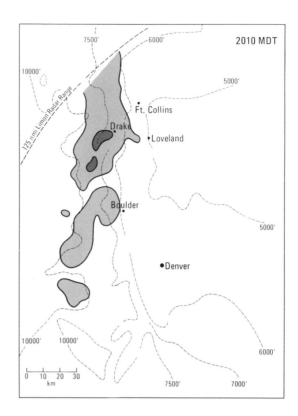

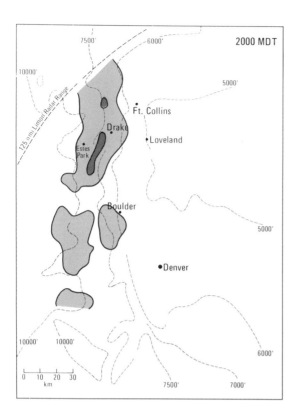

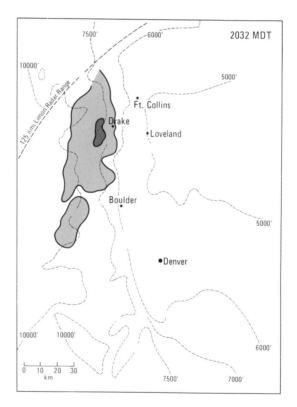

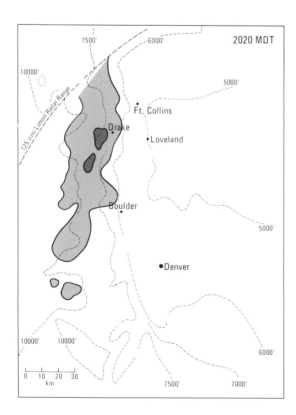

2 are shaded light gray; level 3 is shaded dark gray. A longer sequence appears in Maddox et al. (1977).

29

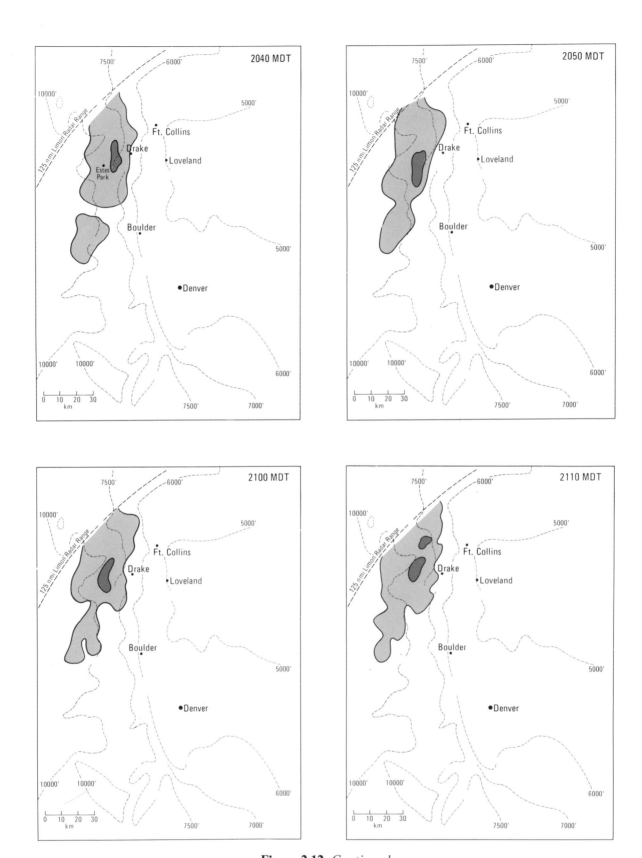

**Figure 2.12.** *Continued.*

only by a key ring inscribed "Colorado State Patrol."

Larimer County Sheriff Bob Watson has vivid memories of the night, when his on-duty ordeal began. The Sheriff's Department began emergency preparations in case cloudbursts hit the upper reaches of the Big Thompson and its north fork, or the big watershed of Buckhorn Creek.

Deputies and patrolmen responded to calls and warned drivers, campers, and residents. The mounting waters altered constructions in the canyon and some of its natural features as well. Within the canyon the floodwaters swept away homes and motels along the stream's edge (Fig. 2.15). Nothing was left of the Loveland hydroelectric plant after the flood. Much of U.S. Highway 34 was washed out. Campgrounds were inundated. Hundreds of automobiles were pulled into the current, then ground up by tumbling rocks.

At the mouth of the canyon a battering ram of debris, including big propane tanks emitting an eerie whistle as they lost pressure through their broken sides, crashed into and dislodged the structure supporting a huge water siphon (part of a U.S. Bureau of Reclamation water-diversion project). The north end of the steel pipe, weighing 1,000 lb/running ft, or 227,000 lb total, and full of an estimated 873,000 lb of water, was pulled from its connection and crashed into the maelstrom. The siphon, deeply embedded in the mountainside, "came out like a big soda straw," said Watson.

According to Watson, the river rose rapidly, but a wall of water did not form until the huge mass of water and debris was crowded into The Narrows portion of the canyon. At this point a wall of water about 19 ft above the original stream bed formed. It dispersed rapidly when freed from the narrow canyon, but the huge buildup of water continued to devastate the landscape as it spread eastward over the flatlands downstream.

Recovery and rescue operations continued for days after the flood; months were needed to repair Highway 34 through the canyon. Cleanup activities were continuing a year later and rebuilding even after that. One hundred and thirty-nine people died in the flood, and several bodies were never recovered. Property damage was estimated at $35 million.

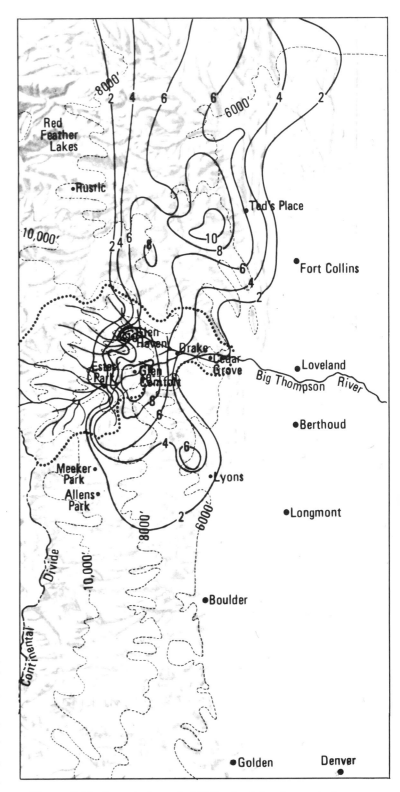

**Figure 2.13.** Cumulative rainfall (inches) for the period 31 July-2 August 1976. Terrain contours (ft) are indicated by dashed lines (Maddox et al., 1977). The Big Thompson river drainage is indicated by a dotted line.

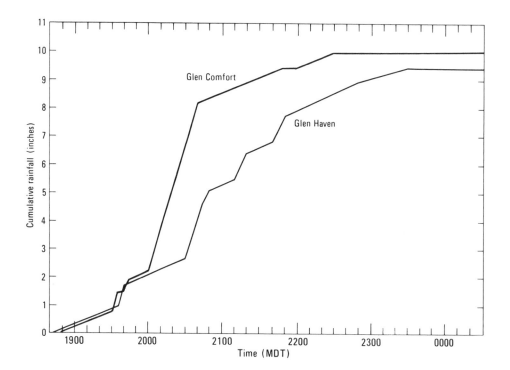

**Figure 2.14.** Accumulated rainfall curves developed from the Limon, Colo., radar data (after Maddox et al., 1977).

**Figure 2.15a-c.** The Big Thompson Canyon, a few days after the flood. 2.15a. (Above) Drake, Colo. (Photos courtesy of U.S. Geological Survey, Denver, Colo.)

**Figure 2.15b.** Debris deposited on a bridge.

**Figure 2.15c.** U.S. Highway 34.

## The National Flash-Flood Problem

Although most flash floods are caused by strong thunderstorms, only recently have the environmental conditions associated with these storms been systematically defined (Mogil and Groper, 1976; Maddox et al., 1979). In addition to geographic and topographic influences, the following characteristics typify many flash-flood thunderstorm events (Maddox et al., 1979):

1. Storms occur in regions where surface dew-point temperatures are high.
2. The moisture content is high through a deep tropospheric layer.
3. The horizontal wind does not vary significantly through the cloud depth.
4. Convective storms and/or cells repeatedly form and move over the same area.
5. The storm area is often near the large-scale ridge shown by charts of the middle atmosphere.
6. A weak short-wave trough acts to destabilize the atmosphere and trigger and focus the storm.
7. Storms often occur during the night.
8. Tornadoes, hail, and strong wind gusts are often absent from the heavy-rain area.

Rains that produce flash floods sometimes occur with other weather patterns:

1. Slow-moving decaying tropical storms.
2. Slow-moving extratropical storms.
3. Heavy rains falling on melting snow.
4. Steady nonthunderstorm precipitation produced by sustained flow over topographic barriers.

The National Weather Service Forecast and Warning programs for flash floods and for severe thunderstorms are similar (Mogil et al., 1978). From indicators like those in the lists above, local and state forecast offices are responsible for issuing both watches (alerts in advance of an actual event) and warnings (advice concerning events in progress) (see also Chapter 9). However, the problem represented by the need for timely communication of watches and warnings to the threatened population is compounded by the fact that many storms, and therefore many flash floods, occur at night, when people are asleep. In fact, Maddox et al. (1979) found that nearly 70% of 151 significant flash floods east of the Continental Divide occurred during the night.

Furthermore, watches and warnings on flash floods are generally not as precise and timely as necessary to allow property to be protected and people evacuated in an orderly manner. The United States river and rainfall reporting network, which continually analyzes precipitation and stream-flow data to provide river forecasts and flood warnings, often cannot detect thunderstorms that can produce torrential rains in small areas. Satellite and radar observations show promise of yielding useful rainfall estimates but do not yet provide estimates of maximum rainfall that are reliable and accurate enough for routine warnings of localized floods. And the indicators on medium and large scales serve only to alert the forecaster; they often do not provide data relevant for timely warnings to threatened areas. In this situation of limited forecasting capability, the difference between life and death often depends on an effective community warning system. Information must be relayed very rapidly when it becomes available, and recipients must often respond quickly. But response as well as warning is often inadequate.

Many communities hit by flash floods have no semblance of a warning system. The inhabitants believe that floods cannot happen in their communities, and local officials are often unwilling to put resources into nonstructural defenses.

The response of people to a warning system is the main reason for such a system, yet this response has received the least attention in setting up hazard warnings (White, 1975; White and Haas, 1975; Mileti, 1975). Response is defined as the protective behavior adopted by those who receive warning: individuals, small groups, organizations, and the community. Recent studies of the response of those warned of disaster have found the following:

1. The credibility attached to a warning is related to one's ability to confirm it. Most people will try to confirm a warning for a time before acting on it, especially after early-warning messages (Mileti, 1974 and 1975).
2. The more warning messages received by an individual, the fewer attempts he will make at confirmation.
3. Messages from friends and relatives are more likely

to produce protective behavior than are those of mass media (Mack and Baker, 1961). A family is more likely than an individual to take action (Drabek and Stephenson, 1971).

4. A person is more likely to believe a warning of impending danger if changes in his physical environment support the warning.

5. Warnings from official sources (police, state patrol, fire department) are more likely to produce protective response than are those from unofficial sources (Drabek and Boggs, 1968; Mileti, 1974).

6. In a number of disasters a disproportionate number of victims are elderly because they are physically less able to move (Hutton, 1976).

7. Personal communication, by such modes as telephones, bullhorns, and face-to-face contact, is much more effective than impersonal communication by radio, television, etc. (Drabek, 1969).

8. Panic is not a typical response to predisaster warnings (Quarantelli, 1960).

People's first response to disaster warning is disbelief—denying danger is one way of dealing with it and is something everyone does to some extent (NOAA, 1976). The actions of the residents of Big Thompson Canyon on the night of 31 July 1976, fit the pattern reported by researchers who investigated other disasters. The law-enforcement officials—the sheriff and his deputies, the State Highway Patrol, the police, and the fire departments—took the warning action, and the warnings were ignored by many, who refused to evacuate. Others moved only when they were told more than once or when they saw the river coming up, saw water cascading down the mountains, heard the hissing of propane tanks, and saw bridges go out and water cover the roadway. Others left when they heard rumors of a dam failure. Most people, particularly residents, were slow to realize that they were not safe.

Patrolman Littlejohn, directing traffic at Drake and warning campers and residents, summed it up by saying that residents looked at him as if he were crazy. He had to turn on his lights and siren and turn back six or seven cars about three-fourths of a mile above Drake. He has said, "I don't think any of us fully understood the magnitude of this until it was on top of us."

A resident of Glen Comfort told a NOAA survey team that he had never been able to under-

stand how people faced with imminent danger and warned that floodwaters or a hurricane surge was about to hit could disregard the advice. "And yet when they came to the door warning us to get out, I said 'Why? We've had hard rain before and we got through it.'" He added, "We just don't get those kinds of storms, and we felt that we had no reason to leave our home. . . . You can just bet I won't be that foolish the next time."

Grunfest (1977) found that persons with recent disaster experience are more likely to take protective action when warnings are issued than are those without recent disaster experience. She found that one-fourth of those who died in the Big Thompson were more than 60 years old. The proportion over age 60 in the canyon at the time of the flood was not noted but was presumably much smaller. She agreed with the finding that evacuations are directly related to the number of warnings. Many responded to environmental cues such as the rising river, the severity of the rainfall, or a change in the sound of the river.

The Grunfest report notes that, when threatened with a flood people tended to get in their cars and drive out of the canyon to escape the water. For many people in the Big Thompson and in other flash floods this action was fatal. If they had abandoned their cars and climbed 25 ft up the canyon wall, they might have survived. The Grunfest observation about cars was supported by observations of the Kansas City flash flood of 1977, in which 17 of the 25 deaths occurred in automobiles.

## Summary

Our account of one flood discusses elements common to many. An unusually severe storm developed locally, in a broad region of thunderstorm activity. Shower activity was foreshadowed 12-24 hours in advance, but the phenomenal local episode was appreciated only after it was under way. When it became apparent that the amount of rain was dangerous, heroic efforts were made to carry this information to persons in threatened areas. Some heeded the warnings; some did not. Some were washed away before they received any warning.

Flash floods are an act of nature. Death and

damage caused by them are exacerbated by our intensive use of the land, ameliorated by a complex system for conveying current and forecast information to the public, and further modulated by the nature of individual responses to warning. The toll taken by flash floods will be determined in the future, as it has been in the past, by the nature and density of our settlements, the quality of flood-control measures, the systems used by scientists for acquiring and interpreting meteorological observations, the means established for communicating forecasts and warnings, and the factors of society and individual psychology that shape response.

# 3. Tornadoes: The Tornado Outbreak of 3–4 April 1974

*Robert F. Abbey, Jr., and T. Theodore Fujita*

## Introduction

About 100,000 thunderstorms occur each year within the 48 contiguous United States. When they produce tornadoes and other strong winds, hail, and intense lightning, they may be very hazardous. White and Haas (1975) presented statistics for the 15 principal natural hazards in the United States. Thunderstorms with all their components rank first in deaths, second in injuries, and third in property damage.

Approximately 700 to 1,200 tornadoes are reported within the United States each year. The more common type of tornado is small and lasts only a minute or two, causing only slight damage over a track often less than 100 m wide and 2 km long. Because of their rapid development, short duration, and small size, it is difficult to warn the public of them, but these small tornadoes do not usually constitute a major hazard. Most tornado-related deaths, injuries, and property damage are caused by the infrequent large, long-enduring tornadoes, whose paths may be 2 km wide and hundreds of kilometers long. Such destructive tornadoes last up to 3 h and are therefore much easier to track and warn against.

Most physical characteristics and effects of tornadoes are well represented in the 16-h outbreak

**Table 3.1.** Effects of Tornadoes of 3–4 April 1974*

| Category | Total | Ala. | Ga. | Ill. | Ind. | Ky. | Mich. | Miss. | N.C. | Ohio | S.C. | Tenn. | Va. | W.Va. |
|---|---|---|---|---|---|---|---|---|---|---|---|---|---|---|
| Persons | | | | | | | | | | | | | | |
|   Dead | 335 | 86 | 17 | 2 | 49 | 77 | 3 | | 7 | 41 | | 50 | 2 | 1 |
|   Injured | 6,142 | 949 | 104 | 30 | 768 | 1,377 | 20 | 1 | 74 | 2,138 | 1 | 635 | 13 | 32 |
|   Hospitalized | 1,183 | 296 | 37 | 14 | 203 | 280 | 6 | | 17 | 162 | | 155 | 1 | 12 |
| Dwellings | | | | | | | | | | | | | | |
|   Destroyed | 7,512 | 1,078 | 67 | 51 | 1,454 | 1,522 | 50 | 1 | 45 | 2,756 | | 443 | 1 | 44 |
|   Major damage | 5,946 | 780 | 97 | 40 | 1,420 | 1,520 | 30 | 25 | 46 | 1,362 | 6 | 498 | 38 | 84 |
|   Minor damage | 8,390 | 1,076 | 88 | 49 | 2,004 | 1,552 | 60 | 8 | 103 | 2,201 | 3 | 986 | 169 | 91 |
| Mobile homes | | | | | | | | | | | | | | |
|   Destroyed | 2,091 | 421 | 78 | 4 | 584 | 484 | 45 | | 79 | 74 | 4 | 276 | 9 | 33 |
|   Major damage | 909 | 142 | 40 | 2 | 208 | 239 | 20 | 2 | 43 | 87 | 3 | 85 | 5 | 33 |
| Farm buildings | | | | | | | | | | | | | | |
|   Destroyed | 3,996 | 719 | 92 | 18 | 889 | 1,575 | 70 | 1 | 33 | 134 | 2 | 436 | 7 | 20 |
|   Major damage | 2,871 | 299 | 55 | 2 | 754 | 1,231 | 85 | 30 | 9 | 54 | | 340 | 5 | 7 |
| Small businesses | | | | | | | | | | | | | | |
|   Destroyed or | | | | | | | | | | | | | | |
|     major damage | 1,427 | 205 | 10 | 2 | 232 | 230 | | 1 | 5 | 639 | 1 | 85 | | 17 |
| Families | | | | | | | | | | | | | | |
|   Suffering loss | 27,590 | 3,728 | 421 | 158 | 5,966 | 6,625 | 200 | 50 | 347 | 6,959 | 17 | 2,436 | 391 | 292 |

*Casualty and damage survey by American Red Cross. From NOAA (1974)

of 3-4 April 1974, the most severe ever recorded in terms of number of tornadoes, length of tornado tracks, area affected, and damage. More than 5,500 people were injured, and 335 were killed; property losses were estimated at more than $600 million by the U.S. Civil Defense Preparedness Agency, and more than 27,000 families were affected (Table 3.1). Aerial and ground observations located 147 tornadoes, and at one time at least 15 different tornadoes were on the ground simultaneously (Fujita, 1974; Fujita and Forbes, 1974; NOAA, 1974).

Typically, most of the 147 tornadoes of 3-4 April

**Table 3.2.** Tornadoes in the Eastern United States and Canada, 3-4 April 1974

|   |   | F scale[a] | P$_L$[a] | P$_W$[a] | Length (miles) | Duration (minutes) | Touchdown time (CDST) | Lift-off time (CDST) | Confidence[b] | Family[c] | Echo[d] |
|---|---|---|---|---|---|---|---|---|---|---|---|
| 1 | Morris, Ill. | 0 | 0 | 0 | 0.5 | 1 | 1310 | 1311 | B | XX | NN |
| 2 | Carlock, Ill. | 0 | 0 | 0 | 0.5 | 1 | 1407 | 1408 | A | XX | NC |
| 3 | Lincoln, Ill. | 1 | 3 | 1 | 15 | 16 | 1403 | 1419 | A | 1 | 1 |
| 4 | Anchor, Ill. | 3 | 2 | 3 | 8 | 9 | 1448 | 1457 | A | 1 | 1 |
| 5 | Decatur, Ill. | 3 | 3 | 3 | 19 | 20 | 1430 | 1450 | B | 2 | 2 |
| 6 | Farmer City, Ill. | 1 | 3 | 1 | 13 | 13 | 1514 | 1527 | B | 2 | 2 |
| 7 | Owaneco, Ill. | 1 | 2 | 2 | 8 | 9 | 1447 | 1456 | A | 3 | 3 |
| 8 | Pierson, Ill. | 0 | 2 | 1 | 4 | 5 | 1520 | 1525 | B | 3 | 3 |
| 9 | Tolono, Ill. | 3 | 2 | 2 | 8 | 8 | 1544 | 1552 | A | 3 | 3 |
| 10 | Homer Lake, Ill. | 3 | 3 | 3 | 17 | 16 | 1558 | 1614 | A | 3 | 3 |
| 11 | Bismarck, Ill. | 2 | 2 | 3 | 7 | 7 | 1618 | 1625 | A | 3 | 3 |
| 12 | Rainsville, Ind. | 3 | 3 | 4 | 26 | 26 | 1637 | 1703 | B | 3 | 3 |
| 13 | Monticello, Ind. | 4 | 5 | 4 | 121 | 120 | 1647 | 1847 | A | 3 | 3 |
| 14 | Plato, Ind. | 1 | 2 | 3 | 8 | 8 | 1851 | 1859 | B | 3 | 3 |
| 15 | Angola, Ind. | 3 | 4 | 4 | 36 | 36 | 1853 | 1929 | B | 4 | 4 |
| 16 | Hillsdale, Mich. | 2 | 3 | 3 | 21 | 15 | 1944 | 1959 | B | 4 | 4 |
| 17 | Charleston, Ill. | 1 | 3 | 2 | 16 | 13 | 1622 | 1635 | B | XX | 5 |
| 18 | Paris, Ill. | 2 | 2 | 2 | 2 | 2 | 1700 | 1702 | C | XX | 6 |
| 19 | N. Manchester, Ind. | 1 | 2 | 2 | 7 | 10 | 1835 | 1845 | D | XX | NN |
| 20 | Hudson, Mich. | 2 | 3 | 3 | 10 | 10 | 2005 | 2015 | C | XX | NN |
| 21 | Swayzee, Ind. | 2 | 3 | 3 | 19 | 23 | 1845 | 1908 | B | 5 | 8N |
| 22 | Plum Tree, Ind. | 2 | 3 | 3 | 11 | 10 | 1920 | 1930 | C | 5 | 8N |
| 23 | Paulding, Ohio | 2 | 2 | 2 | 7 | 7 | 2016 | 2023 | A | 5 | 8N |
| 24 | Bluffton, Ind. | 2 | 3 | 3 | 12 | 12 | 1915 | 1927 | C | 6 | 8S |
| 25 | Melrose, Ohio | 2 | 2 | 3 | 8 | 8 | 2026 | 2034 | A | 6 | 8S |
| 26 | Decatur, Ind. | 1 | 3 | 3 | 13 | 15 | 1925 | 1940 | C | 6 | 8S |
| 27 | Continental, Ohio | 3 | 3 | 3 | 10 | 10 | 1833 | 1843 | B | XX | 7 |
| 28 | Erie, Mich. | 2 | 0 | 0 | 0.5 | 1 | 2056 | 2057 | A | XX | NC |
| 29 | Estral Beach, Mich. | 1 | 0 | 1 | 0.5 | 1 | 1930 | 1931 | C | XX | NN |
| 30 | Windsor, Mich.-Ont. | 2 | 2 | 2 | 6 | 8 | 2009 | 2016 | B | XX | NN |
| 31 | Fountaintown, Ind. | 3 | 3 | 4 | 17 | 20 | 1450 | 1510 | A | 7 | 9 |
| 32 | Kennard, Ind. | 4 | 3 | 4 | 20 | 23 | 1502 | 1525 | A | 7 | 9 |
| 33 | Parker, Ind. | 4 | 3 | 4 | 22 | 23 | 1535 | 1558 | A | 7 | 9 |
| 34 | Orleans, Ind. | 1 | 3 | 3 | 13 | 17 | 1403 | 1420 | B | 8 | 10 |
| 35 | Medora, Ind. | 3 | 4 | 4 | 38 | 50 | 1415 | 1505 | B | 8 | 10 |
| 36 | Hamburg, Ind. | 4 | 4 | 4 | 37 | 42 | 1500 | 1542 | B | 8 | 10 |
| 37 | Xenia, Ohio | 5 | 4 | 3 | 32 | 37 | 1532 | 1609 | A | 9 | 11 |
| 38 | London, Ohio | 2 | 3 | 2 | 15 | 19 | 1601 | 1620 | A | 9 | 11 |
| 39 | New Albany, Ohio | 2 | 2 | 2 | 5 | 5 | 1713 | 1718 | C | 9 | 11 |
| 40 | Depauw, Ind. | 5 | 4 | 5 | 62 | 69 | 1416 | 1525 | B | 10 | 12 |
| 41 | Madison, Ind. | 4 | 4 | 4 | 38 | 47 | 1519 | 1606 | B | 10 | 12 |
| 42 | Bear Branch, Ind. | 4 | 3 | 4 | 28 | 25 | 1604 | 1629 | A | 10 | 12 |
| 43 | Sayler Park, Ohio | 5 | 3 | 3 | 21 | 23 | 1628 | 1651 | B | 10 | 12 |
| 44 | Mason, Ohio | 4 | 3 | 3 | 20 | 22 | 1652 | 1714 | B | 10 | 12 |
| 45 | Lebanon, Ohio | 2 | 3 | 3 | 10 | 10 | 1712 | 1722 | B | 10 | 12 |
| 46 | Frewsburg, N.Y. | 0 | 0 | 0 | 0.5 | 1 | 2157 | 2158 | A | XX | NIS |

**Table 3.2.** *Continued*

| | | F scale[a] | $P_L$[a] | $P_W$[a] | Length (miles) | Duration (minutes) | Touchdown time (CDST) | Lift-off time (CDST) | Confidence[b] | Family[c] | Echo[d] |
|---|---|---|---|---|---|---|---|---|---|---|---|
| 47 | Brandenburg, Ky. | 5 | 4 | 4 | 34 | 52 | 1530 | 1622 | A | 11 | 13 |
| 48 | Louisville, Ky. | 4 | 3 | 3 | 21 | 22 | 1637 | 1659 | A | 11 | 13 |
| 49 | New Castle, Ky. | 1 | 3 | 2 | 21 | 23 | 1704 | 1727 | B | 11 | 13 |
| 50 | Circleville, Ohio | 0 | 1 | 0 | 1 | 1 | 1718 | 1719 | A | XX | NC |
| 51 | Peebles, Ohio | 3 | 3 | 3 | 16 | 17 | 1920 | 1937 | B | UU | NC |
| 52 | Caneyville, Ky. | 4 | 3 | 2 | 28 | 34 | 1600 | 1634 | B | 12 | 14 |
| 53 | Elizabethtown, Ky. | 4 | 4 | 4 | 42 | 50 | 1643 | 1733 | A | 12 | 14 |
| 54 | Frankfort, Ky. | 4 | 4 | 4 | 36 | 38 | 1750 | 1828 | B | 12 | 14 |
| 55 | Cynthiana, Ky. | 3 | 3 | 4 | 25 | 26 | 1855 | 1921 | B | 12 | 14 |
| 56 | Aberdeen, Ky.-Ohio | 1 | 2 | 3 | 9 | 10 | 1910 | 1920 | E | UU | NC |
| 57 | Georgetown, Ky. | 2 | 3 | 4 | 14 | 15 | 2013 | 2028 | B | XX | 16 |
| 58 | Harrodsburg, Ky. | 2 | 3 | 5 | 18 | 20 | 1915 | 1935 | A | 13 | 15 |
| 59 | Valley View, Ky. | 2 | 2 | 1 | 9 | 10 | 1945 | 1955 | C | 13 | 15 |
| 60 | Springfield, Tenn. | 0 | 2 | 1 | 6 | 6 | 1605 | 1611 | B | 14 | 18 |
| 61 | Franklin, Ky. | 3 | 3 | 3 | 25 | 31 | 1634 | 1705 | B | 14 | 18 |
| 62 | Mannsville, Ky. | 4 | 3 | 4 | 29 | 28 | 1740 | 1808 | B | 14 | 18 |
| 63 | Danville, Ky. | 3 | 3 | 5 | 18 | 21 | 1835[e] | 1855 | B | 14 | 18 |
| 64 | Richmond, Ky. | 4 | 4 | 4 | 35 | 39 | 1918 | 1957 | B | 14 | 18 |
| 65 | Camargo, Ky. | 1 | 2 | 3 | 7 | 8 | 2005 | 2013 | B | 14 | 18 |
| 66 | Somerset, Ky. | 3 | 3 | 3 | 24 | 30 | 2235 | 2305 | B | XX | NN |
| 67 | Nashville, Tenn. | 2 | 3 | 3 | 12 | 13 | 1707 | 1720 | A | 15 | 19 |
| 68 | Taylorsville, Tenn. | 3 | 3 | 3 | 21 | 23 | 1750 | 1813 | A | 15 | 19 |
| 69 | Ida, Ky. | 4 | 3 | 4 | 30 | 29 | 1835 | 1904 | B | 15 | 19 |
| 70 | Parnell, Ky. | 3 | 3 | 4 | 24 | 28 | 1856 | 1924 | B | 15 | 19 |
| 71 | Rally Hill, Tenn. | 1 | 3 | 2 | 10 | 12 | 1725 | 1737 | C | 16 | 20 |
| 72 | Lascassas, Tenn. | 3 | 3 | 2 | 19 | 23 | 1803 | 1826 | C | 16 | 20 |
| 73 | First Livingston, Tenn. | 1 | 2 | 3 | 4 | 5 | 2020 | 2025 | C | 17 | 21 |
| 74 | Cumberland, Ky. | 4 | 3 | 5 | 26 | 28 | 2004 | 2032 | R | 16 | 20 |
| 75 | Laurel Ridge, Tenn. | 2 | 3 | 4 | 20 | 20 | 2015 | 2035 | C | 16 | 20 |
| 76 | Honeybee, Ky. | 2 | 3 | 3 | 13 | 15 | 2030 | 2045 | R | 16 | 20 |
| 77 | London, Ky. | 0 | 3 | 2 | 3 | 4 | 2105 | 2109 | R | 16 | 20 |
| 78 | Cedar Grove, Tenn. | 1 | 3 | 3 | 15 | 20 | 1814 | 1834 | C | 17 | 21 |
| 79 | Farmington, Tenn. | 1 | 3 | 3 | 26 | 31 | 1814 | 1845 | B | 17 | 21 |
| 80 | Dowellton, Tenn. | 3 | 3 | 3 | 15 | 18 | 1917 | 1935 | C | 17 | 21 |
| 81 | Dodson Branch, Tenn. | 1 | 3 | 2 | 10 | 12 | 1955 | 2007 | C | 17 | 21 |
| 82 | Moodyville, Tenn.-Ky. | 4 | 3 | 3 | 19 | 25 | 2025 | 2050 | B | 17 | 21 |
| 83 | Alpine, Ky. | 3 | 3 | 4 | 29 | 35 | 2035 | 2100 | C | 17 | 21 |
| 84 | Daniel Boone, Ky. | 3 | 3 | 5 | 30 | 35 | 1955 | 2030 | C | 15 | 19 |
| 85 | Second Livingston, Tenn. | 3 | 3 | 3 | 13 | 15 | 2330 | 2345 | C | XX | NN |
| 86 | Cookeville, Tenn. | 4 | 4 | 4 | 32 | 34 | 2005 | 2039 | C | 18 | 22 |
| 87 | Obey River, Tenn. | 4 | 3 | 4 | 13 | 16 | 2041 | 2057 | C | 18 | 22 |
| 88 | Corbin, Ky. | 3 | 3 | 2 | 21 | 25 | 2055 | 2120 | B | 16 | 20 |
| 89 | Black Oak, Tenn. | 2 | 3 | 2 | 12 | 13 | 2348 | 0001 | B | XX | NN |
| 90 | Board Valley, Tenn. | 1 | 2 | 2 | 4 | 5 | 0030 | 0035 | D | XX | NN |
| 91 | Ostella, Tenn. | 1 | 3 | 2 | 28 | 30 | 2300 | 2330 | D | XX | NN |
| 92 | Midway, Tenn. | 1 | 3 | 1 | 11 | 13 | 2333 | 2346 | B | 19 | NN |
| 93 | Crossville, Tenn. | 3 | 3 | 3 | 26 | 30 | 0030 | 0100 | C | 19 | NN |
| 94 | Coal Hill, Tenn. | 3 | 3 | 3 | 12 | 15 | 0050 | 0105 | C | XX | NN |
| 95 | Phil Campbell, Ala. | 2 | 3 | 2 | 12 | 14 | 1801 | 1815 | B | 20 | 23 |
| 96 | First Tanner, Ala. | 5 | 4 | 3 | 51 | 61 | 1820 | 1921 | B | 20 | 23 |
| 97 | Harmony, Tenn. | 4 | 4 | 3 | 36 | 40 | 1945 | 2025 | B | 20 | 23 |
| 98 | Second Tanner, Ala.-Tenn. | 4 | 4 | 3 | 50 | 55 | 1930 | 2025 | B | 21 | 37 |
| 99 | Rutledge Hill, Tenn. | 3 | 3 | 2 | 20 | 22 | 2040 | 2102 | B | 21 | 37 |
| 100 | Shiloh, Tenn. | 3 | 3 | 3 | 16 | 18 | 2104 | 2122 | B | 21 | 37 |

**Table 3.2.** *Continued*

| | | F scale[a] | $P_L$[a] | $P_W$[a] | Length (miles) | Duration (minutes) | Touchdown time (CDST) | Lift-off time (CDST) | Confidence[b] | Family[c] | Echo[d] |
|---|---|---|---|---|---|---|---|---|---|---|---|
| 101 | Guin, Miss.-Ala. | 5 | 5 | 3 | 102 | 122 | 2025 | 2257 | B | 22 | 24 |
| 102 | Huntsville, Ala. | 3 | 4 | 4 | 41 | 58 | 2229 | 2327 | A | 22 | 24 |
| 103 | Jasper, Ala. | 4 | 5 | 3 | 103 | 124 | 1844 | 2048 | A | 23 | 29 |
| 104 | Concord, Ala. | 2 | 1 | 3 | 1 | 1 | 1615 | 1616 | C | XX | 30 |
| 105 | Laurel, Miss. | 3 | 3 | 1 | 12 | 19 | 1700 | 1719 | C | XX | 31 |
| 106 | Big Ridge, Tenn. | 0 | 2 | 3 | 9 | 10 | 0220 | 0230 | C | XX | NN |
| 107 | Sunrise, Tenn. | 2 | 2 | 2 | 4 | 4 | 0030 | 0035 | C | XX | NN |
| 108 | Mill Springs, Tenn. | 0 | 2 | 1 | 5 | 5 | 0155 | 0200 | C | XX | NN |
| 109 | Meadow View, Tenn. | 1 | 2 | 1 | 6 | 7 | 1533 | 1540 | C | XX | NN |
| 110 | Greenback, Tenn. | 2 | 1 | 2 | 2 | 2 | 1709 | 1711 | A | XX | NN |
| 111 | Prospect, Tenn. | 1 | 1 | 1 | 1 | 1 | 1509 | 1510 | C | XX | NN |
| 112 | First Etowah, Tenn. | 1 | 2 | 1 | 4 | 5 | 1400 | 1405 | D | XX | 25 |
| 113 | First Cleveland, Tenn. | 3 | 3 | 3 | 13 | 23 | 1403 | 1426 | B | XX | 27 |
| 114 | Cleveland-Etowah, Tenn. | 3 | 3 | 3 | 24 | 31 | 1555 | 1626 | A | 24 | 26 |
| 115 | Ball Play, Tenn. | 1 | 2 | 1 | 9 | 13 | 1637 | 1650 | C | 24 | 26 |
| 116 | Appalachia Dam, N.C. | 0 | 1 | 1 | 3 | 4 | 1955 | 1959 | B | 26 | 33 |
| 117 | Stecoah, N.C. | 2 | 3 | 3 | 12 | 15 | 1910 | 1925 | C | XX | 28 |
| 118 | Weiss Lake, Ala. | 3 | 3 | 2 | 14 | 13 | 1735 | 1748 | B | 26 | 33 |
| 119 | Resaca, Ga. | 4 | 3 | 2 | 26 | 30 | 1830 | 1900 | C | 26 | 33 |
| 120 | Blue Ridge, Ga. | 3 | 3 | 1 | 17 | 26 | 1940 | 2006 | B | 25 | 32 |
| 121 | Murphy, Ga.-N.C. | 4 | 3 | 3 | 22 | 30 | 2015 | 2045 | B | 25 | 32 |
| 122 | Cherrylog Creek, Ga. | 0 | 1 | 0 | 1 | 1 | UUUU | UUUU | U | UU | UU |
| 123 | Cherrylog, Ga. | 2 | 3 | 3 | 19 | 30 | 1350 | 1420 | B | 33 | 35 |
| 124 | First Brasstown, N.C. | 0 | 0 | 0 | 0.5 | 1 | 1440 | 1441 | C | 33 | 35 |
| 125 | Stanley Creek, Ga. | 0 | 0 | 0 | 0.5 | 1 | 0500 | 0501 | E | XX | NN |
| 126 | Duke, Ala. | 1 | 1 | 4 | 1 | 1 | 1721 | 1722 | B | 26 | 33 |
| 127 | Acworth, Ala.-Ga. | 2 | 4 | 2 | 65 | 91 | 1729 | 1900 | B | 27 | 36 |
| 128 | Juno, Ga. | 4 | 3 | 3 | 24 | 31 | 1922 | 1953 | B | 27 | 36 |
| 129 | Second Brasstown, N.C. | 0 | 0 | 0 | 0.5 | 1 | 0800 | 0801 | D | XX | NN |
| 130 | Mountain City, Ga. | 0 | 0 | 0 | 0.5 | 1 | 1409 | 1410 | D | XX | NN |
| 131 | Dillard, Ga. | 0 | 0 | 0 | 0.5 | 1 | 2100 | 2101 | C | 27 | 36 |
| 132 | East Fork, N.C. | 0 | 1 | 0 | 1 | 1 | 1600 | 1601 | D | XX | NN |
| 133 | Del Rio, Tenn. | 0 | 0 | 0 | 0.5 | 1 | 0945 | 0946 | D | XX | NN |
| 134 | Rogersville, Tenn. | 0 | 0 | 0 | 0.5 | 1 | 0250 | 0251 | D | 30 | NIS |
| 135 | Leonard Town, Tenn.-Va. | 0 | 3 | 5 | 26 | 30 | 0320 | 0350 | C | 30 | NIS |
| 136 | Beckley, W.Va. | 1 | 1 | 1 | 2 | 2 | 0326 | 0328 | B | 28 | NIS |
| 137 | Meadow Bridge, W.Va. | 3 | 4 | 5 | 35 | 40 | 0330 | 0410 | C | 28 | NIS |
| 138 | Breaks, Va. | 1 | 2 | 1 | 5 | 5 | 0200 | 0205 | D | 29 | NIS |
| 139 | Mullensville, W.Va. | 1 | 2 | 1 | 9 | 10 | 0300 | 0310 | C | 29 | NIS |
| 140 | Shady Spring, W.Va. | 3 | 3 | 3 | 12 | 14 | 0314 | 1328 | B | 29 | NIS |
| 141 | Welch, W.Va. | 0 | 0 | 0 | 0.5 | 1 | 0300 | 0301 | D | 31 | NIS |
| 142 | Hinton, W.Va. | 1 | 0 | 0 | 0.5 | 1 | 0340 | 0341 | B | 31 | NIS |
| 143 | Jonesville, Va. | 0 | 2 | 0 | 8 | 9 | UUUU | UUUU | U | XX | NIS |
| 144 | Saltville, Va. | 3 | 2 | 3 | 9 | 11 | 0315 | 0326 | B | XX | NIS |
| 145 | Staunton, Va. | 1 | 3 | 1 | 18 | 20 | 0607 | 0627 | C | XX | NIS |
| 146 | Roanoke, Va. | 2 | 2 | 3 | 9 | 11 | 0452 | 0503 | A | XX | NIS |
| 147 | Morganton, N.C. | 1 | 1 | 0 | 1 | 5 | 0830 | 0835 | E | 32 | NIS |
| 148 | Baton, N.C. | 2 | 2 | 1 | 5 | 5 | 0845 | 0850 | E | 32 | NIS |

[a] F, $P_L$, and $P_W$ are maximum intensity, mean length, and mean width in categories from 1 to 5.

[b] Time-list confidence:

| A | within 3 minutes |
|---|---|
| B | 7 |
| C | 15 |
| D | 30 |
| E | 60 |
| R | fit to agree with radar |

[c] XX = none; UU = unknown.

[d] NN = not distinctive; NC = not covered; NIS = not in survey area.

[e] The Danville tornado touched down momentarily from 1810 to 1811.

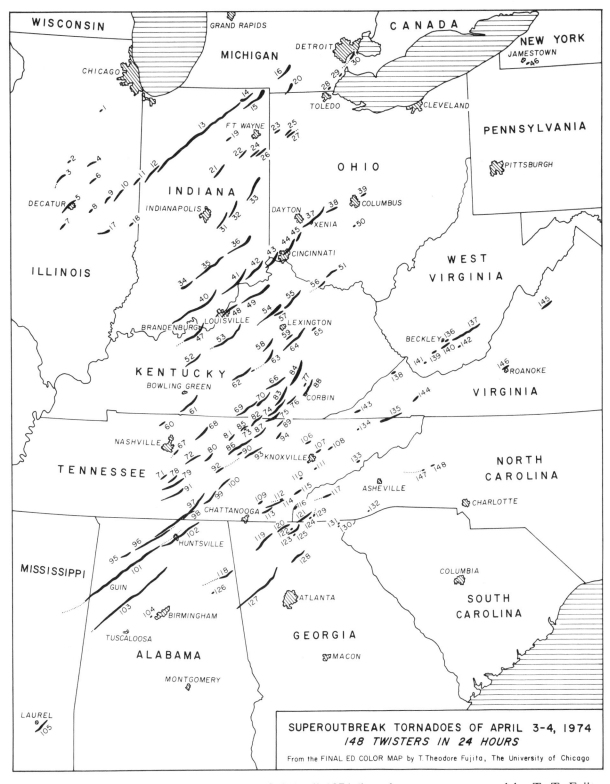

**Figure 3.1.** Paths of the 148 tornadoes on 3-4 April 1974 (based on a map prepared by T. T. Fujita at the University of Chicago).

caused relatively little damage. More than half of the deaths were caused by less than 5% of the tornadoes; the worst single tornado struck Xenia, Ohio, killing 34 persons and injuring 1,150. Each of the six most destructive tornadoes had paths longer than 50 km; the path lengths of two exceeded 160 km.

Fujita (1975) plotted the paths of 148 tornadoes and surveyed their damage (Fig. 3.1; one of these storms was subsequently reclassified as a tornado cyclone, i.e., a whirlwind that is larger but less intense than a tornado and is often a tornado spawning ground). The statistical aspects of each tornado that touched down between 1310 CDT on 3 April and 0520 CDT on 4 April are listed in Table 3.2; numbers are assigned in relation to eastward and southward progression of tornado and tornado-family occurrences, as shown in Fig. 3.1. The total length of the paths was 2,572 miles for 32 tornado families (Table 3.3) and one additional long-track tornado (Jasper, 103).

The classification scheme developed by Fujita and Pearson (the FPP scale, 1973) rates tornadoes with three numbers (e.g., 3, 2, 3) to describe maximum intensity as estimated from damage done, path length, and path width; 5 is the most intense (i.e., greatest damage, hence strongest inferred winds), the longest and the widest, respectively. Estimated winds range from 40 to about 250 mi/h, the path length from less than 1 to more than 100 mi, and path widths from less than 50 ft to more

than 3 mi. The first number in the classification is often used alone as a gross description of a tornado, since damage done is its most essential attribute; the mean F-scale intensities of groups of tornadoes are shown in Fig. 3.2. Figure 3.3 depicts the distribution of tornadoes and deaths by intensity; 99% of the deaths resulted from violent (F4-F5) tornadoes.

Fujita rated six tornadoes F5; that is, they produced some of the extreme damage characterized as 5: Xenia, Ohio (number 37 in Table 3.2); De-Pauw, Indiana (40); Sayler Park, Ohio (43); Brandenburg, Kentucky (47); First Tanner, Alabama (96); and Guin, Alabama (101). Five cities were struck twice by major tornadoes: Etowah, Tennessee (at 1505 and 1705); Tanner, Alabama (1900 and 1930); Harvest, Alabama (1915 and 1945); Huntsville, Alabama (2255 and 2305); Livingston, Tennessee (1930 and 2330; all times are CDT unless otherwise indicated).

Distributions of duration of individual tornadoes and tornado families are shown in Figs. 3.4 and 3.5. The median duration was 15 min, the mean duration was 20 min, and the longest was 124 min (number 103). The median family duration, from first touchdown to last lift-off, was 92 min with a maximum of approximately 252 min. As computed by Forbes (1978), 76% of the individual tornadoes occurred in families, and more than 95% of the deaths were from tornadoes in families. Nevertheless, the longer duration of tornado families sug-

**Table 3.3.** Tornado Families

| Family and associated tornadoes* | Echo† | Max F | Time of first tornado | Time of last tornado | Family duration (minutes) | Cumulative tornado duration (minutes) |
|---|---|---|---|---|---|---|
| 1 Anchor 3, 4 | 1 | 3 | 1403 | 1457 | 54 | 25 |
| 2 Decatur 5, 6 | 2 | 3 | 1430 | 1527 | 57 | 33 |
| 3 Monticello 7–14 | 3 | 4 | 1447 | 1859 | 252 | 199 |
| 4 Angola 15, 16 | 4 | 3 | 1853 | 1959 | 66 | 51 |
| 5 Swayzee 21–23 | 8N | 2 | 1845 | 2023 | 98 | 40 |
| 6 Melrose 24, 26, 25 | 8S | 2 | 1915 | 2034 | 79 | 35 |
| 7 Parker 31–33 | 9 | 4 | 1450 | 1558 | 68 | 66 |

**Table 3.3.** *Continued*

| Family and associated tornadoes* | Echo† | Max F | Time of first tornado | Time of last tornado | Family duration (minutes) | Cumulative tornado duration (minutes) |
|---|---|---|---|---|---|---|
| 8  Hamburg<br>34-36 | 10 | 4 | 1403 | 1542 | 99 | 109 |
| 9  Xenia<br>37-39 | 11 | 5 | 1532 | 1718 | 106 | 61 |
| 10  Depauw<br>40-45 | 12 | 5 | 1416 | 1722 | 186 | 196 |
| 11  Louisville<br>47-49 | 13 | 5 | 1530 | 1727 | 117 | 97 |
| 12  Elizabethtown<br>52-55 | 14 | 4 | 1643 | 1921 | 158 | 148 |
| 13  Harrodsburg<br>58, 59 | 15 | 2 | 1915 | 1955 | 40 | 30 |
| 14  Franklin<br>60-65 | 18 | 4 | 1605 | 2013 | 248 | 133 |
| 15  Nashville<br>67-70, 84 | 19 | 4 | 1707 | 2030 | 203 | 128 |
| 16  Lascassas<br>71, 72, 74-77, 88 | 20 | 4 | 1725 | 2120 | 235 | 127 |
| 17  Dowellton<br>78, 80, 81, 73, 82, 83, 79 | 21 | 4 | 1814 | 2135 | 201 | 146 |
| 18  Cookeville<br>86, 87 | 22 | 4 | 2005 | 2057 | 52 | 50 |
| 19  Crossville<br>92, 93 | NN | 3 | 2333 | 0100 | 87 | 43 |
| 20  First Tanner<br>95-97 | 23 | 5 | 1801 | 2025 | 144 | 115 |
| 21  Second Tanner<br>98-100 | 37 | 4 | 1930 | 2122 | 112 | 95 |
| 22  Guin<br>101, 102 | 24 | 5 | 2025 | 2327 | 182 | 180 |
| 23  Jasper<br>103, long-track | 29 | 4 | 1844 | 2048 | 124 | 124 |
| 24  Cleveland-Etowah<br>114, 115 | 26 | 3 | 1555 | 1650 | 55 | 44 |
| 25  Murphy<br>120, 121 | 32 | 4 | 1940 | 2045 | 65 | 56 |
| 26  Duke<br>126, 118, 119, 116 | 33 | 4 | 1721 | 1959 | 158 | 48 |
| 27  Acworth<br>127, 128, 131 | 36 | 4 | 1729 | 2101 | 212 | 123 |
| 28  Beckley<br>136, 137 | NIS | 3 | 0326 | 0410 | 44 | 42 |
| 29  Shady Spring<br>138-40 | NIS | 3 | 0200 | 0328 | 88 | 29 |
| 30  Leonard Town<br>134, 135 | NIS | 0 | 0250 | 0350 | 60 | 31 |
| 31  Hinton<br>141, 142 | NIS | 1 | 0300 | 0341 | 41 | 2 |
| 32  Baton<br>147, 148 | NIS | 2 | 0830 | 0850 | 20 | 10 |
| 33  Cherrylog<br>123, 124 | 35 | 2 | 1350 | 1441 | 51 | 31 |

*Numbers under the family name refer to tornadoes that belong to the family, as numbered in Table 3.2.
†NN = not distinctive; NIS = not in survey area.

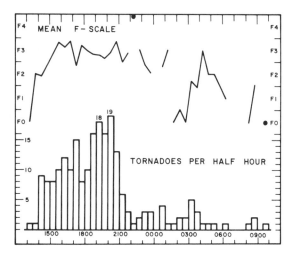

**Figure 3.2.** Rate of tornado occurrence 3-4 April 1974 and the mean F-scale intensity of each group.

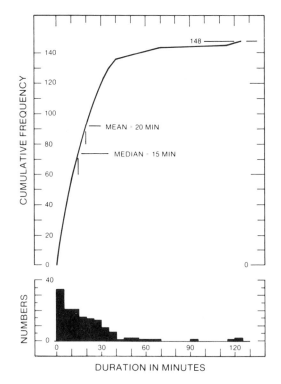

**Figure 3.4.** Duration of individual tornadoes and cumulative frequency of individual tornadoes.

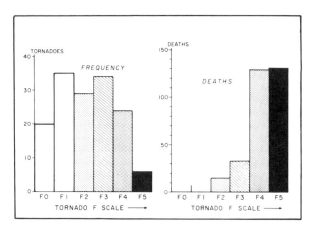

**Figure 3.3.** Tornado frequency and deaths as a function of F-scale intensity.

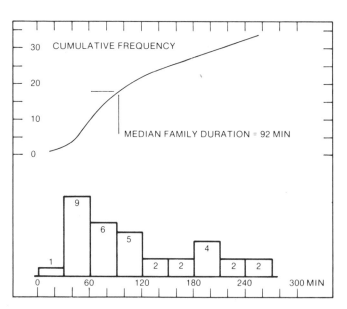

**Figure 3.5.** Duration of tornado families. The horizontal axis indicates the duration of tornado families whose number is indicated by the height of the bars and the numeral within. The cumulative frequency of tornado-family durations is indicated by the sloping line at top.

gests that warnings are likely to be more effective for tornado families than for individual tornadoes.

Mortality data are given in Figs. 3.6-3.9. Deaths peak more strongly after 1800 (Fig. 3.6) than does the frequency of tornado occurrence (Fig. 3.2), suggesting greater vulnerability of population during evening than afternoon. Figure 3.7 indicates the relatively great vulnerability of rural areas; only about 40% of the population in the affected states live in rural areas and in communities of

(conditionally unstable air overturns following a substantial upward impulse).

The intense surface low moved from north-central Kansas northeastward to the Iowa-Illinois border during the day on 3 April. The strong fields of convergence at low altitudes and rising motion associated with this storm system entered the Ohio and Tennessee valleys, northern Gulf states, and southern Appalachian areas. Low-level heating over most of the region combined with the large-scale forcing and triggered intense convection and resultant severe weather.

Purdom (1974), Fujita and Forbes (1974), and Agee et al. (1975) analyzed the ATS-III satellite pictures taken every 13 min during this time. The positions of major tornadoes on the ATS-111 satellite photos are illustrated in Figs. 3.11a-c. At 1406 CDT, each squall line in Fig. 3.11a is producing tornadoes. The DePauw (F5) tornado (number 40 in Table 3.2) forms in line B. By 1512 CDT (Fig. 3.11b) the Pierson tornado (number 8) of the Monticello family is occurring within line A (this largest family in the superoutbreak is charted in Fig. 3.13). At 1538 CDT (Fig. 3.11c) line B is producing the Xenia (F5, number 37, in Table 3.2), Parker (F4, number 33), Hamburg (F4, number 36), Madison (F4, number 41), and Brandenburg (F5, number 17) tornadoes. All superoutbreak tornadoes occurred within the area of these distinct squall lines. Most tornadoes were located within the large active thunderstorm cells characterized by rapidly growing anvils and a clear area to the west.

In addition to information from analysis of the ATS-III satellite photos, photographs of radar plan position indicators (PPI) provide insight into the behavior and characteristics of tornadoes. Investigations using PPI photographs deal with (1) radar echo shape as an indicator of tornado occurrence; (2) systematic differences in the movement of tornadic and nontornadic storms as revealed by the radar echoes; and (3) thunderstorm-scale features associated with formation of left- or right-turn tornado families. For example, a prominent hook-shaped echo is often associated with a tornado in the same area (Forbes, 1975). The radar screen in Fig. 3.12 shows a hook echo of classic shape associated with the Hamburg, Indiana, tornado storm, as photographed on the radar display at Covington, Kentucky, at 1521 CDT on 3 April. In the

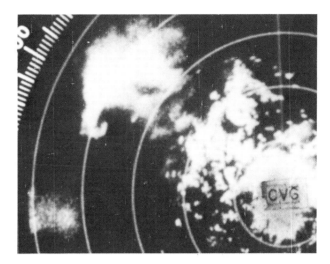

**Figure 3.12.** Hamburg, Ind., F4 tornado storm as seen by radar at Covington, Ky., 1521 CDST, 3 April 1974. Range marks are at 10-mi intervals.

superoutbreak such hook echoes were associated with 81% of the 93 tornadoes studied. Of the hook echoes, 72% were associated with at least one tornado, and all F4- and F5-intensity tornadoes were associated with hook echoes. The mean intensity of all tornadoes identified with hook-shaped echoes

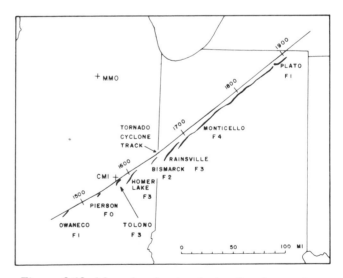

**Figure 3.13.** Map showing track details of tornadoes constituting the Monticello family. The centroid of the parent storm moved from the southwest along the path indicated by the solid line and produced tornadoes intermittently.

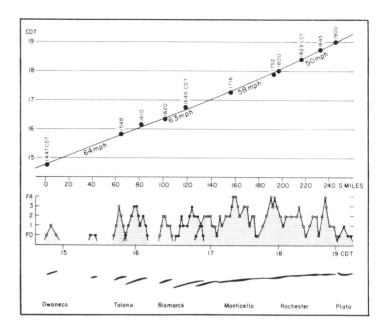

**Figure 3.14.** (Below) Intensity variation with time of the eight tornadoes constituting the Monticello family. (Above) Some locations of particular tornadoes in time and position along the family path.

was F3, whereas the tornadoes not associated with a hook echo on radar had a mean intensity of F1. The tornadic hooklike echoes moved to the right of the nontornadic echoes representing squall lines and formed lines of tornadoes in advance. Fujita (1975) found that several of the stronger tornadoes (Brandenburg, Sayler Park, Louisville, and Xenia) moved out of their parent hook on reaching maturity or slightly thereafter, but the movement of the tornadoes did not appear to follow any systematic direction relative to the motion of the parent echo. Figures 3.13 and 3.14 depict variations in forward speed of storms and of intensity in the Monticello tornado family, which was associated with a spiral echo pattern.

Darkow and Livingston (1975) used hourly reports of the network of surface stations located at airports to examine the evolution of the surface static-energy fields on 3 April 1974. Small-scale variations in the surface static-energy fields were resolvable in the airways network data, and had an important relationship to the location and timing of severe storms as revealed by satellite and radar data.

**Warning Dissemination and Response**

All phases of the tornado warning system, from detection at the various NOAA offices, through communications and dissemination of warnings, to the public response to warning by the community and individual, were examined shortly after the 3-4 April tornado disaster (NOAA, 1974).

The warning system starts with observations and analyses. Thousands of observations are made each day at many locations, including NOAA's Weather Service Offices; Department of Defense installations; FAA-manned stations; special stations and networks such as spotter groups, cooperative observers, and law-enforcement officials; radar stations and upper-air observing sites; and satellite platforms. Basic severe-weather forecasts are prepared by the Severe Local Storms Unit (SELS) of the National Severe Storms Forecast Center (NSSFC) in Kansas City. These forecasts are termed Severe Thunderstorm Outlooks, Severe Thunderstorm Watches, and Tornado Watches. Local Weather Service Forecast Offices, which have designated county areas of responsibility, are charged with issuing specialized severe-weather forecasts for local use and preparing and issuing severe-weather warnings.

The potential threat of the April tornado out-

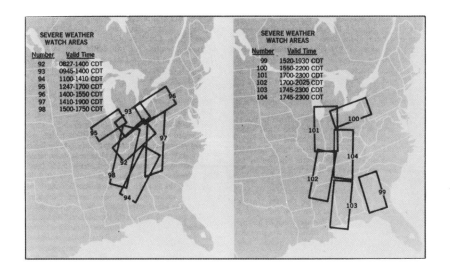

SEVERE WEATHER
WATCH AREAS

| Number | Valid Time |
|---|---|
| 92 | 0827-1400 CDT |
| 93 | 0945-1400 CDT |
| 94 | 1100-1410 CDT |
| 95 | 1247-1700 CDT |
| 96 | 1400-1550 CDT |
| 97 | 1410-1900 CDT |
| 98 | 1500-1750 CDT |

SEVERE WEATHER
WATCH AREAS

| Number | Valid Time |
|---|---|
| 99 | 1520-1930 CDT |
| 100 | 1550-2200 CDT |
| 101 | 1700-2300 CDT |
| 102 | 1700-2025 CDT |
| 103 | 1745-2300 CDT |
| 104 | 1745-2300 CDT |

**Figure 3.15.** Severe-weather watches issued on 3 April 1974. Watches 99 to 104 apply to the period of maximum storm activity (NOAA, 1974).

break was perceived as early as 0730 CDT on 2 April. Thus the 24-h outlook for the period beginning a day later at 0700 CDT on 3 April included almost all areas where tornado and severe-weather activity occurred in that 24-h period. The first Severe Thunderstorm Watch was issued at 0827 on 3 April. By noon, CDST, portions of 11 states were included in tornado or severe-thunderstorm-watch areas (Fig. 3.15); two tornado warnings and nine severe-thunderstorm warnings had been issued.

Although severe thunderstorms developed in Indiana as early as midmorning on 3 April and hail the size of golf balls was reported in South Carolina as late as evening 4 April, most tornadoes and resulting deaths and destruction occurred in the 12-h period between noon and midnight on 3 April. During this period 172 tornado warnings or extensions, 133 severe-thunderstorm warnings, and 15 tornado watches were issued in 18 states. Almost three-fourths of the tornado warnings were released in the 6-h period between 1400 and 2000. Between 1900 and 2000 alone, 26 tornado warnings or extensions were issued for portions of nine states. Figure 3.16 shows the total area covered by Severe Weather Watches, and Fig. 3.17 depicts the counties in 14 states for which tornado warnings were issued 3–4 April 1974. There were only weak tornadoes on the borders of two states where tornado warnings had not been issued, and one state for which warnings were issued gave no evidence of tornado occurrences.

The dissemination portion of a warning system comprises a complex mix of communication channels. In the April outbreak most radio and television stations interrupted normal programming to announce warnings as they were received. In Brandenburg the announcer at FM station WMMG observed the tornado coming and broadcast a warning continuously until the station was destroyed. The National Warning System, operated by the Defense Civil Preparedness Agency, provided an effective communication link during the outbreak. The NOAA Weather Radio with its tone alert was valuable for sending warnings rapidly from the

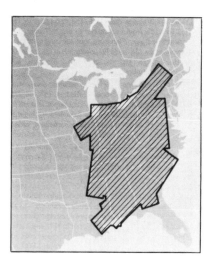

**Figure 3.16.** Total area covered by severe weather watches 92-119 (NOAA, 1974).

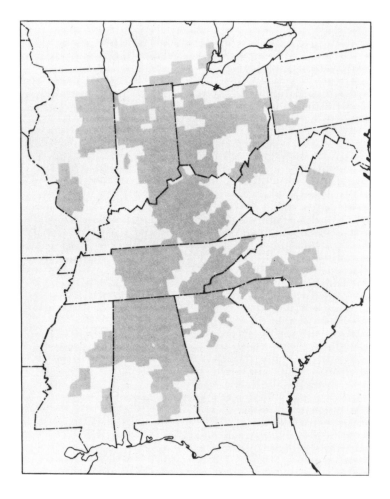

**Figure 3.17.** Geographic areas by counties for tornado warnings issued 3-4 April 1974 (NOAA, 1974).

warning office to the general public, schools, hospitals, local-action officials, and mass media for immediate rebroadcast.

The public response to severe-weather watches broadcast over radio and television probably reduced loss of life. In the hardest-hit areas, only a few of those interviewed had been unaware that severe weather threatened.

The value of prior education was demonstrated by individual actions when the tornadoes came. People went to basements or storm cellars if possible and shared them with neighbors. Others went into closets, under furniture or stairwells, or into halls of large, well-constructed brick buildings. They got out of gymnasiums and large open rooms, stayed away from windows, and protected their heads from flying debris.

As behavioral scientists have noted, the actions of the people and organizations seemed to be directly related to their experience. Where tornadoes are frequent, as in Alabama, community and individual readiness was high, preparations were made earlier, and people tended to be responsive to warnings. Of course, there are always some people who, for various reasons of training or the lack of it and personal psyche, ignore warnings and seek safety only as a tornado is in sight and approaching.

## Photogrammetric Analyses of Three Violent Tornadoes

Photographs reveal the spatial arrangement of condensation boundaries, i.e., cloud edges, that can be linked qualitatively and mathematically to the associated motions and forces. By tracking dust and debris tags, windspeeds along the outer edge of the tornado can be calculated, and measurements on the photographs can be related to associated damage along the tornado track (Fujita et al., 1976; Golden, 1976).

Of the 147 tornadoes on 3-4 April 1974, three of the most violent, at Xenia and Sayler, Ohio (both F5), and Parker (Muncie), Indiana (F4), were photographed along part of their paths of destruction. Each of these tornadoes exhibited suction vortices, or small-scale multiple-vortex phenomena, discussed by Fujita (1971) and modeled experimentally by Ward (1972).

In Xenia, Ohio, there was no evidence that the funnel reached the ground during the most destructive period. The storm started as two small funnel clouds twisting around each other (Fig. 3.18a). As the storm intensified, the funnel took on various shapes like those in Figs. 3.18b and 3.18c. Twin vortices can be seen in Fig. 3.18d. One of the vortices was moving right to left (west to east) at about 90 m/s (200 mi/h). The dust column, about 10 m across, was spinning up to 45 m/s. The damage of the Xenia tornado (Fig. 3.19) was most severe in swaths identified with the suction vortices.

The apparent dust motion (Fig. 3.20) was computed by tracking clusters of dust clouds in successive motion-picture frames (Fujita et al., 1976).

**Figure 3.18a-d.** Xenia, Ohio, tornado. a, 1630 CDST; b, 1635; c, 1639; d, 1640. Note twin suction vortices. (Photo a by K. W. Ross; photos b, c, and d by Terry Hess.)

**Figure 3.19.** Damage path of Xenia, Ohio, tornado through Arrowhead subdivision.

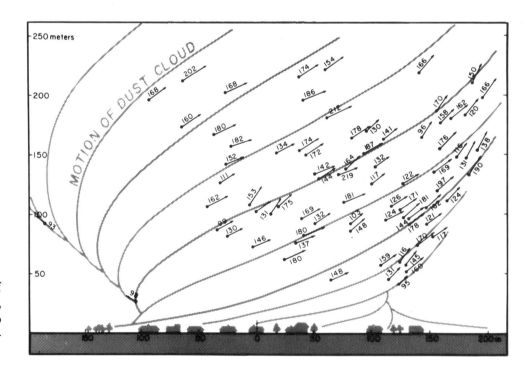

**Figure 3.20.** Speeds of dust aggregates in mi/h, in Xenia, Ohio, tornado tracked photogrammetrically.

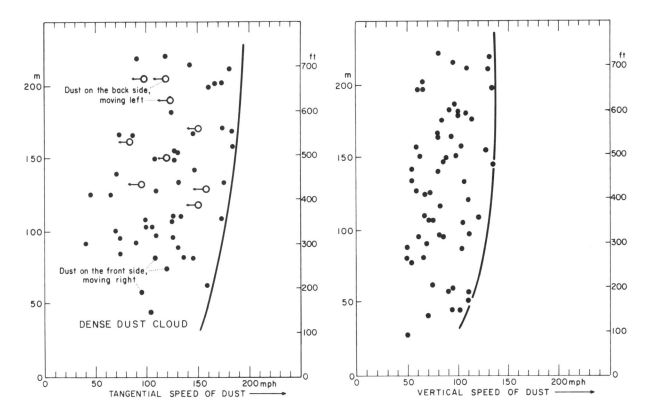

**Figure 3.21.** (Left) Tangential speeds of dust as a function of height in the Xenia, Ohio, tornado. The vertical-trending line is the envelope of maximum observed velocities. (Right) Vertical speeds of dust in the same tornado.

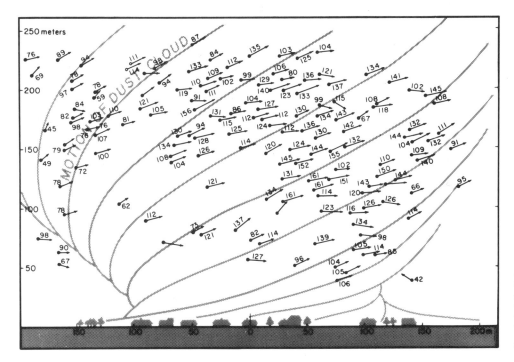

**Figure 3.22.** Speeds of debris in mi/h, in the Xenia, Ohio, tornado, tracked photogrammetrically.

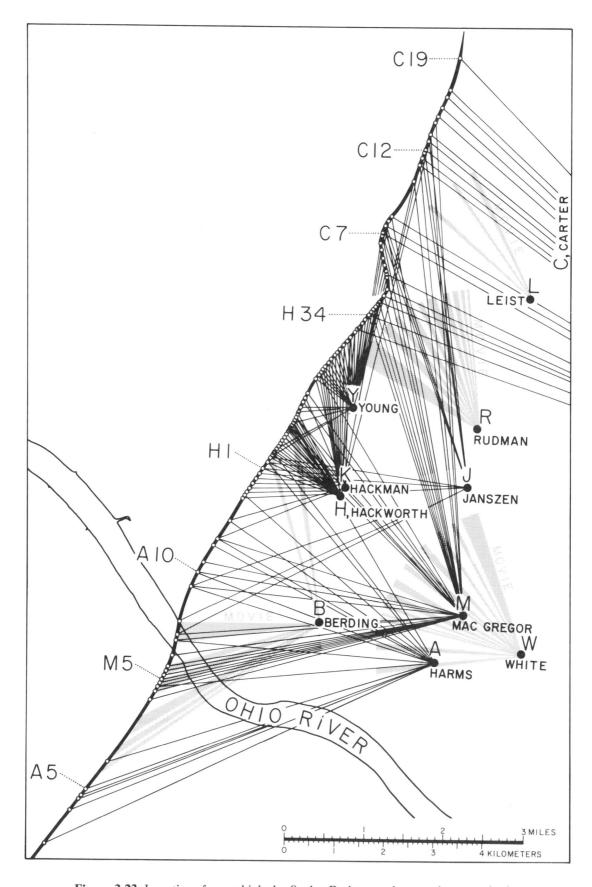

**Figure 3.23.** Locations from which the Sayler Park tornado was photographed.

**Figure 3.24.** The Sayler Park, Ohio, tornado exhibited a lowering and expansion of the cloud mass as it crossed the Ohio River. (Photo by Andrew MacGregor.)

The maximum 1-s windspeed (219 mi/h) appears at a height of 140 m. The tangential speeds relative to the tornado center were plotted versus the height above the ground (Fig. 3.21). The heavy line represents the highest tangential speeds of the dust clouds (150 to 190 mi/h). The high tangential speeds of suction vortices are likely to exist down to the level of building and treetops if not to the ground. The vertical speeds, computed as the vertical component of the apparent dust motion in Fig. 3.20, are also presented.

Additional data of this kind would provide a

**Figure 3.25.** Sayler Park, Ohio, tornado exhibiting characteristic ropelike structure just before its dissipation. (Photo by Jay Carter.)

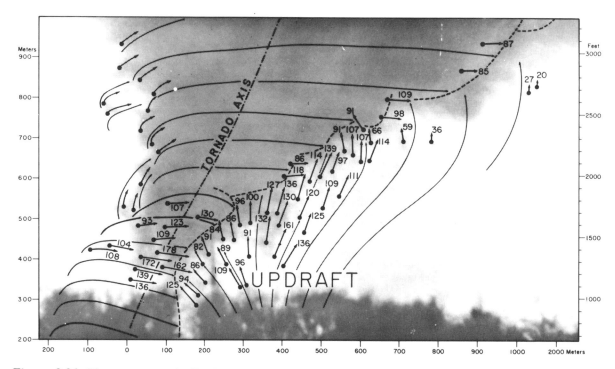

**Figure 3.26.** Photogrammetrically determined windspeeds in mi/h in the Sayler Park, Ohio, tornado as it crossed the Ohio River. The updraft is located in advance of the funnel cloud.

basis for firm assessment of wind that is characteristic of strong tornadoes. It appears from the photogrammetric measurements of the Xenia tornado that an F5 wind near the ground may be experienced only inside suction vortex swaths on the right side of the tornado path. Thus, an F5 wind will persist for less than 2 s in a very narrow swath, probably only 20 m wide. Detailed analysis of damage patterns can be found in Abbey and Fujita (1975, 1978).

The behavior of debris in tornadic wind fields depends on the shape, size, and density of particles, with grains of dust most nearly tracing the path of the wind. Figure 3.22 shows the vectors of apparent debris motion in the Xenia tornado. Most debris trajectories appear to be more horizontal than the dust aggregates, and the debris usually moves at a slower velocity. The maximum measured 1-s debris speed was 161 mi/h at a height of about 120 m.

The Sayler Park tornado was the only tristate tornado in the superoutbreak and was the most photographed (Fig. 3.23a,b). While crossing the

Ohio River, the visible cone-shaped funnel became very wide, partly because of the moist air above the river. The two views in Fig. 3.24 show this change in shape as the funnel crossed the river. Occurring between 1730 and 1755, the tornado finally entered a classic dissipating stage as an elongated rope. Eventually it disintegrated outside the parent cloud, even while its ropelike funnel was on the ground (Fig. 3.25). Results of the photogrammetric analysis of this F4 tornado as it crossed the Ohio River are shown in Fig. 3.26. Strong vertical motions (updrafts) in excess of 160 mi/h are evident ahead of the funnel.

The third tornado analyzed photogrammetrically by Fujita occurred at Parker, Indiana (F4). Figure 3.27 shows the evolution of the visible funnel. The photos cover a path about 5 mi long; the diameter of the tornado funnel at treetop level (10 m) increased from 150 m to 800 m as the tornado became a giant dust cloud. At the time represented in Fig. 3.28, the diameter increased from about 300 m at the ground to nearly 800 m at a height of 400 m, and the tornado was advancing

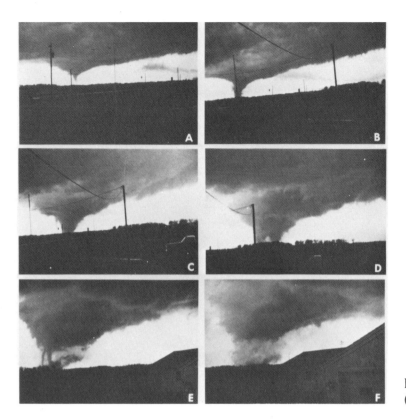

**Figure 3.27.** Evolution of Parker, Ind., tornado. (Photos by Doyle Anderson.)

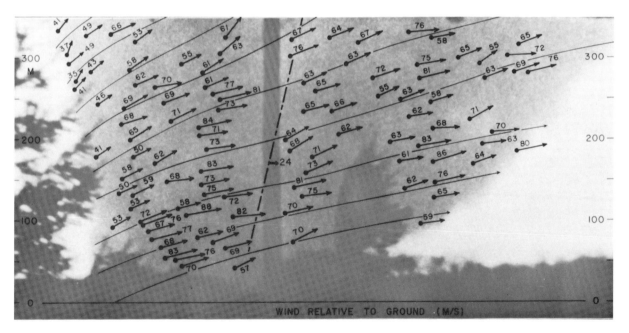

**Figure 3.28.** Parker, Ind., tornado as it appeared just before suction vortices became visible, with sectors and velocities superimposed. (From motion picture by Wally Hubbard.)

**Figure 3.29.** Parker, Ind., tornado with multiple vortices. (From motion picture by Wally Hubbard.)

horizontally at a nearly constant speed of about 24 m/s. The maximum velocity measured from photographs was 88 m/s. Figure 3.29 shows the Parker tornado with multiple vortices when it was near Monroe Central High School and associated with winds more than 200 mi/h (89.4 m/s).

### Special Features of Tornado Paths

#### Topography

Effects of topography on tornado formation, intensification, and decay have long been conjectured by meteorologists. Attempts have been made to establish a relationship between tornado behavior and the underlying terrain features, but the evidence of 3–4 April 1974 indicates that violent (F4-5) tornadoes are little influenced by topographic variations; they cross rivers and climb mountain and canyon walls. The largest-scale dynamical forcing of the tornado system appears to override the smaller-scale influence of ground roughness. Among

the more notable river-crossing tornadoes in the superoutbreak were the Sayler Park (F5) and the Brandenburg (F5) tornadoes. Figure 3.30 shows part of the damage path of the Brandenburg tornado.

The Blue Ridge, Georgia, tornado climbed 3,300-ft Betty Mountain (Fig. 3.31). The Murphy, Tennessee, tornado climbed straight up a mountain, and the Campbellsville, Alabama, tornado descended a 200-ft cliff into Robinson Creek (Fig. 3.32). The Obey River, Tennessee, tornado crossed the 100-ft-deep Obey River canyon and apparently became stronger after crossing the canyon while maintaining a rectilinear path. The Stecoah, N.C., tornado touched down on top of a 3,300-ft ridge and then descended 1,200 ft to the valley community of Stecoah, killing two people.

#### An Unusually Narrow Path

The Guin, Alabama (F5), tornado left a path of great damage (Fig. 3.33) and killed 13 persons, though it was extremely narrow. Six months later

**Figure 3.30.** Damage path of Brandenburg, Ky., tornado. Tornado crossed the Ohio River (left).

**Figure 3.31.** Path of Blue Ridge, Ga., tornado on Betty Mountain.

**Figure 3.32.** Campbellsville, Ala., tornado path.

the narrow tornado track through the William T. Bankhead National Forest could be clearly seen in a satellite photograph (Fig. 3.34).

### Cycloidal Ground Marks

Cycloidal ground marks were replete in the super-outbreak. Figure 3.35 illustrates the small cycloidal swaths of the Anchor, Illinois, tornado and the giant cycloidal swaths of the Homer Lake, Indiana, tornado. In the latter the double swaths indicate the paths of twin suction vortices. Such swaths are well marked in fields of grain or stubble and on bare soil where the path of the wind is well traced by fine particles. Swaths are not as clear in built-up areas because of heavier debris there.

### Applications of 3–4 April 1974 Tornado Data

The data now available from comprehensive studies provide useful detail on conditions that spawn large and severe tornado outbreaks and on storm

**Figure 3.33.** Damage path of Guin, Ala., tornado.

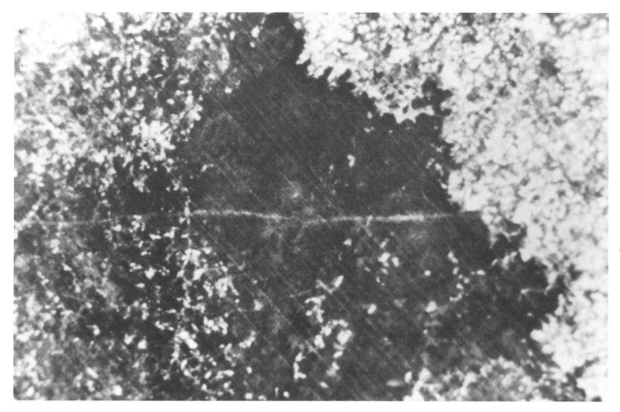

**Figure 3.34.** Guin, Ala., tornado track 6 mo after tornado, prepared from data transmitted by an Earth Resources Technology Satellite.

**Figure 3.35.** Cycloidal ground marks left by tornadoes in (left) Anchor, Ill., and (right) Homer Lake, Ind.

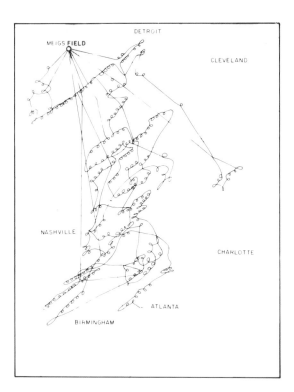

**Figure 3.36.** Flight paths of T. T. Fujita for aerial surveys of 3-4 April 1974 tornadoes.

behavior. Tornado-damage analysis is also contributing to safe engineering practice and building design and to statistical hazard assessments.

Detailed damage surveys provide a basis for more accurate assessments of tornado hazard probabilities. Thus, a tornado of intensity category F5 produces some damage in all categories from F0 to F5 along its path, an F4 tornado produces damage in all categories from F0 to F4, etc. The probability of local occurrence of the hazard represented by F5 windspeeds, for example, can be estimated from a base in surveys that define the actual area having such damage in representative intense tornadoes. The observed area of F5 damage must be multiplied by a number representative of the overall occurrence of such strong tornadoes, and the product divided by the total area in which the incidence of such tornadoes is defined, to arrive at a probability of local occurrence of the meteorological conditions productive of the damage observed (Abbey and Fujita, 1975; Abbey, 1976).

Thus, for example, immediately after the disastrous events of 3-4 April 1974, Fujita and others conducted exhaustive aerial surveys (Fig. 3.36), taking thousands of aerial photographs (Fig. 3.37). The damage photos allow both the limits of damage and the distribution of damage by F-scale categories to be defined (Fig. 3.38). The tabulated results from photographs of the damage wrought during 3-4 April 1974 are presented in Table 3.4, explained as follows:

Table 3.4 uses a kind of shorthand notation. The columns are labeled with F classifications of damage. Thus column F3 contains information on all tornadoes studied that produced some damage as high as the F3 category (of course, these tornadoes are also referred to as having F3 intensity and corresponding F3 winds, although the connection between numerical values of windspeed and the damage done by the wind is best made with engineering analysis). In the first row, labeled $L_0 \leq$, the entry under F3 is 710, the total length in miles of the path of F3 tornadoes on 3-4 April 1974. As noted above, this path is characterized by damage in all categories from F0 to F3. Now, in the fifth row of the third column the number 486 is, for F3 tornadoes, the length of their path in miles along which the damage done was in categories F1 to F3. The difference $(710 - 486 = 224)$ is the length in miles along the F3 tornado tracks where the damage was only slight, i.e., in the category F0. All other numbers in the table should be understood in terms of the same rules implicit in the illustrations above. W refers to path width in miles and A to area in square miles. D is the DAPPLE index, the damage area per unit path length, A/L. Thus, for example, referring to the first column in Table 3.4, the total length of path of F5 tornadoes on April 3-4 was 302 mi, their average width was 0.487 mi, and the area they damaged was $302 \times 0.487 = 147.1$ mi$^2$. This area embraces damage in all categories F0 to F5. In the lower left of the table, we see that only along 39 of the 302 mi identified with F5 tornadoes was damage in the extreme F5 category; the average width of damage in the F5 category was 0.006 mi (32 ft), and the total area of F5 damage was 0.23 mi$^2$. These numbers reflect the fact that the F5 damage within F5 tornadoes was generally concentrated in narrow swaths. The DAPPLE index D5 shows

**Figure 3.37.** Part of the damage path of Xenia, Ohio, tornado.

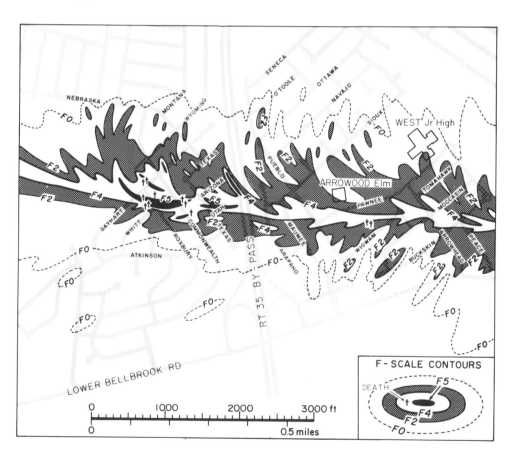

**Figure 3.38.** Isolines of intensity categories in the path of the Xenia, Ohio, tornado, based on the nature of the damage observed.

**Table 3.4.** Extent of Damage Associated with Tornadoes of the 3-4 April 1974 Outbreak

| Dimension* | Extent of damage by tornado category | | | | | |
|---|---|---|---|---|---|---|
| | F5 | F4 | F3 | F2 | F1 | F0 |
| $L_0 \leq$ | 302.0 | 858.0 | 710.0 | 360.0 | 295.0 | 46.0 |
| $W_0 \leq$ | 0.487 | 0.457 | 0.366 | 0.185 | 0.062 | 0.028 |
| $A_0 \leq$ | 147.1 | 392.1 | 259.9 | 66.6 | 18.3 | 1.3 |
| $D_0 \leq$ | 0.487 | 0.457 | 0.366 | 0.185 | 0.062 | 0.028 |
| $L_1 \leq$ | 233.0 | 643.0 | 486.0 | 187.0 | 91.0 | |
| $W_1 \leq$ | 0.203 | 0.190 | 0.153 | 0.077 | 0.026 | |
| $A_1 \leq$ | 47.3 | 122.7 | 74.4 | 14.4 | 2.4 | |
| $D_1 \leq$ | 0.157 | 0.142 | 0.105 | 0.040 | 0.0080 | |
| $L_2 \leq$ | 203.0 | 526.0 | 356.0 | 103.0 | | |
| $W_2 \leq$ | 0.085 | 0.079 | 0.064 | 0.032 | | |
| $A_2 \leq$ | 17.3 | 41.6 | 22.8 | 3.3 | | |
| $D_2 \leq$ | 0.057 | 0.048 | 0.032 | 0.0092 | | |
| $L_3 \leq$ | 155.0 | 331.0 | 187.0 | | | |
| $W_3 \leq$ | 0.035 | 0.033 | 0.026 | | | |
| $A_3 \leq$ | 5.4 | 10.9 | 4.9 | | | |
| $D_3 \leq$ | 0.018 | 0.013 | 0.0068 | | | |
| $L_4 \leq$ | 86.0 | 175.0 | | | | |
| $W_4 \leq$ | 0.015 | 0.014 | | | | |
| $A_4 \leq$ | 1.3 | 2.5 | | | | |
| $D_4 \leq$ | 0.0043 | 0.0029 | | | | |
| $L_5 \leq$ | 39.0 | | | | | |
| $W_5 \leq$ | 0.006 | | | | | |
| $A_5 \leq$ | 0.23 | | | | | |
| $D_5 \leq$ | 0.0008 | | | | | |

*$L$ = path length in miles; $L_0 \leq (L_1 \leq)$ = length with F0 (F1) or more damage.
 $W$ = path width in miles; $W_0 \leq$ = width with F0 or more damage.
 $A$ = path area in square miles; $A_0 \leq$ = area with F0 or more damage.
 $D$ = DAPPLE index (A/L); $D_0 \leq = A_0/L_0$.

that F5 damage was wrought at the average rate of 8/10,000 unit area per unit path length. By way of further explanation, note that damage in the F3 category, for example, is done by tornadoes of rank F3 and above; to find the total area of F3 damage on 3-4 April, add the three numbers appearing to the right of $A_3 \leq$ in the table, to obtain 21.2 mi².

The results of the damage survey can be combined with historical statistics on tornado path length, path width, and intensity, with windspeed estimates based on photogrammetry and on engineering analyses to provide point estimates of windspeed probability, for application to actuarial problems. In doing this, Abbey (1976) used historical statistics assembled and classified by Fujita (1971) and assumed that the area ratios applicable to the historical record are the same as those derived from the sample of 3-4 April 1974. Abbey's results are of particular relevance to cost-benefit analyses of construction plans for critical facilities such as nuclear reactors, hospitals, and schools.

# 4. Thunderstorms in Agriculture and in Forest Management

*D. G. DeCoursey, W. L. Chameides, J. McQuigg, M. H. Frere, and A. D. Nicks*

## Introduction

Precipitation can be divided into two general types: that associated with weak ascending air currents on a scale of about 1,000 km and that associated with rapid overturning of a local air mass with large variability of air motion and precipitation on a scale of tens of kilometers. The first type is light but persistent, covers large land areas, and tends to recur at intervals of several days or a week. It includes much snowstorm activity. Such precipitation is beneficial to agriculture because its low intensity seldom exceeds infiltration rates of soil (Chow, 1964; see pp. 9-22). The showers and thunderstorms identified with the second type can be beneficial or harmful to agriculture depending on such factors as amount and intensity of rainfall, time of year, previous rainfall, crop and tillage conditions, and soil type.

## Beneficial Effects of Thunderstorms

Many texts on botany and agricultural crops describe plant growth and the climatic adaptations of various crops. For example, Leonard and Martin (1963) report on the physiology and culture of grains around the world. Here we cite a few illustrations of the function of thunderstorms in agriculture. Thunderstorms benefit agriculture by supplying large quantities of water directly to the soil and to reservoirs. Lightning converts gaseous nitrogen, which cannot be used by plants, into nitrogen compounds essential to formation of plant tissues and development of the seeds that provide proteins essential to animal life, and means for plant reproduction.

### Moisture for Crop Production

Most nonirrigated crops depend on two sources of moisture during the growing season: water collected from precipitation during the nongrowing season and stored in the root zone and water from storms during the growing season. Soil moisture bridges the gap between storms, although it cannot completely replace timely rains.

Only a few studies have indicated the percentage of annual precipitation from thunderstorms. Changnon (1957) wrote that the percentage of normal annual precipitation from thunderstorms in Illinois ranges from 37% to 50%. Osborn and Hickock (1968) claimed that thunderstorm rainfall is responsible for 70% of all precipitation in the southwestern United States.

Local agricultural economy probably has evolved to fit closely with area climatology, including thunderstorms. Thus corn and soybeans are grown in Illinois, where the maximum number of thunderstorm days and the maximum amount of thunderstorm rainfall occur at the time of year when corn and soybeans are most sensitive to lack of precipitation. In middle latitudes thunderstorms are frequent in the grain-producing areas. On the other hand, world thunderstorm data show that thunderstorms are most frequent in some less-productive tropical regions. Low agricultural productivity in warm, moist regions results from rapid decomposition of organic materials and leaching of soluble nutrients from the soil by the abundant precipitation.

Crop sensitivity to moisture depends on crop variety and stage of growth. For most crops, limiting moisture after planting delays seed germination; however, if the delay is short, depending on crop variety, it may not affect yield. Yields of fall-planted winter-wheat crops are similar even though planting and germination dates range over several weeks. On the other hand, in the spring a 10-day delay in planting corn may reduce yields by 10% to 20% (Pendleton, 1965).

Plants suffer stress when the rate of transpiration from leaf surfaces exceeds the rate that roots can take the water from the soil. This stress is intensified by water shortage and high temperature. Plants in water stress have closed stomates (openings) in the leaves to reduce water loss, but stomate closure also reduces the amount of carbon dioxide absorption and thus limits photosynthesis. A plant's water requirements depend on its size, but availability of water for its use depends on its root size. Small plants require small amounts of water, but that water must be available to the root zone in the upper soil layers. Therefore, frequent rains are needed when plants are small, especially when temperature is high, to replace rapid evaporative losses from the upper soil layers. As a plant grows, its greater demand for water is paced by its growing root system, which removes water from greater depths and a larger volume of soil.

Moderate water stress during vegetative growth usually reduces fruit yield only slightly. Lack of adequate moisture during flowering, fruit set, and fruit development, however, can greatly reduce yield, typically by 25% to 50% (Shaw and Laing, 1965). The plant is usually least sensitive to moisture supply during the period of fruit ripening and maturation.

Although the relationships of crop yield to temperature and precipitation are complex, models of plant growth have been developed that range from simple statistical regression relationships for crop yield to large models based on knowledge of plant physiology. These models could be used to study the impact of thunderstorm type variability in frequency, amount, and intensity on crop yield (see Curry and Chen, 1971, and McKinion et al., 1975a, for a general discussion of plant-growth modeling). Crops for which models have been described include the following: cotton—Jones et al. (1975), McKinion et al. (1975a and b); corn—Baker and Horrocks (1975); soybeans—Curry et al. (1975); alfalfa—Miles et al. (1973).

Recently, complex hydrologic models have been developed to evaluate environmental problems such as nonpoint source pollution and the effects of erosion on soil productivity. CREAMS (Knisel, 1980) is a model for simulating the movement of chemicals, water, and sediment in response to changes in management on a field-scale area. EPIC (Williams, 1982), also a field-scale model, is intended to evaluate the long-term effects of erosion on soil productivity. Both of these models could be used to study the effect of rainfall variability on hydrologic response. The crop model in EPIC was developed to estimate crop yield, whereas the one in CREAMS is designed to simulate crop size and its impact on erosion and use of plant nutrients. If desired, the plant components in EPIC and CREAMS could be replaced by some of the more complex plant-growth models mentioned in the previous paragraph.

A problem in using regression models is selecting appropriate weather variables, since the variables typically are not independent but are correlated in space and time. Such correlation makes it difficult to evaluate significance of selected variables. The modeler may begin by trying to identify functions of technology and weather that he theorizes are related to crop yield. Thus, he may consider an equation of the form

$$y = f(\text{technology}) + g(\text{weather}),$$

where $y$ is yield and $f$ and $g$ are functions to be defined from analysis of the historical record, supplemented by direct experimentation and theory. In some cases excellent historical yield and weather data are available and can be used in a statistical regression model. Figures 4.1–4.3 show effects of weather variability and an upward trend that reflects improving technology and crop varieties. With appropriate techniques these individual influences can be evaluated separately and represented in mathematical model equations, illustrated by the nonlinear relationships between crop yields and precipitation shown in Figs. 4.4–4.6. Table 4.1 shows the months of greatest yield sensitivity to precipitation variability as defined by yield models for wheat, corn, soybeans, and grain sorghum in several states where these are major crops. Although these models do not show the ef-

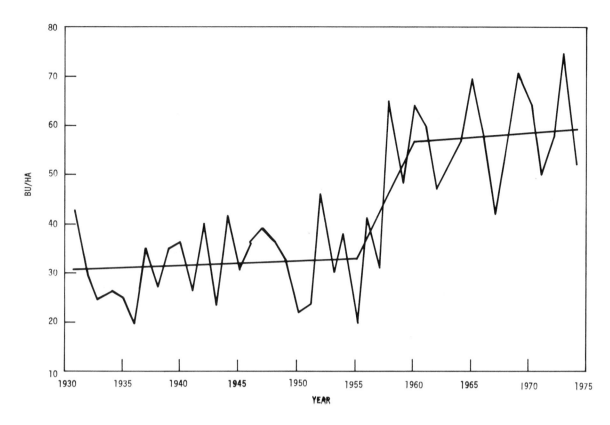

**Figure 4.1.** Oklahoma wheat yields, showing result of weather variability (year-to-year fluctuations) and effect of increased use of chemical fertilizers and improved plant varieties (long-term trends).

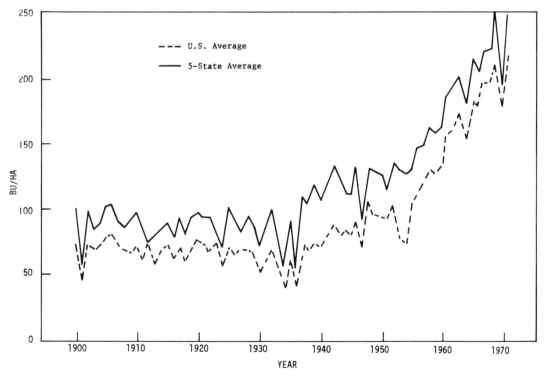

**Figure 4.2.** Average corn yields by year. Five-state average includes Iowa, Illinois, Indiana, Ohio, and Missouri.

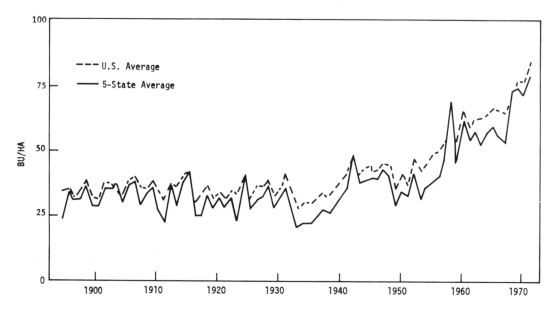

**Figure 4.3.** Average wheat yields by year. Five-state average includes North Dakota, South Dakota, Nebraska, Kansas, and Oklahoma.

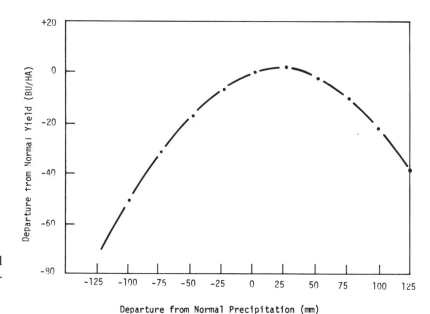

**Figure 4.4.** Second-order polynomial fitted to Iowa corn yields in relation to July rainfall.

fects of thunderstorms explicitly, such effects are implicit in the major contribution of thunderstorms to summer rains.

Although there is no simple relationship between the frequency of thunderstorm occurrences and agricultural yields, it is obvious that agricultural yields are closely though complexly related to precipitation. The crops of choice in a given region are those that give satisfactory results with the weather typical of the region. During growing sea-

sons over much of the Earth, thunderstorms are an important determinant of that weather and major contributors to the rainfall.

### Farm and Ranch Water Supply

Thunderstorms are important sources of livestock water. Excessive rainfall, that amount which does not infiltrate the soil, can be trapped in small ponds and reservoirs such as those built in the Great Plains

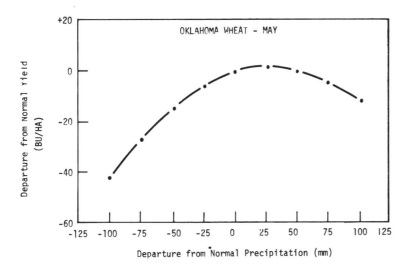

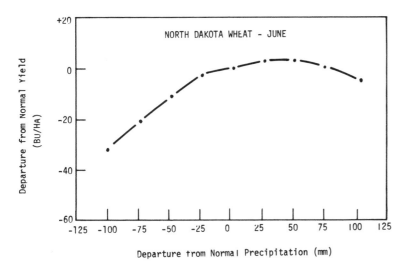

**Figure 4.5.** Model results illustrating wheat yields in Oklahoma and North Dakota in relation to rainfall anomalies in May and June.

**Table 4.1.** Months of Greatest Yield Sensitivity to Precipitation Variability

| State | Crop | March | April | May | June | July | August | September | October |
|-------|------|-------|-------|-----|------|------|--------|-----------|---------|
| Colorado | Wheat | | | | × | | | | |
| Kansas | Wheat | × | | | | | | | |
| Nebraska | Wheat | | | | | | | | |
| North Dakota | Wheat | | | × | | | | | × |
| Oklahoma | Wheat | × | | | | | | | |
| Iowa | Corn | | | | | × | | | |
| Ohio | Corn | | | | | × | | | |
| Indiana | Corn | | | | | × | | | |
| Missouri | Corn | | | | | × | | | |
| Illinois | Corn | | | | | × | | | |
| Iowa | Soybeans | | | | | × | | | |
| Ohio | Soybeans | | | | | × | | | |
| Indiana | Soybeans | | | | | × | | | |
| Missouri | Soybeans | | | | | × | × | | |
| Illinois | Soybeans | | | | | × | | | |
| Kansas | Grain sorghum | | | | | × | | | |

71

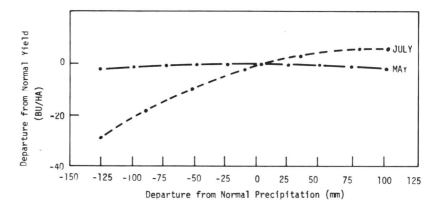

**Figure 4.6.** Model results for soybean yields in Illinois in relation to May and July rainfall.

and areas of low rainfall farther west (Fig. 4.7). Almost all of this runoff is from thunderstorms (Osborn and Hickock, 1968), and in some areas nearly 20% may be saved. In recent years attempts have been made to increase runoff into some catchments by making the watershed above the ponds impervious (Myers, 1975). Where these small storage reservoirs hold the only water supply available for livestock, as in areas where streamflow is intermittent and there is no groundwater, relatively dry summers with infrequent thunderstorms may force early marketing of livestock.

### Irrigation Water Supply

The amount of thunderstorm rainfall in a region affects soil moisture and influences total irrigation water needed. Thunderstorm rainfall also contributes directly to irrigation-supply reservoirs. In arid lands where irrigated agriculture is prevalent, the large variability of rainfall makes it difficult to develop and forecast water needs (Soil Conservation Service, 1960).

### Nitrogen Fixation

Nitrogen fixation is the process of converting nitrogen gas into nitrogen compounds by bonding nitrogen to an atom of another element. Such fixed nitrogen is usable by plants.

Although 80% of the Earth's atmosphere is nitrogen gas, nitrogen compounds are seldom abundant enough in the soil to allow plants to grow at maximum rates. The chemical conversion of nitrogen gas in air to ammonia ($NH_3$) fertilizer, usually

through a process that uses natural gas, is known as *anthropogenic fixation.* In 1969 manufactured fertilizer provided 46% of the nitrogen input to United States agriculture (Frere, 1976). Biological fixation accounted for 20%, lightning and rain 10%, and manure and plant residue the remainder.

Several microorganisms metabolize atmospheric nitrogen into organic nitrogen compounds. Thunderstorms contribute indirectly to this 20% by improving conditions for microbiological growth. Such growth in soil is best near temperatures of 35°C, with water in about 80% of a typical soil's intergranular spaces. Free-living organisms in range- and forest land are estimated to produce about 10 kg/ha (kilograms per hectare) of fixed N per year. Fixation by symbiotic organisms and crops is an order of magnitude higher and can produce as much as 600 kg/ha (Allison, 1973). Integrating over all land area, the annual rate of biological fixation is estimated to be about $175 \times 10^{12}$g of N. By comparison, blue-green algae are estimated to produce about $40 \times 10^{12}$g of fixed N per year in the world's oceans, implying a global natural fixation rate of about $200 \times 10^{12}$g of N per year, or, on average, about 4 kg/ha.

The fixed nitrogen provided by lightning discharges is created as nitrogen oxides and later hydrolyzed to nitric acid and brought to Earth by rain. Although von Liebig (1827) first proposed that lightning might convert molecular nitrogen $N_2$ to fixed nitrogen in the form of NO, the magnitude of the fixation rate and its importance to the global nitrogen cycle are still subjects of investigation by atmospheric scientists.

NO and its related compounds are referred to

**Figure 4.7.** A typical small surface-water impoundment or water-supply reservoir.

as $NO_x$ in atmospheric photochemistry. The first studies assessing the amount of nitrogen as nitrate in atmospheric $NO_x$ generally searched for a correlation between nitrates in rainwater and lightning intensity. Since they did not show a strong correlation, the consensus was that lightning was not a major source of atmospheric $NO_x$. For example, Hutchinson (1954) concluded that less than 20% of the nitrate in rain is produced by lightning. However, current understanding of the atmospheric $NO_x$ system points to a basic misconception of these experiments. Although rainwater probably acquires most of its nitrate by dissolving gaseous $HNO_3$, NO is the form of $NO_x$ initially produced by electrical discharge (Chameides, 1975) and converted to $HNO_3$ by a chain reaction that usually takes about 24 hours:

$$NO + O_3 \rightarrow NO_2 + O_2$$
$$NO_2 + OH + M \rightarrow HNO_3 + M,$$

where M represents any gaseous species taking part in the three-body reaction by absorbing the excess energy released in the chemical reaction. The long conversion time, coupled with the typical 1-h lifetime of a thundercloud, leads one to expect

that the observations do not necessarily mean that lightning does not produce large quantities of $NO_x$ as NO. In fact, the enhanced concentrations of gaseous $NO_2$ in thunderclouds observed by Noxon (1976) imply that lightning may produce significant quantities of $NO_x$.

Lightning channels are associated with high pressures and temperatures that cause a radially propagated cylindrical shock wave that dissipates most of the discharge energy in the form of heat and mechanical energy. The surrounding air is momentarily heated to temperatures as high as 30,000 K (kelvins; about 54,000°F) in the immediate vicinity of the discharge channel but to lower temperatures at greater distances. By heating the air within about 7 cm of the discharge to temperatures above 2,000 K, the shock wave leads to the production of NO from $N_2$ and $O_2$ from the overall forward-and-backward chemical reaction:

$$N_2 + O_2 \rightleftarrows NO + NO.$$

Although at atmospheric temperatures the $N_2$ and $O_2$ are thermodynamically stable, as the temperature increases the equilibrium shifts toward NO. Thus if NO remained in equilibrium, its concentration would increase to several percent at temperatures greater than 4,000 K and would then decrease to negligibly small values as temperatures returned to normal atmospheric levels. However, as the temperature and the equilibrium NO concentration decrease, the rate of reactions that convert NO to $N_2$ and $O_2$ becomes slow, thereby blocking the reconversion. At some concentration, which depends on the cooling rate, the NO is "frozen," chemical equilibrium is not maintained, and thus a net amount of NO remains after cooling has been completed. For cooling times of about a second or less typically encountered in atmospheric discharges, the final NO concentration is a low percent by volume, corresponding to the equilibrium NO abundance between 2,000 and 4,000 K.

The mechanism for producing NO at high temperatures as by lightning was first described by Zel'dovitch and Raizer (1966) and has been used to calculate the production of NO in several high-temperature processes, including the internal-combustion engine and nuclear explosions. Chameides

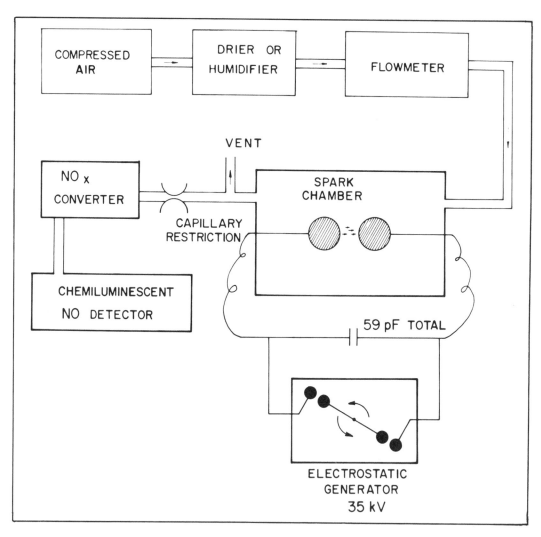

**Figure 4.8.** Schematic diagram of the experimental system used by Chameides et al. (1977) to measure the fixation of nitrogen in electrical discharges. A regulated flow of air was subjected to electric sparks about 1 cm long and about $4 \times 10^{-2}$ J, passed through an $NO_x$ converter which converts all nitrogen oxides to NO, and then through a detector which measures the NO concentration by a chemiluminescent technique. The experiment indicated that $(6\pm1) \times 10^{16}$ NO molecules are produced per joule of discharge.

et al. (1977), using a simple cylindrical shock-wave model, estimated the NO produced by this mechanism from electrical discharges. These calculations, coupled with laboratory experiments using sparks of 1 cm to 1 m (Fig. 4.8), indicate that about $(6 \pm 1) \times 10^{16}$ NO molecules are produced per joule of electrical discharge. This yield is in approximate agreement with those of other investigators who used different approaches (Noxon, 1976; Zipf and Dubin, 1976; Griffing, 1977). Estimating that about $8 \times 10^{11}$ watts are dissipated by lightning globally, Chameides et al. (1977) concluded that about $30 \times 10^{12}$g of N as NO are produced annually. A more recent evaluation of the energy dissipated by lightning has caused this estimate to be revised downward to about $6 \times 10^{12}$g/yr N (Kowalczyk and Bauer, 1982), equivalent to a globally averaged annual fixation rate of about 0.12 kg/ha yr. However, the rate of energy dissipation by lightning remains a highly uncertain parameter, and as a result, the global fixation rate by lightning will probably be subject to further revision.

Biological processes fix atmospheric $N_2$ at an annual global rate of about $200 \times 10^{12}$g (about 4 kg/ha of land and ocean), and anthropogenic fixation and resultant concentrated application in agricultural regions occur at a rate of about $60 \times 10^{12}$g/yr. Thus on the basis of the above estimate it would appear that lightning is responsible for only a small percent of the Earth's total nitrogen fixation. On the other hand, lightning, by producing about $6 \times 10^{12}$g N as NO per year, apparently represents one of the major natural sources of gaseous $NO_x$ compounds to the atmosphere. These compounds play an important role in the photochemistry of the Earth's lower atmosphere. In regions strongly affected by anthropogenic activities, however, this natural source of $NO_x$ is completely swamped by $NO_x$ production from the burning of fossil fuels, wood, and vegetation, which amounts to about $30 \times 10^{12}$g N/yr on a globally averaged basis.

**Harmful Effects of Thunderstorms on Agriculture**

Harmful effects of thunderstorms can be grouped into five major areas: (1) damage directly to rangeland and crops by hail, flooding, or wetting an air-dried product; (2) erosion of cropland caused by

**Figure 4.9.** Part of a cornfield virtually destroyed by hail. (Photo courtesy of Illinois State Water Survey, Urbana, Ill.)

excessive runoff rates; (3) leaching of plant nutrients from the soil profile; (4) polluting surface waters; (5) flooding of cropland along major streams.

Crop Damage

Thunderstorms can greatly damage agricultural production, especially if they include hail (Fig. 4.9). For example, hail damage to crops in Colorado and Wyoming during 1978 was estimated at nearly $100 million. Hail losses amount to about 1% of overall agricultural production in the United States. The burden of many individual crop losses is distributed by hail insurance under-written by private companies and by government-sponsored crop-insurance programs.

During the planting season, storms create several problems. If fields are too wet, they cannot be negotiated by tractors, and the soil suffers harmful compaction when turned; thus planting may be delayed and yields of crops that require a long growing season are reduced. Or the soil may form a crust which, in fields already planted, may significantly reduce seedling emergence and hence crop yield, especially of crops with small seeds such as lettuce and beans (Evans and Boul, 1968; Ahmad and Robin, 1971). Cotton and corn are examples of plants less susceptible to harm from crust formation. Finally, seeds may rot or plants drown in ponded areas, particularly on flatlands and in alluvial valleys.

Storms may also cause crop losses at harvest. Rain and heavy winds flatten many crops, especially those near maturity. This results in poor or difficult harvest. Ripe grain can be shattered from the head by wind, rain, and hail. Unless a crop is relatively dry when harvested, it must be dried before storage to prevent decay. In addition, harvesting machines, expensive to buy and maintain, are subject to greater wear and are more likely to fail if the crop is damp when harvested.

One or two days of drying are required to prepare hay crops such as alfalfa for baling. If rain falls on drying hay, the drying process is interrupted, valuable nutrients are leached out of the hay, and some plant material decomposes. After a heavy rain, windrowed hay must be turned over to prevent rotting. Indeed, untimely rains cause substantial losses to the hay crop in the United States each year.

Frequent rains during the growing season contribute to prevalence of weeds and insects, and pesticides for insect and weed control may be washed off plants before they are effective. If shifting winds during thunderstorms are improperly accounted for during spraying operations, pesticide accidents can occur; i.e., insecticides and herbicides may be carried to nontarget areas, where they may produce unwanted effects (Fred and Kessler, 1980).

## Erosion of Farmlands

Most erosion damage occurs when large amounts of precipitation fall at high intensities. Heavy rain, usually associated with thunder, produces large volumes of surface runoff, with resulting loss of soil (Fig. 4.10) and associated pollutants, including sediment, nutrients, and pesticides.

Runoff occurs whenever rainfall intensity exceeds the infiltration rate of water into soil. Infiltration rate varies greatly, even between areas of similar or the same soil type, and is a function of soil moisture, previous cultivation, and wetting and drying. In dry soil, the infiltration rate can exceed several centimeters per hour; in saturated soil, it can be as low as 1 mm/day or even less.

Soil losses from watershed areas increase nonlinearly with surface runoff. Studies of small plots throughout the country have shown that one-third of the total soil loss is caused by events occurring less frequently than once in 2 years; another third is lost in severe storms with return periods between 1 and 2 years, and the final third is caused by more frequent, less extreme storms with return periods less than 1 year (Wischmeier, 1962; Wischmeier and Smith, 1965). In a related study, Piest (1963) found that 75% of local soil loss is caused by only about four storms per year. Similar studies of watersheds less than 1 km$^2$ and larger show about one-fifth of the soil loss associated with large storms, one-tenth with moderate-size storms, and seventenths with small storms (Piest, 1963).

The erosion of soil particles from the Earth's surface begins when raindrops strike and detach particles by splash (Fig. 4.11). The erosive potential of these drops depends on fall velocities, size distribution, and total mass of droplets at impact. Raindrop-fall speed varies approximately as the square root of diameter, from 1 m/s for 0.25-mm diameter to about 9 m/s for 5-mm diameter (List, 1958). Wind adds a significant horizontal-velocity component and causes raindrops to impact the soil at a glancing angle. Studies of drop-size distribution by Laws and Parsons (1943), Marshall and Palmer (1948), Hudson (1971), and McGregor and Mutchler (1977), for example, provide bases for assessing the actual impact energies of rains of different types and intensities. The number of drops commonly decreases rapidly as the drops increase in size from 0.5 to 5 mm and increases slowly as the rainfall rate increases.

The erosive potential of raindrops is enormous. In an area where annual rainfall is about 750 mm, the impact energy (i.e., the dissipation of kinetic energy of falling rain) amounts to about 160 million J-m/ha/yr or the equivalent of 35 t (metric tons) of TNT per hectare (ha) per year (1 t/ha = 892 lb/acre) (Meyer, 1971). The amount of soil displaced by the intermittent application of the forces of rain

**Figure 4.10.** Typical example of field erosion caused by thunderstorm rainfall.

**Figure 4.11.** Soil particles being detached from the soil surface by raindrop impact.

depends critically on the soil microstructure. On an unprotected saturated soil surface, detachment of soil particles results from the dissipation of impact energy. Particle movement by raindrop impact is not significant until the soil surface becomes saturated. Then soil is transported to small channels of flowing water (rills) by both splash action and acceleration of the very thin surface flow caused by raindrop impact. Mutchler and Young (1975) described raindrop splash and soil detachment in detail. Wind action can substantially increase detachment of soil particles. Thus Lyles (1977) showed that, for similar rainfall duration and intensity and similar clod size, winds of 40 km/h increase detachment by about 2.7 times, and minor amounts of surface mulch that normally reduce loss are almost completely ineffective.

Not all soil is detached and moved by raindrops directly; much is dislodged and moved by water flowing in small channels (Fig. 4.12) or through erosion and caving of stream banks. However, rainfall is responsible for the large quantities of water and sediment that concentrate into rills and ultimately into streams and rivers. The amount of material dislodged and moved by flowing water is a function of soil texture and slope and the velocity and volume of water. For example, in an experiment on two soils, the interrill erosion (i.e., that dislodged and moved by rainfall and shallow overland flow) was about 7 kg/h/m of plot length for both soils on plots 12 m wide. However, because rill erosion is caused by both the velocity and the mass of water flowing in a channel, it tends to increase with length of the channel or plot. For the two soils, rill erosion rates were negligible at the head of the rows but were more than 50 and 150 kg/m at a point between 30 and 40 m from the head of the row. Net losses for the plots 12 m wide and 40 m long were 1,310 and 3,320 kg for a 1-h event. Rill erosion was responsible for 79% and 92% of the total loss (Meyer et al., 1976).

In many soils, raindrop impact creates a crust on an unprotected surface, thereby enhancing runoff and reducing crop productivity. The crusts range in thickness from 1 mm to 2 cm, have very low permeabilities, and are harder and more brittle than the soil beneath them (Fig. 4.13). Raindrop impact creates these crusts from suspended material by breaking down the soil aggregates, moving fine particles into pores in the upper layer of the soil surface, and compacting the soil surface to form a thin film of very fine particles deposited on the surface. Both the amount and the intensity of rainfall influence the thickness, density, and character of the crust. Extremely low hydraulic conductivity (the rate of water movement through the soil) in crusts is responsible for reductions in infiltration rates. McIntyre (1958) observed values of $5 \times 10^{-7}$ cm/s for the skinlike surface and $5 \times 10^{-6}$ cm/s for the 2-mm-thick washed-in layer. These values are compared with those of about $10^{-3}$ cm/s for the cultivated soil (fine sandy loam). Soil crust reduces the infiltration rate to only one-third to one-eighth of the rate for uncrusted soil (Mannering and Wiersma, 1970). The decrease in infiltration is accompanied by a decrease in accumulated evaporation; thus the overall response to crust development is a large increase in surface runoff and soil loss after thunderstorm rains.

Through use of a formula that combines factors of rainfall, soil erodibility, slope length and gradient, crop management, and erosion control practices, the Soil Conservation Service estimates that annual losses of cropland soil in the United States average about 20 t/ha (Cutler, 1977). Of course, this soil loss reduces the productivity of cropland.

The amount of soil that actually leaves an area can be estimated from surveys of reservoirs and streamflows. Most reservoirs trap more than 85% of inflowing suspended materials, and some trap more than 95%. Dendy et al. (1973) and Dendy and Bolton (1976) analyzed records of sedimentation in about 1,500 reservoirs and ponds in the United States with drainage areas varying from a few hectares to more than 70,000 km². Using an average density of 0.96 t/m³ for sedimentary deposits, they found that average annual values of sedimentation ranged from about 6.4 t/ha from drainage areas of about 2.5 km², to 1.5 t/ha for areas of about 25,000 km².

The net effect of rainfall erosion in the United States is to produce an estimated 3.6 billion t of suspended soil particles annually. However, only about 0.9 billion t are discharged to the oceans (Glymph and Storey, 1967; Wadleigh, 1968). Thus nearly 2.7 billion t are deposited as sediment in valleys, channels, lakes, and reservoirs. The source of this sediment is estimated to be as follows: agri-

**Figure 4.12.** Site where water flowing in a small rill has dislodged surface soil and organic material.

**Figure 4.13.** Soil crusts formed by raindrop impact on unprotected soil.

cultural lands, 40%; pasture-, range-, and forest lands, 25%; stream channels, 26%; urban, road, mining, and miscellaneous sources, 9% (Dow Chemical Co., 1972). The rate of soil loss from these sources is variable and ranges from less than 0.1 t/ha for well-protected timber- and rangeland to maximum rates of nearly 600 t/ha for gullied areas and construction sites. Soil losses from croplands range from negligible amounts to nearly 200 t/ha; most fields average less than 30 t/ha. Holeman (1968), analyzing records from major rivers throughout the world, estimated that the average amount of suspended materials reaching the oceans annually amounts to about 1.9 t/ha (the rate of erosion from Asia is estimated to be higher than the rate from any other continent; Asia contributes nearly 80% of all material that moves to the oceans). Thus rainfall is responsible for moving nearly 20 billion t to the oceans annually; this is enough material to cover France, Belgium, the Netherlands, Luxembourg, Switzerland, and Portugal with a 2.5-cm layer.

## Leaching of Plant Nutrients and Other Chemicals

Excessive rainfall is responsible for loss of crop nutrients from soil and potential downstream pollution caused by both nutrients and pesticides that are transported with the water and soil particles. Soil eroded from the surface is particularly important because (1) many pesticides and nutrients that create water-quality problems downstream are adsorbed (attached to the surface) on organic matter and on the soil-particle surface; (2) the fine-grained soil, which is most easily detached and transported, is responsible for most of the adsorption and transport of the chemicals; (3) fine-grained soil particles are least likely to settle out in the field and thus are transported long distances downstream to lakes or reservoirs or ultimately the ocean.

Lakes, reservoirs, and farm ponds require nutrients to produce plankton growth for fish production. However, the supply of nutrients may be so increased by runoff from rainfall on intensively farmed land and feedlots that an undesirable growth of algae and other nuisance aquatic plants is produced (Fig. 4.14). This leads to eutrophication, a form of pollution associated with an oxygen deficiency caused by the degradation of plant material

and excessive biochemical oxygen demand (McDowell and Grissinger, 1976). Nitrogen, phosphorus, carbon, and other elements have been considered responsible for eutrophic conditions, though the role they play in development of eutrophic conditions is not fully understood (Frere, 1976).

Nitrite carried to sources of municipal water supply by nutrient-laden runoff may appear in drinking water. If the concentration is high enough, it can be converted to toxic nitrate in the stomachs of animals and human beings. In children, the resulting illness is called methemoglobinemia or blue-baby syndrome. Dissolved ammonia, a pH-dependent form of nitrogen present in runoff, can be toxic to fish at relatively low concentrations.

Soils normally contain 2 to 10 kg/ha N, mostly as organic N, in the top 15 cm. A small and variable contribution of 1 to 3 kg/ha of nitrogen as nitrate and ammonium ion is added each year by rainfall (since atmospheric $NH_3$ is derived primarily from the evaporation of $NH_3$ in soils, the presence of $NH_4+$ in rain does not actually represent a net source of nutrients to the soil but rather represents a recycling of the nutrient). Since this form of nitrogen is very soluble, it is easily leached into the soil by infiltration during the first part of a storm and is found both in groundwater and interflow (the groundwater returned to the channel by lateral flow shortly after a storm has ceased). The amount of nitrate found in surface runoff is a function of the amount present near the soil surface (whether natural or added as fertilizer), the amount of rainfall, and the soil-moisture conditions.

The total phosphorus present in soils ranges from 100 to 1,300 ppm; however, the phosphate concentration in soil solution is only 0.01 to 0.2 mg/l (i.e., thousands of times smaller) because of its very low solubility and high absorbtivity to soil particles, especially clay. It is estimated that 0.2 to 16 kg/ha/yr are added from dust in rainfall. Phosphorus is transported largely by soil particles, except under conservation tillage practices (minimum or very little tillage associated with crop residues at the soil surface), where the soluble phase of phosphorus predominates; crops and crop residues can contribute significant amounts of soluble phosphorus to runoff, particularly from the leaching of standing crops at senescence (old age) and from the rupturing and subsequent release of P from plant

**Figure 4.14.** Eutrophic conditions in a farm pond, caused by excessive nutrients in incoming water.

cells during freezing and thawing cycles of winter (McDowell and Grissinger, 1976). Figure 4.15 shows some ranges in concentrations and spatial rates of nitrogen and phosphorus from croplands and noncroplands.

### Pollution of Surface Waters

Rainfall and resulting runoff from cropland not only wash out soil nutrients but also wash into stream systems the agricultural chemicals that have been applied to control plant diseases, insects, weeds, or undesirable plant growth. The pesticides most commonly found in surface waters are persistent chlorinated hydrocarbons, such as the insecticides dieldrin, DDT, DDE, endrin, and toxaphene (Merkle and Bovey, 1974). Even where they are no longer used, they are often found in surface waters because of their slow degradation rates in soils and bottom sediments of lakes. Chemicals applied directly to water to control mosquitoes, water weeds, or other pests may appear downstream when ponds are flushed by heavy rain. All these chemicals move in solution and adsorbed to sediment and organic material, with the persistent chemicals causing most pollution problems. Although some chemicals are highly toxic and even

at low levels can cause fish kills (Fig. 4.16), many problems of chemical pollution are associated with continuous exposure of aquatic organisms to low concentrations of pesticides, which are magnified to toxic levels by accumulation along the food chain.

The time of a storm with respect to a chemical application is important in determining the effect of rainfall on the movement of the chemicals into streams and lakes. When a storm occurs immediately after pesticide application, concentration of the chemical in runoff obviously is high, whether or not the chemical degrades rapidly. Method of chemical application, its solubility in water, slope of the land, soil characteristics, permeability, vegetative cover, and amount and intensity of rainfall influence the concentration of the chemical in runoff. The distance downstream from the area treated is also significant because of dilution and chemical changes with time (McDowell and Grissinger, 1976; Merkle and Bovey, 1974).

### Flooding of Cropland Along Major Streams

Large, intense thunderstorm systems can create serious downstream problems, including overbank flooding of cropland, channel degradation, and ex-

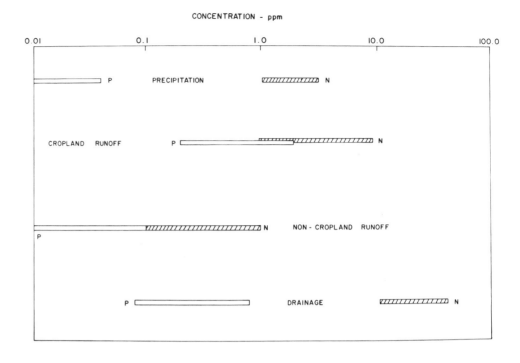

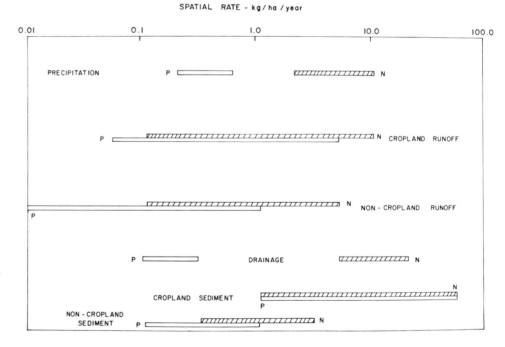

**Figure 4.15.** (Above) Range of nitrogen and phosphorus concentration in different waters. (Below) Range of spatial rates of nitrogen and phosphorus in water and sediments (Frere, 1976).

tensive sediment deposition (Fig. 4.17). Overbank flooding on a typical stream is estimated to occur once in 1 to 4 years (Leopold et al., 1964). Thus, the mean annual flood is frequently assumed to be a bank-full condition. Depending on the size of the watershed and the gradient of the stream-channel system, periods of inundation can last for less than 1 hour or as long as several days or weeks. Quite often, flooded areas include the most productive soils planted with high-yield crops. Thus, overbank flooding with sediment deposition can result in substantial financial loss.

**Figure 4.16.** Typical fish kill in a lake, caused by a highly toxic chemical.

Erosion of stream channels and gullies indirectly resulting from heavy rains is a major problem (Fig. 4.18). In the United States, 500,000 to 800,000 km of stream banks produce more than 450 million t of sediment each year (McDowell and Grissinger, 1976). This erosion adversely affects water quality, stream-channel capacity, and land use adjacent to the channels. In the uplands, much of the damage is attributable to loss of valuable cropland.

Human activity increases soil losses along streams. Thus, in northern Mississippi, two natural channels whose banks are contributing 5% and 19% of their total measured sediment discharge have loss rates of 70 and 150 t/km/yr, respectively. But a dredged channel of similar capacity in the same area is contributing nearly 3,200 t/km/yr from its banks. The extremely high rates from the dredged channel are caused by "increased channel conveyance and attendant increases in runoff velocities and tractive forces, reduced vegetative cover on dredged streambanks, and a change in the sediment content of (upland) runoff due to land use changes" (Piest and Bowie, 1974).

In the lower reaches of river systems, both channel degradation from floods and sediment deposi-

tion caused by lower stream velocities can occur. For example, in the Yazoo River, the U.S. Army Corps of Engineers estimated that 200 km of the stream channel need bank protection, yet sediment carried into the channel from the tributary areas is so great that barge traffic requires continuous dredging.

**Figure 4.17.** Out-of-bank flooding on Sugar Creek in Oklahoma following rainfall of up to 9 inches in 6 hours on 20-21 September 1965.

**Figure 4.18.** Destruction of valuable farm land by stream bank erosion.

**Figure 4.19.** Typical small reservoir nearly filled by deposition of sediment.

# 5. Effects of Wind on Buildings

*Joseph E. Minor*

## Introduction

Damage to buildings and other structures during windstorms is becoming a major problem. Urban sprawl has increased the number of windstorm-related damage incidents, and the quality of certain types of building construction has declined. Windstorm losses generally include physical losses (such as property damage), social costs (such as loss of life, loss of income, or loss of business time), and insured losses, which may be a combination of the first two. Losses attributed to hurricanes, tornadoes, and local winds are estimated to total $0.5 to $2.0 billion a year in the United States (OEP, 1972; Wiggins, 1974; Brinkmann, 1975). Single events, such as the great tornado outbreak of 3-4 April 1974, have caused damage estimated at $0.4 billion or more (Brinkmann, 1975). Wiggins (1974) has estimated the sudden-loss potential from a single windstorm event to be $2 billion.

Improving the wind resistance of buildings and thus decreasing losses involves two steps concerned with technique: (1) clear understanding of the effects of winds on buildings and (2) alteration of construction and other practice in accordance with new technical knowledge. These needs are discussed here, but, critical as they are, they represent only part of a rather complex problem attending improvement of wind resistance in buildings. Construction practice includes intricate relationships among designers, builders, codes, insurers, and the public and has been slow to react to the availability of technical knowledge. For example, the effect of wind on mobile homes is well understood, and tie-downs and shelters in mobile-home parks have proved effective in reducing property damage and injury caused by wind. Nevertheless, they are not in widespread use. According to Langston (1977) mobile-home residents in Illinois chose not to install tie-downs because of economic factors and because they were not required by ordinance. He also found that residents and managers did not believe that shelters were an attractive alternative.

## Building Failure Caused by Airflow

When winds approach and envelop a structure, the direction of airflow is changed, and several phenomena become apparent near building surfaces. The effects of wind on a rectangular building are related to features of the building's geometry, as depicted in Fig. 5.1. The overall pattern of airflow produces an inward-acting pressure across the windward wall and outward-acting pressures across the two sidewalls, the leeward wall, and the roof (Fig. 5.2). Outward-acting pressures across four of the five surfaces result from acceleration of the airflow as the air travels the longer distance around or over the structure, in accordance with the Bernoulli effect (see Appendix A to this chapter below). The smooth flow of air cannot negotiate many of the sharp angles; hence, the airflow streamlines separate from some surfaces (Fig. 5.3), with relatively low pressures occurring immediately downstream. Locally severe, outward pressures act on the surfaces separated from the airflow and are the principal initiation forces for failures in many buildings.

In addition to Bernoulli and flow-separation phenomena, pressure differences across roofs and walls occur when openings appear in the structure, either by design or through component failure (Fig. 5.4).

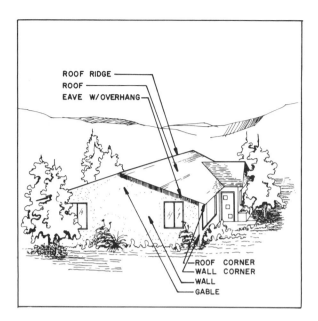

**Figure 5.1.** Building components affected by wind. These parts of a building often are failure-initiation points.

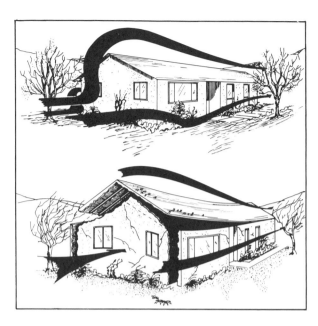

**Figure 5.2.** Overall flow patterns. Air flowing over and around a building (above) may induce wall and roof failures (below).

Windward wall openings cause an increase in pressure within the building. This pressure increase combines with outward pressures already acting across the roof, the leeward wall, and the sidewalls to intensify the net, outward-acting pressures on these surfaces. Conversely, an opening in a sidewall or the leeward wall causes a decrease in pressure within the building because air is drawn out. Such a pressure decrease combines with the external pressure across the windward wall to increase the outside-external pressure on this surface, but the decrease of internal pressure reduces the net force on the roof, sidewalls, and leeward walls.

The decision to open a window when a windstorm is imminent depends on the direction of the wind and the window placement. In a given windstorm the window left open may become a windward-wall window or a leeward-wall window. Although opening a leeward-wall window has advantages, opening a windward-wall window increases the risk to the structure. In a hurricane, cyclone, or typhoon where the direction of wind attack can be fairly well estimated in advance, the open leeward-wall window helps hold the roof on but produces an increase in net pressure across the

windward wall. One-story buildings, particularly housing, tend to have weaker roof-to-wall connections than wall strength; hence, opening a window on the leeward wall may be advisable.

The action of winds when they come in contact with buildings can be illustrated by specific examples. Wind lifted the roof of the house in Fig. 5.5 and caused the side and leeward walls to fall outward. The windward wall was pushed inward. A building damaged in this way often appears to have exploded, fostering a conclusion that the windstorm contained a tornado. More often, engineering analysis reveals that the roof was lifted first, and the walls, no longer supported at the top and restrained from falling inward, toppled outward, all influenced by wind-induced pressures.

The windward wall of the gymnasium in Fig. 5.6 fell inward. This failure resulted from inward-acting pressure across a large vertical surface. A weak roof-to-wall connection may have been a factor in the failure. If the roof rose first because of local, upward-acting pressures along the windward eave, the wall would have been freestanding, in effect, between the two vertical construction joints.

The effects of winds on a commercial building

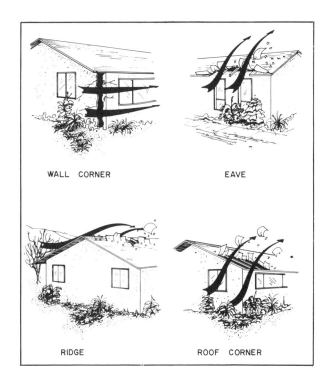

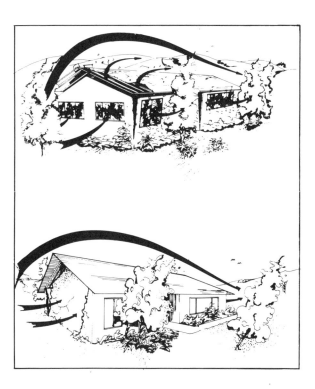

**Figure 5.3.** Local flow patterns. Air flow separations cause locally severe, outward-acting pressures and can cause component failure.

**Figure 5.4.** Effects of internal pressure. Openings in windward wall (above) compound outward-acting pressures on roof and sidewalls; openings in leeward wall (below) make more severe the inward-acting pressures on the windward wall.

**Figure 5.5.** Effects of airflow around buildings. Wind-induced pressures pushed windward wall (far side) inward, side and leeward walls outward, and the roof upward.

**Figure 5.6.** Windward-wall failure. Wind pressure on this unreinforced masonry wall pushed it inward. Vertical construction joints are indicated with arrows.

**Figure 5.7.** The results of internal pressure. Failure of the windward wall allowed pressure to increase inside the building, causing roof to lift and walls (foreground) to fall outward.

**Figure 5.8.** Failures of roof components. Roof ridges, roof corners, and eaves experience high concentrations of pressure.

can be seen in Fig. 5.7. The windward wall fell inward, the sidewalls fell outward, and the roof was lifted. Failure of the windward wall allowed pressure to increase inside the structure. Thus, an increase in pressure inside the building contributed to damage by augmenting outward-acting pressures across the walls and roof caused by air flowing over and around the building. The mode of failure shown in Fig. 5.7 is common when large glass windows or overhead doors in the windward wall are left open or are broken by the wind.

Air streamlines over the church building in Fig. 5.8 separated from the surfaces at roof corners, eaves, and roof ridges, causing locally severe, outward-acting internal pressures at these locations. Eaves with overhangs are particularly vulnerable to wind effects.

## Building Performance in Windstorms Related to Degree of Engineering Attention

Studies of wind-induced damage indicate that the wind resistance of buildings is related to the amount of engineering attention given to them. Buildings classified as fully engineered, pre-engineered, marginally engineered, and nonengineered are, in that order, increasingly susceptible to wind damage.

### Fully Engineered Buildings

Buildings that are individually designed by professional architects and engineers are called fully engineered. Such buildings usually withstand extreme winds very well. The hospital hit directly by a tornado (Fig. 5.9) illustrates this. Such a structure, even when in a tornado's path, often escapes damage while adjacent buildings are destroyed. It is sometimes assumed that the storm skipped over the engineered building, when, in fact, the building simply was better able to withstand the wind-induced pressures. Similarly, windspeed estimates are sometimes made on the basis of cursory examinations of extensive damage regardless of construction, when windspeed could be more accurately

**Figure 5.9.** Fully engineered building that survived a severe tornado with only slight damage (at the left).

estimated by examining the limited damage to a fully engineered building (see Appendix B).

### Pre-engineered Buildings

Pre-engineered buildings are planned as a group by engineers before construction and are marketed as individual units throughout the country (MBMA, 1976). Many manufacturers design their buildings so that all components are equally strong. Nevertheless, windstorm events have revealed certain weaknesses in some of these buildings. Failures in overhead doors allow winds to enter the building, increasing internal pressure on wall and roof components (Fig. 5.4). Another possible failure is loss of cladding along wall and roof corners, eaves, and ridges, the locations of localized low pressures and outward-acting forces. Both of these failures can occur at relatively low windspeeds, i.e., less than 125 mi/h (56 m/s), if the structures are not properly designed and constructed.

### Marginally Engineered Buildings

Damage to marginally engineered buildings presents the largest category of loss in windstorms. Commercial buildings, light-industrial buildings, schools, and motels and apartments that are built with combinations of masonry, light-steel framing, open-web steel joists, wood framing, wood rafters, and concrete constitute this group. Although combinations of these materials can be used effectively in engineered designs, they are often carelessly assembled and provide only minimal resistance to wind-induced pressures.

Buildings containing masonry are particularly susceptible to damage in windstorms. Two types of buildings containing masonry are common: buildings in which the roof system is supported by the walls, making the walls "load-bearing," and buildings with light-steel framing (often steel-pipe columns and light I-beams) with masonry walls between columns, called fill-in walls or nonload-bearing walls. Wind-induced pressures push masonry walls inward or outward, depending on wind-approach direction and the type of windward-wall openings. In the case of load-bearing masonry, the roof system falls when the walls collapse. Collapse of nonload-bearing walls does not always produce collapse of the roof system, but the contents of the affected building are destroyed. Although these failures illustrate severe damage and appear to be caused by large pressures from extreme windspeeds, they are often induced by winds under 125 mi/h (56 m/s).

Motel and apartment units that are framed mainly with wood usually receive only limited engineering attention and thus are vulnerable to wind-induced pressures. Roofs are commonly lifted because of inadequate connection to walls or fail when overhangs over walkways are lifted by wind-induced pressure increases beneath. In such failures damage is severe and is usually described as total destruction, although the windspeeds causing the damage are usually nominal, i.e., 125 mi/h (56 m/s) or less.

## Nonengineered Buildings

Single- and multiple-family residences, certain apartment units, and many small commercial buildings receive no engineering attention at all. Largely of wood-frame construction, these buildings generally offer little resistance to lateral and uplift pressures induced by the wind. Weak roof-to-wall and wall-to-foundation connections, little resistance to lateral loads, and inadequate overall structural integrity typify these buildings. They can be damaged by winds of 75 mi/h (33 m/s), and total destruction may occur when winds reach 125 mi/h (56 m/s).

## Performance of Housing in Windstorms

### Factors Affecting Resistance to Wind

Five factors strongly influence the behavior of housing in windstorms: construction, house orientation with respect to the wind, house geometry, shielding by adjacent structures or trees, and terrain (Minor et al., 1977). Construction significantly influences the resistance of a house to winds. Examinations of housing throughout the Southeast, South, Southwest, and Midwest have led investigators to conclude that (1) unzoned rural construction is inferior to construction within cities that have active building-code-enforcement programs,

(2) traditional methods of housing construction evolve differently in different cities, and (3) these differences in construction practice often lead to large variations in housing damage during windstorms. Rural housing is often characterized by light framing, poor foundation anchorage, and minimum attention to connections, because no city or zoning authority enforces strict building codes. City builders have developed habits of housing construction (Walker, 1976) that have become almost traditional, and are rarely changed until a major event, such as a windstorm or an earthquake, compels corrective action. For example, in Omaha, Nebraska, little or no anchorage was generally used between the superstructure and the perimeter foundation of housing. Figure 5.10 shows that an entire unanchored superstructure unit was moved intact from its foundation, probably at a relatively low windspeed, 100 mi/h (45 m/s) or less. In Plainview, Texas, gabled roofs are usually constructed with rafters only, leaving open space in the attic. When gable spans are large, winds can remove large segments of roof as shown in Fig. 5.11. In Birmingham, Alabama, concrete-block foundations common to split-level housing often did not contain vertical reinforcing steel; hence, many foundation failures were evident in a 1977 windstorm (Fig. 5.12).

Investigations have shown that house orientation is an important determinant of damage. With an attached garage facing the approaching wind a house is more susceptible to damage than a house without an attached garage or with a garage that does not face approaching winds. Houses with porches or large overhanging eaves that face the wind and houses oriented so that gables face the approaching wind are also more vulnerable to wind than similar houses in other orientations. For example, houses in Xenia, Ohio, with garages facing west incurred greater damage from a tornado than similar housing oriented differently (Fig. 5.13).

Hip and mansard roofs (Fig. 5.14) appear to offer better wind resistance than gable and flat roofs. Besides their favorable aerodynamic shape the hip roofs have better anchorage since the roof is tied to the wall around the entire perimeter of the house.

Shielding by trees also mitigates wind damage in residential areas and in mobile-home parks. Mutual shielding in a group of houses is a recognized but not well-understood effect. Single houses in the

**Figure 5.10.** House (above) that was moved from foundation because no house-to-foundation anchorage was employed (below). The structure merely rested on the foundation shown.

**Figure 5.11.** Wind damage to residential roof system constructed without internal bracing.

**Figure 5.12.** Wind damage to house with concrete-block perimeter foundation. Absence of vertical reinforcing steel made house more vulnerable.

**Figure 5.13.** Wind damage to houses in Xenia, Ohio, 3 April 1974. Houses with garages facing west (toward bottom of photo) sustained more damage.

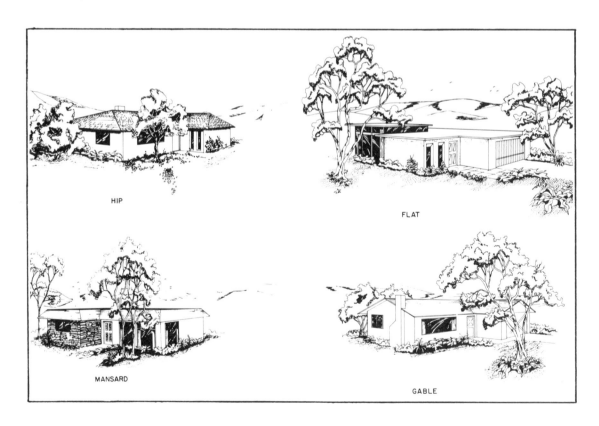

**Figure 5.14.** Typical roof styles. Hip and mansard roofs are less vulnerable to wind damage.

**Figure 5.15.** Hurricane clips (arrows) used to fasten roof beams to wall.

open (such as rural houses) and houses at the windward edge of a group feel the full effects of a windstorm. For houses in the interior and leeward side of a group, some protection through mutual shielding may be realized, although effects of wake turbulence and missiles may increase damage.

Some recent tornado events have shown that terrain undulations do not necessarily afford protection from tornadoes. Many of the tornadoes of 3-4 April 1974 had long tracks, some of which followed hilly, even mountainous, terrain quite closely. The Omaha tornado of 6 May 1975 also followed closely the hills within the city.

## Methods of Strengthening Wind Resistance of Houses

The most important consideration in building wind resistance into a house is maintaining the overall integrity of the structure. The roof should be anchored securely to the wall, and the walls should be tied securely to the foundation. Roof systems must remain integral, and wall strength must not be compromised by openings that are weak relative to wall strength. Specific suggestions for strengthening housing are advanced below:

*Roofing Systems:* Hip- and mansard-roof geometries offer the best wind resistance. Regardless of geometry, roof systems more than 20 ft wide should be constituted of roof trusses, and care should be taken to assure that the trusses and roofing material (battens, shingles) form an integral unit.

*Roof-to-Wall Connection:* The roofing system must be firmly attached to the walls. This connection is best achieved by framing the walls integral with the roof (e.g., letting wall studs extend into the roofing system to form parts of the roof trusses). Using positive fasteners such as hurricane clips (Fig. 5.15) for rafter-to-wall connection is far superior to nailing.

*Wall Systems:* Stud walls should contain sheathing that is missile-resistant (e.g., brick veneer or metal paneling). If brick veneer is used, the brick should be anchored to the walls. Openings such as windows and doors should be "storm" quality

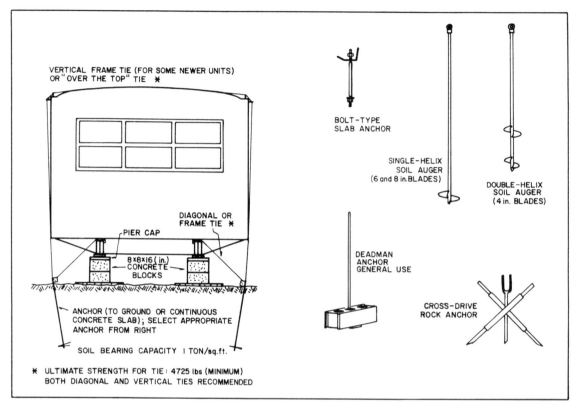

**Figure 5.16.** An effective tie-down system for mobile homes.

or should be protected by screens designed to withstand winds and reject missiles.

*Wall-to-Foundation Connection:* Wall-to-foundation anchorages should be positive (e.g., anchor bolts). To resist large lateral forces there should be a substantial number of anchorage points.

*Foundation:* Foundations should extend at least 2 ft into the soil. Concrete-block foundations should be reinforced with vertical reinforcing steel.

Mobile homes present special problems. Authorities agree that mobile homes should be vacated when a windstorm threatens. To mitigate property damage, a well-engineered and properly installed tie-down system is essential. Figure 5.16 illustrates a recommended method. Anchorages should be selected in light of local soil conditions. Vann and McDonald (1978) discuss technical aspects of mobile homes in windstorms.

## Designing Shelters for Wind Resistance

Extensive studies of wind-caused building damage and increased understanding of wind dynamics gained from wind-tunnel studies have produced innovations in building design and construction. Engineers can now build shelters that will virtually assure survival of people and property from the direct effects of windstorms, including tornadoes.

### Protection of People

Investigations of wind-caused damage to residences have shown that the interior portions of houses have a good chance of surviving even severe tornadoes (Fig. 5.17). The relatively compact interior walls that frame closets, halls, bathrooms, and other small rooms are strong enough to resist extreme winds and thus provide the best shelter if a basement or interior storm shelter is not available (Eagleman et al., 1975; Kiesling and Goolsby,

**Figure 5.17.** An interior portion of a house, the only part surviving a severe windstorm.

**Figure 5.18.** Interior shelter being constructed in a residence. This windstorm-proof room cost the homeowner only $700 (1978 prices) more than he would otherwise have paid for the same space.

1974). To protect lives, a stormproof above-ground shelter located in the center of a residence is preferable to an underground, outside shelter because of its accessibility and relatively low cost. A small interior room can be turned into such a shelter with materials commonly used in residential construction and at reasonable cost. The typical interior shelter is constructed with concrete blocks, reinforcing steel, and concrete and costs little more than a conventional room (Fig. 5.18). An interior shelter should be designed to resist the maximum winds possible in a tornado, to vent changes in atmospheric pressure, and to withstand missiles that may be propelled against the walls or roof (see DCPA, 1975a, for further details on residential-shelter designs).

Design principles that apply to residential shelters are also applicable to shelters in schools and public buildings. Interior halls, usually the surviving building space, provide the best sites for shelter construction. The design in Fig. 5.19 is one of several detailed shelter designs for schools available from the federal government (DCPA, 1975b).

**Figure 5.19.** Reinforced construction in a school hallway. This shelter concept employs available interior space and common construction materials.

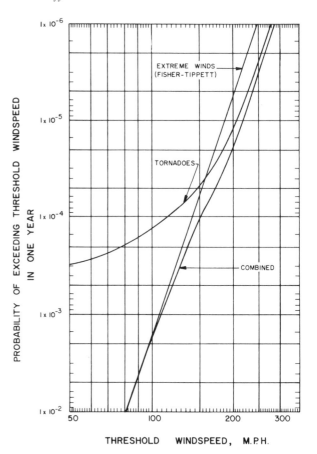

**Figure 5.20.** Sample hazard-probability model for wind. Probabilistic models of this type enable engineers to design buildings and facilities for windspeeds consistent with appropriate levels of risk.

## Protection of Property

Contents of buildings can be protected by proper construction for wind resistance. Perhaps the most common weakness in building construction is the roof-to-wall connection. In commercial construction this weakness often results from inattention to detail, and a few anchor bolts or welds would strengthen the connection. As noted above, the use of a hurricane clip in residential construction (Fig. 5.15) is superior to the common practice of toenailing rafters to the wall. Appropriate engineering attention to overhead door and window components can increase their wind resistance to the level of the rest of the structure. Vertical reinforcing steel within walls constructed of concrete blocks substantially increases wind resistance at small cost.

## Protection of Building Function

Computer facilities, facilities housing radioactive and toxic materials, and buildings such as hospitals and emergency centers often require special engineering to ensure uninterrupted function. For design of such a building, a hazard-probability model for winds is usually developed. In graphic form, the model indicates the probability of exceedance, i.e., the probability that a given windspeed will be exceeded in a given period, usually a year (Fig. 5.20). The extreme-wind curve is developed using a procedure advanced by Thom (1968), who recommends a Fisher-Tippett (Type II) probability distribution to characterize extreme winds. The tornado curve is developed by using procedures proposed by McDonald (1975). Once a hazard-probability model has been established for a geographic location, only the risk consistent with the facility being designed remains to be specified. Facilities that

**Figure 5.21.** Wind damage to housing in Darwin, Australia (1974).

house or process nuclear materials are commonly assigned risk levels of $1 \times 10^{-7}$; i.e., they are designed to withstand a wind that has a 1-in-10-million chance of being exceeded in a given year. Facilities such as hospitals, central computers, and refineries are assigned risk levels of $1 \times 10^{-2}$ (1-in-100 chance) or less. Conventional buildings are usually designed for winds that have a probability of exceedance of $2 \times 10^{-2}$, or a 1-in-50 chance of being exceeded in a given year.

### Improvements in Building Practice

Many myths and misconceptions surround windstorms produced by thunderstorms, particularly those producing tornadoes. Many believe, for example, that buildings cannot be built to resist a tornado and that the very large pressure deficits in the core of the tornado produce unmanageable forces on building components. Even though many professionals are now aware that in large percentages (90% or more) of all tornadoes windspeeds are survivable (150 mi/h [67 m/s] or less) and

atmospheric pressure changes are 60 mb or less, building owners and the public often remain doubtful.

The first step in improving building practice is making the public aware of the magnitude of the wind-damage problem and the availability of technology to solve it. Disasters such as the Darwin, Australia, catastrophe of Christmas Day 1974 (Fig. 5.21) helped alert Australians to the problem (Walker, 1976). Public awareness in the United States, however, was not altered by the Australian event, and many of our cities are vulnerable to disasters by hurricanes, tornadoes, and other severe windstorms.

Once the public is aware of the need for change, the design professional and the building official can effect appropriate changes in building codes. Building practices will improve when the knowledge of wind engineers and meteorologists has been assimilated by the building industry. The national building standard that embodies much of this knowledge (ANSI, 1972) is finding increased acceptance among design professionals; changes in building codes will follow this acceptance.

## Concluding Remarks

The demand for environmentally safe facilities for the nuclear-reactor industry and an increasing concern about the magnitude of losses from strong winds have spurred valuable research into the thunderstorm, with implications for construction practices. Tornado-proof shelters and wind-resistant buildings can be constructed at reasonable cost to provide safety in windstorms.

Perhaps the most important revelations of research into thunderstorms and the damage their winds produce are those about the magnitude and character of damaging winds. Conventional buildings, especially housing, are damaged by wind speeds as low as 75 mi/h (33 m/s). Most of the damage to conventional buildings by thunderstorms, including tornado-producing thunderstorms, is caused by winds with speeds less than 125 mi/h (56 m/s). Only very small areas are affected by winds exceeding these values, and these extreme winds occur in a very small percentage of thunderstorms. Maximum thunderstorm-produced windspeeds probably do not exceed 250 to 275 mi/h (112 to 123 m/s).

# Appendix A

## Phenomena Affecting Interaction Between Wind and Buildings

### Bernoulli Effect

Bernoulli's equation characterizes fluid flow in a statement of the energy principle, the essential balance between kinetic energy and potential energy over every part of a streamline (Rouse, 1938). For steady, inviscid, incompressible flow, we have

$$\rho \frac{V^2}{2} + p + \gamma h = \text{constant}, \qquad (5.1)$$

where $\rho$ = mass density, $V$ = velocity, $p$ = pressure intensity, $\gamma$ = specific weight, and $h$ = elevation. The pressure intensity varies along a streamline with change in velocity and in elevation. Where air flows over and around a low-rise building, effects of changes in elevation of a streamline are negligible; hence, the $\gamma h$ term can be neglected. Thus, regions of accelerated (higher velocity) flow (e.g., flow over a roof or along a wall) are regions of lower pressure, relative to pressure in the free stream in advance of the building. If the building is enclosed and contains air at ambient pressure $p$, a pressure differential acts upward or outward on the roof and sidewalls. A change in velocity toward zero along a streamline causes the pressure to increase by $\frac{1}{2}\rho V^2$. The pressure increase experienced by a windward wall of a building may approach this value if the wall is very large, because airstream velocity is brought to near zero in front of the wall.

### Flow Separation

Under many conditions of flow over surfaces, and particularly flow over bluff bodies, the flow separates from the surface of the body (Davenport, 1960). This is a phenomenon related to fluid viscosity, which precludes application of the Bernoulli equation discussed above. The point of separation is a point of stagnation on the streamline that divides the oncoming flow from a localized reverse flow along the surface downstream from the flow-separation point. Behind the body is the wake region, characterized by energy dissipation. The wake is a region with small pressure gradients and a pressure comparable with that existing at the separation point. The pressure in the wake finds expression in a dimensionless pressure coefficient

$$C_{pw} = \frac{p_w - p_0}{\frac{1}{2}\rho V_0^2}, \qquad (5.2)$$

where $p_w$ = pressure in wake, $p_0$ = free stream pressure, and $V_0$ = free-stream velocity.

The coefficient $C_{pw}$ is defined experimentally with the aid of models and wind tunnels and can be applied to evaluation of pressure forces on real structures. With very sharp corners and certain angles of wind incidence $C_{pw}$ values can be very large, ranging up to 5 or more. Such values for $C_{pw}$ mean that pressures acting upward along eaves and corners of roofs can be as large as five times the value $\frac{1}{2}\rho V^2$, which is the largest average inward-acting pressure on a windward wall.

# Appendix B

# Windspeeds in Thunderstorms

In recent years estimates of maximum tornadic windspeeds have dropped from about 500 mi/h (224 m/s) to 250 to 300 mi/h (112 to 134 m/s) (Kessler, 1976). This reduction has profound engineering implications. Buildings will be more economically designed to be tornado-proof if windspeeds of 300 mi/h (134 m/s) are considered the upper limit. In addition, since only a small percentage (2% or less) of all tornadoes possess windspeeds approaching the maximum, many conventional buildings can be made tornado resistant.

Windspeeds in thunderstorms, including tornadoes, have been estimated through coordinated efforts of engineers and meteorologists. Meteorologists estimate tornadic windspeeds by using theoretical modeling, laboratory work, and photogrammetric evaluations. Engineers rely mainly on calculations of wind-induced pressures that have produced damage to buildings to estimate windspeeds. Examples of engineering calculations are provided below.

## Approach to Windspeed Calculations

Many studies of procedures for assessing the response of structures to strong gusty winds are reported in the literature (Davenport, 1961; Smart et al., 1967; Handa, 1971). Generalized treatment of the interaction of gusty winds with elastically responding structures leads to two response functions: (1) a function in which the classic $\frac{1}{2}\rho V^2 C_D$ term relates drag force to the square of wind velocity (described as the drag term) and (2) a function in which the reaction of the structure is associated with the acceleration of the wind (described as the acceleration term). The coefficients of drag $C_D$ in the drag term can be associated with a mean windspeed value if the wind turbulence and structural response are governed by probabilistic processes that are stationary, i.e., independent of the duration of the wind record. The acceleration term

is more important for winds whose speed and direction change rapidly relative to fundamental frequencies of structural vibration.

Windfield conditions in severe thunderstorms may violate the assumptions of stationarity fundamental to the formulations, but this is important only where the vibration periods are long. Usually, however, the systems of interest are structural components (e.g., walls, wall panels, roof panels) with short periods of vibration. In these situations, the assumptions of stationarity are valid, and the drag term evaluations are applicable.

Engineering analysis defines the pressure $p$ that causes a given building or building component to fail. The windspeed that produces this pressure is then calculated from an expression that relates the pressure, windspeed and drag coefficient (see ASCE, 1961). Thus, for example,

$$p = \frac{1}{2}\rho V^2 C_D, \qquad (5.3)$$

where $p$ = wind-induced pressure, $V$ = wind velocity, $\rho$ = mass density of air, and $C_D$ = drag, shape, or pressure coefficient. With $\rho = 0.00237$ slug/ft$^3$ (air at 60°F, standard atmospheric pressure at sea level), $p$ in lb/ft$^2$, and $V$ in mi/h, unit conversion yields $p = 0.00256 C_D V^2$, which is widely used in engineering calculations of wind pressures on bluff objects.

## Examples of Windspeed Calculations

A single-track, simple-span, dual-girder bridge carries a railroad over the Tippecanoe River in Monticello, Indiana. The tornado that struck Monticello on 3 April 1974 traveled northeast across the center of town and crossed the east-west railroad bridge near its east end. Four spans were pushed sideways into the river. The simple spans were resting on steel pins and steel rollers (Fig. 5.22) in such a way that they

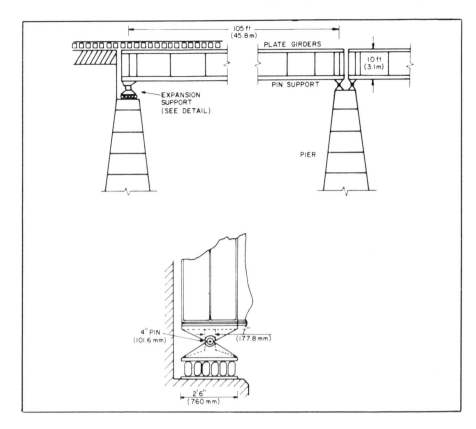

**Figure 5.22.** Construction of spans of railroad bridge. Steel-plate girders were resting on steel pins and rollers.

would experience no resistance to lateral load other than through frictional forces. Windspeed is calculated as follows (Mehta et al., 1976):

1. Total weight $W$ of a single span (from plans) is 223,300 lb (101,290 kg).

2. Assumed steel-on-steel coefficient of friction $\mu$ is 0.35.

3. Net pressure coefficient $C_D$ for rectangular bridge cross section is 1.3 (ANSI, 1972).

4. Depth and span of plate girder is 10 ft (3 m) × 105 ft (32 m).

5. Force required to slide the span $F$ is $F = \mu W$ (lb) = (0.35) (223,000) = 78,160 lb (347 kN).

6. Uniform wind pressure required to develop force $F$ is $p = F/[(10) \times (105)] = 74.4$ lb/ft² (3.6 kN/m²); 74.4 = 0.00256 (1.3) $V^2$ (from Eq.53).

7. $V = 150$ mi/h (67 m/s).

This calculated windspeed must be considered a conservative estimate because (1) the analysis assumes that maximum winds act normal to the plate girders, and (2) the windspeed value corresponds to windspeeds necessary to start motion only. However, the value of 150 mi/h (67 m/s) seems reasonable as a probable maximum windspeed when compared with estimates from other damage analyses in the Monticello area (Mehta et al., 1975).

The roof of a junior high school in Xenia, Ohio, sustained damage by uplifting of precast roof beams during the 3 April 1974 tornado (Mehta et al., 1976) (Fig. 5.23). The structure had enough venting area (through windows) to eliminate net forces caused by atmospheric pressure change. Lifting of the precast beams could occur through aerodynamically induced pressures as air flowed over the roof. The precast, double-T beams were 8 ft (2.4 m) wide and 12 in (305 mm) deep; they spanned 26 ft (8 m) between supports and had a 2-ft (0.6 m) overhang. Each beam was anchored by fillet welds ¼ × 2 in (6 × 51 mm) at the beam's supports. Since beams lifted only in one corner of the roof, it is possible to estimate a minimum windspeed that was experienced by the roof. The minimum width w of the building is 138 ft (42 m); thus local pressure coefficients for roof corner and roof eave apply for a distance 13.8 ft (4.2 m), or 10% of w from the edge of the building, including the overhang (ANSI, 1972). The breakage of window glass indicates that internal pressure and aerodynamically induced pressure acted in combination. Wind pres-

**Figure 5.23.** Wind damage to junior-high-school building in Xenia, Ohio. Precast concrete roof beams were lifted.

sures necessary to break the welds along the beams in the roof-corner area can be determined by taking moments about interior support.

Windspeed calculations are as follows for the corner beam:

1. Anchorage weld capacity = $(0.25 \times 0.707 \times 4)$ $(36,000) = 25,500$ lb (11,570 kg).

2. Dead weight (including beam, insulation, and built-up roofing) is $47 \times 8 = 376$ lb/ft (560 kg/m).

3. Local pressure coefficient for a corner of a flat

**Table 5.1.** Credence Levels for Windspeed Calculations

| Component of windspeed calculation | Credence level | | |
|---|---|---|---|
| | Good (G) | Acceptable (A) | Questionable (Q) |
| Structural system | Free-standing structures | Certain framed structures | Typical residences |
| | "Clean" structures | Conventional buildings | Rural buildings |
| Material strengths | Steel | Concrete | Missiles |
| | Steel connections | Masonry | Glass |
| | | Timber | Nailed connections |
| | | Precast concrete | |
| | | Engineered connections | |
| Gust sensitivity | Rigid structures (e.g., low-rise reinforced concrete) | Nonrigid structures (e.g., certain framed buildings) | Flexible structures (e.g., flagpoles) |
| Pressure-coefficient values | Net pressure coefficients | External and internal pressure coefficients | Local pressure coefficients |
| Location of windspeed estimate | At point of failure | Near point of failure | Points away from point of failure |

**Table 5.2.** Credence Levels for Selected Windspeed Estimates

| Windstorm | Reference | Analyzed item | Calculated windspeed in mi/h (m/s) | Credence ratings* 1 2 3 4 5 | | | | | Remarks |
|---|---|---|---|---|---|---|---|---|---|
| Worcester, Mass., tornado 1953 | Booker (1954) | Transmission tower | 330-350 (134-156) | G | G | Q | G | Q | Reported windspeeds based on assumed windspeed profile; did not occur at towers |
| Dallas, Tex., tornado 1957 | Segner (1960) | Freight cars | 83-217 (37-97) | Q | - | G | G | G | Freight cars became missiles |
| Monticello, Ind., tornado 1974 | Mehta et al. (1976) | Bridge girders | 150 (67) | G | G | G | G | G | Rectangular girders on simple supports |

*Numbers correspond to components in the first column of Table 5.1.

roof is $C = 5.0$ (ANSI, 1972), acting on an area $13.8 \times 13.8$ ft ($4.2 \times 4.2$ m), including 2 ft (0.6 m) of the overhang.

4. Pressure coefficient for the eave of a roof is $C = 2.4$ acting on the remaining part of the corner beam (ANSI, 1972).

5. Internal pressure coefficient for openings mainly in windward wall (e.g., broken window) is $C = 0.8$, and it applies in conjunction with external pressure coefficients (ANSI, 1972).

6. Taking moments about interior support yields $(25,500 \times 26) + (376 \times 28 \times 14) - q[(8 \times 13.8 \times 21.1 \times 5.8) + (8 \times 14.2 \times 7.1 \times 3.2)] = 0$; $q = 50.3$ lb/ft² (2.3 kN/m²).

7. If we use Eq. 5.3, $50.3 = 0.00256 V^2$, and $V = 140$ mi/h (63 m/s).

Assumptions are implicit in these analytical proce-

dures, and therefore the reliability of the calculated windspeeds varies. To account for such variability, credence levels are assigned to windspeed estimates, in accord with a process developed by Mehta (1976). Important components of the windspeed-calculation process that can influence credence levels are (1) the character of the structural system, (2) material strengths and construction practices, (3) gust sensitivity (the acceleration term is considered here), (4) pressure-coefficient values, and (5) the location of windspeed estimate with respect to failure origin point. Table 5.1 notes the three credence levels that can be assigned to windspeed estimates as a function of assumptions inherent to the five components of the calculation process. Table 5.2 summarizes credence levels that have been assigned to several windspeed estimates found in the literature.[1]

[1]I wish to acknowledge contributions by my close associates at Texas Tech University, Kishor C. Mehta and James R. McDonald, who, with me have worked for eight years to develop the perspectives contained in this chapter. This work has been sponsored by the National Science Foundation; the National Severe Storms Laboratory, NOAA; the Nuclear Regulatory Commission; and the Civil Defense Preparedness Agency (now the Federal Emergency Management Agency), with the support of Texas Tech University. Ernst W. Kiesling, chairman of the Department of Civil Engineering in Texas Tech University, and Michael P. Gaus, of the National Science Foundation, deserve special acknowledgment as individuals whose perceptions and policies assured the success of the wind-engineering program. Colleagues within the university—Richard E. Peterson and Donald R. Haragan—and outside the university—Edwin Kessler, Robert F. Abbey, Jr., Allen D Pearson, R. P. Davies-Jones, and T. T. Fujita—have also assisted in developing important understandings of the thunderstorm; these contributions are gratefully acknowledged.

# 6. Lightning Damage and Lightning Protection

*E. Philip Krider*

## Introduction

Lightning is a transient, high-current electric discharge whose path length is measured in kilometers. The most common cause of lightning is the electric charge that is generated by thunderstorm clouds, and well over half of all discharges occur within the clouds. Cloud-to-ground lightning is less frequent than intracloud but flashes to ground are the primary hazard to people or objects on the ground. A recent estimate of the annual frequency of cloud-to-ground flashes, based on thunderstorm-hour statistics, is given in Fig. 6.1 (Maier, 1983). Note that most of the continental United States has at least two cloud-to-ground flashes per square kilometer per year on average and that half of the United States has at least 4 $km^{-2}$ $yr^{-1}$. In more familiar units, a flash density of 4 $km^{-2}$ $yr^{-1}$ is equivalent to about 10 discharges per square mile per year. Altogether, an average of about 50 million cloud-to-ground flashes strike the United States each year, and, as Chapter 1 indicates, lightning is among the nation's most severe weather hazards.

In this chapter I briefly review the luminous development of a cloud-to-ground lightning flash, the mechanisms of lightning damage, and the fundamentals of lightning protection. References to more detailed discussions of these subjects are given in the text. Although the interactions of an individual lightning flash are discussed, it is worth noting that the overall phenomenology of lightning in thunderstorms—e.g., the total number of flashes, the fraction of all discharges that strike the ground, the time evolution of the flashing rates, etc.—needs further research (see, for example, Livingston and Krider, 1978). The questions of whether the characteristics of individual flashes depend on the geo-graphical location, the ground characteristics, the season, the meteorological environment, etc., are also still to be answered. Although the average flash is probably similar throughout the world, there are important differences within a given region. For example, frontal storms are thought to produce higher flashing rates and more strokes per flash than air-mass storms (Schonland, 1956); topography affects the channel lengths and perhaps other properties of the discharges (McEachron, 1939; Winn et al., 1973); and there are important seasonal effects, such as in the frequency of positive discharges to ground (Brook et al., 1982).

## Cloud-to-Ground Lightning

Here it may be helpful to review the terminology used to describe the luminous processes that occur in a typical cloud-to-ground lightning flash (for more detailed discussions of these phenomena, see Viemeister, 1961; Schonland, 1964; Uman, 1969, 1971; Salanave, 1980; and Uman and Krider, 1982). A typical discharge begins within the cloud with a process called the *preliminary breakdown.* The preliminary breakdown usually lasts several tens of milliseconds and eventually initiates an intermittent, highly branched discharge, called a *stepped leader,* that propagates downward. The stepped leader usually lowers negative charge, and the direction of the branches in a photograph indicates the direction of stepped-leader propagation. Successive stages in the geometrical development of a stepped leader are shown in Fig. 6.2.

When the tip of any branch of the stepped leader comes close to the ground, the electric field at the surface under the leader becomes very large,

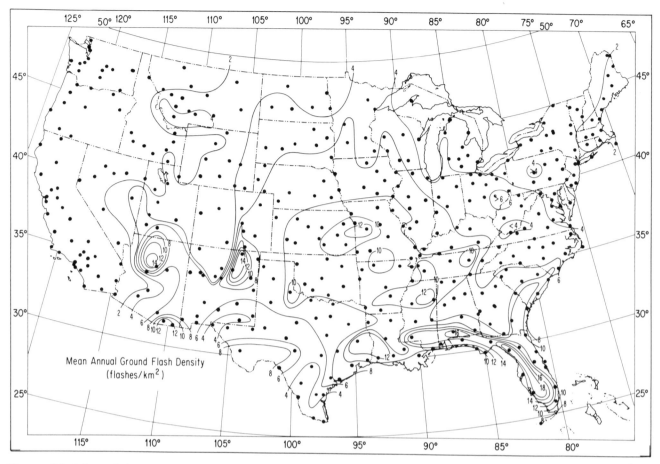

**Figure 6.1.** Map of the annual frequency of cloud-to-ground lightning over the continental United States, based on thunderstorm hour statistics. (Courtesy of M. W. Maier.)

and one or more upward propagating discharges form at the ground and start the *attachment process* (see Fig. 6.2c). These upward-propagating discharges rise until one or more attach to the leader a few tens of meters above the surface. When

contact occurs, the first *return stroke* begins. The return stroke is a very large current pulse that starts at the ground and propagates back up the previously ionized leader channel to the cloud. The peak currents in return strokes are typically

**Figure 6.2.** Sketch of the time development of a lightning stepped leader and the ensuing return strokes.

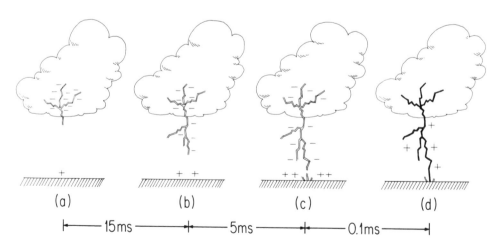

(a)  (b)  (c)  (d)

|— 15ms —|— 5ms —|— 0.1ms —|

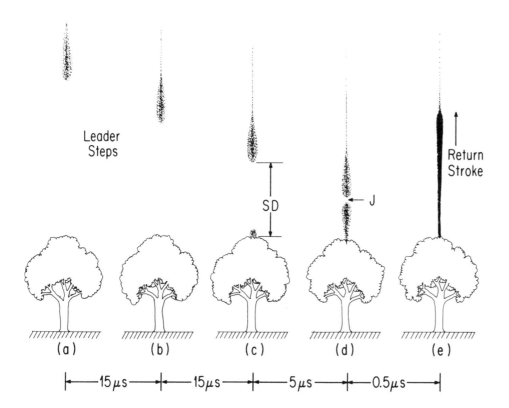

**Figure 6.3.** Sketch of the luminous processes that occur during a lightning strike. An upward-connecting discharge forms in (c) when the stepped leader is at the striking distance, SD.

tens of kiloamperes, and the speed of upward propagation is usually about one-third the speed of light.

The last few steps of the stepped leader, the onset of a connecting discharge, and the beginning of the return stroke are illustrated in Fig. 6.3. The distance between the object that is about to be struck and the tip of the leader when the connecting discharge is initiated is called the *striking distance* and is an important consideration in lightning protection. The distance to the actual junction between the leader and the connecting discharge is often assumed to be about one-half the striking distance. In Fig. 6.3c the striking distance is labeled SD, and in Fig. 6.3d the junction point is labeled J.

A photograph showing upward streamers near the ground during two strikes to mountainous terrain is reproduced in Fig. 6.4. There point d shows what is probably the striking distance (about 39 m above the ground); point e is the junction between the connecting discharge and the leader (16 m); and points a, b, and c are upward discharges that did not contact the leader (8, 10, and 10 m long,

respectively). Further details about this photograph are given in Krider and Ladd, 1975.

After a pause of typically 40 to 80 ms most cloud-to-ground flashes produce a *dart leader* that propagates, without stepping, down the previous return-stroke channel and initiates a subsequent return stroke. Most flashes contain two to four return strokes, and lightning often appears to "flicker" because the human eye can just resolve the time intervals between these bright components. In roughly 20 to 40 percent of all cloud-to-ground flashes the dart leader propagates down only a portion of the previous return-stroke channel and then forges a different path to ground. In these instances the lightning actually strikes the ground in two places, and the channel has a characteristic forked appearance that can be seen in many photographs.

The currents in return strokes have been measured in direct strikes to instrumented towers. Peak currents of typically 20 to 40 kA usually occur within 1 to 3 $\mu$s, and the maximum rate of rise of current during the initial onset may be 150 kA/$\mu$s or higher (Weidman and Krider, 1980). The cur-

**Figure 6.4.** Photograph of upward streamers near the strike points of two flashes in mountainous terrain. Point d: striking distance; e: junction between the connecting discharge and the leader; a, b, and c: upward discharges that did not contact the leader (Krider and Ladd, 1975).

rent falls to about half the peak value in about 50 μsec, and following this, many strokes have a *continuing current* on the order of hundreds of amperes that persists for tens of milliseconds after the stroke peak. Table 6.1 shows a summary of the current characteristics of return strokes that lower negative charge toward ground. Flashes that lower positive charge are much less frequent than those that lower negative charge; positive flashes do sometimes transfer very large amounts of charge to ground (Berger et al., 1975; Brook et al., 1982).

Recent analyses of the broadband electromagnetic power radiated by lightning indicate that the peak power during a first return stroke is at least $2 \times 10^{10}$w and that subsequent strokes produce at least $3 \times 10^9$w (Krider and Guo, 1983). These are large power values, but since the duration of a stroke is limited to just a few tens of microseconds, the total energy is thought to be on the order of $10^8$ to $10^9$ J, or roughly $10^4$ to $10^5$ J per meter of channel (Hill, 1979; Few, 1981).

During a return stroke the large current heats

**Table 6.1.** Parameters of Return Strokes That Lower Negative Charge to Ground*

| Parameters | Unit | Percentage of cases exceeding tabulated value | | |
|---|---|---|---|---|
| | | 95% | 50% | 5% |
| Peak current (minimum 2 kA): | | | | |
|   First stroke | kA | 14.0 | 30.0 | 80.0 |
|   Subsequent stroke | kA | 4.6 | 12.0 | 30.0 |
| Total charge: | | | | |
|   First stroke | C | 1.1 | 5.2 | 24.0 |
|   Subsequent stroke | C | 0.2 | 1.4 | 11.0 |
|   Entire flash | C | 1.3 | 7.5 | 40.0 |
| Impulse charge: | | | | |
|   First stroke | C | 1.1 | 4.5 | 20.0 |
|   Subsequent stroke | C | 0.22 | 0.95 | 4.0 |
| Stroke duration: | | | | |
|   First stroke | $\mu$s | 30.0 | 75.0 | 200.0 |
|   Subsequent stroke | $\mu$s | 6.5 | 32.0 | 140.0 |
| Action integral: | | | | |
|   First strokes | A$^2$ s | $6.0 \times 10^3$ | $5.5 \times 10^4$ | $5.5 \times 10^5$ |
|   Subsequent strokes | A$^2$ s | $5.5 \times 10^2$ | $6.0 \times 10^3$ | $5.2 \times 10^4$ |
| Interval between strokes | ms | 7.0 | 33.0 | 150.0 |
| Flash duration: | | | | |
|   Including single stroke flashes | ms | 0.15 | 13.0 | 1,100.0 |
|   Excluding single stroke flashes | ms | 31.0 | 180.0 | 900.0 |

*Adapted from Berger et al., 1975.

the channel to a peak temperature on the order of 30,000 K in a microsecond or less. As a result of this heating, the channel pressure reaches 20 atm or more, and the channel expands behind a strong shock wave. The shock decays rapidly with distance to a weak shock, which then decays to an acoustic wave that we eventually hear as thunder (see Few, 1981). Ultimately most of the input energy to a return stroke probably goes into heating the air and the mechanical work of the channel expansion (Few, 1981).

## Lightning Damage

By the term *lightning damage* we mean any undesirable physical effect caused by any lightning process. Here the discussion is limited to the electrical effects caused by direct and nearby strikes, and we do not discuss the subsequent damage that can occur as a result of lightning-caused fires, lightning-caused power outages, etc., even though this subsequent damage can be very great.

Before we consider damage and methods of pro-

tection, it is useful to estimate how often a normal-sized structure, such as a house, might be struck, on average. We assume that the house is situated in a geographic region that has about four cloud-to-ground flashes per square kilometer per year (see Fig. 6.1). We also assume that the physical area of the house is about $10 \times 20$ m$^2$ and that there will be a direct strike any time a leader comes within about 10 m of this area. In this instance the effective area of attraction is about $30 \times 40$ m$^2$, and the house will be struck, on average, $(1200)(4)(10^{-6}) = 4.8 \times 10^{-3}$ times a year, or roughly once every two hundred years. Another way to think of this hazard is that under these conditions, on average, one house in two hundred will be struck directly at least once a year.

The electrical effects induced by a nearby flash can often be severe. If we assume that any strike within about 100 m of the house can be deleterious, then, in our example, we would expect such a strike about once every five years, on average. Of course, if the geographic region has a higher flash density than 4 km$^{-2}$ yr$^{-1}$, the strike frequency will be higher, and vice versa.

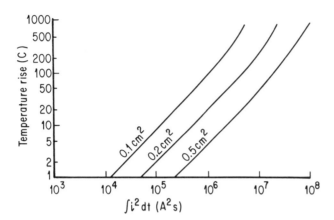

**Figure 6.5.** The temperature rise of copper conductors of various areas versus the action integral of the current (adapted from Golde, 1975, Fig. 23).

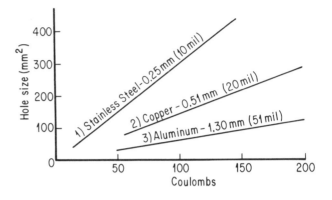

**Figure 6.6.** The hole area burned in metal sheets versus the total charge transfer (adapted from Golde, 1975, Fig. 25).

### Direct Strikes

Most direct lightning strikes cause damage as a result of the large current that flows in the return stroke or the heat that is generated by this and the continuing current. If lightning strikes a person, for example, the current can cause serious burns and damage the central nervous system, heart, lungs, and other vital organs (Lee, 1977; Golde, 1975, Chap. 12). Many types of electronic circuits are damaged or destroyed when exposed to an excess current or to a current of the wrong polarity.

If nearby lightning strikes overhead electric power or telephone lines, large currents flow in one or more of the lines, and these currents can do considerable damage both to power and telecommunications equipment and to anything else that is connected to the system. If a lightning surge enters an unprotected residence by way of a power circuit, the voltages can be large enough to cause sparks in the house wiring or appliances. When these flashovers occur, they short-circuit the power system, and the resulting AC power arc can start a fire. In such cases the lightning does not start the fire directly but causes a power fault; the power system itself does the damage.

The detailed mechanisms whereby lightning currents cause damage are often poorly understood and depend on the specific materials involved. In the human body the current heats the tissue and causes various electrochemical reactions. In metals large currents heat the conductor by electron collisions with the metal lattice, and if this heat is great enough, the metal melts or evaporates. We now examine the thermal effects of lightning on metals and semiconductors in more detail; then we consider mechanical effects. Much of the discussion follows that given by Golde (1975).

*Damage Caused by Heating:* When a current of amplitude, i, is passed through a resistance, R, the electrical heat deposited in the resistance is proportional to the time integral of the power dissipation, $\int i^2 R\,dt$. If we assume that R is independent of current and temperature, and if the duration of the current is short enough that the effects of thermal conduction and convection can be neglected, then the temperature rise in R is proportional to the "action integral" $\int i^2\,dt$. In Table 6.1 we see that a typical action integral for a return stroke is about $5 \times 10^4 A^2$s.

Calculations of the temperature rise of copper wires of varying cross sections for various action integrals are shown in Fig. 6.5. For aluminum conductors the temperature rise is about 1.5 times the values for copper, and for steel it is about 10 times the values for copper. From these curves we can conclude that an action integral of as much as $10^7 A^2$s will raise the temperature of a $50mm^2$ (8mm diameter) steel conductor only about 150° C, a value that is readily acceptable in most situations. If a metal conductor is connected to another con-

**Figure 6.7.** Lightning damage caused by a direct strike to a stone wall (right, rear) and to the ground (Idone and Henderson, 1982).

ductor, it is important that there is good electrical contact or a low resistance at the junction. A high-resistance bond can produce substantial heating and sparking and must be avoided when overlapping metal sheets, corrugated roofing, or similar construction materials are used.

The penetration, or burn-through, characteristics of metal sheets are important when there is a direct strike to a metal roof or to the skin of an aircraft. If a lightning current, i, strikes a metal surface, the heat deposited at the point of contact is approximately $\int Vidt = vQ$, where v is the surface potential of the metal, usually about 10 to 15V, and Q is the charge transferred by the lightning current. Therefore, we might expect that the amount of melting damage will be proportional to the charge transfer, Q, at least to first order.

Figure 6.6 shows the relation between the size of holes burned in metal sheets and the total charge transfer, Q. In Table 6.1 we see that lightning can transfer several tens of coulombs; therefore, we can expect millimeter-sized holes burned in thin sheets. If the duration of the charge transfer is long, the effects of thermal conduction reduces

the damage, and the time required for a burn-through increases (see Golde, 1975, Fig. 26).

If lightning strikes a relatively poor conductor or an insulator, the point of contact can be raised to a very high temperature and result in a burn-through. There are, for example, many reports of centimeter-sized holes burned in glass windows (McIntosh, 1973). If the insulator contains a trace of water or some other conducting material, the current tends to follow the path of least resistance. When moisture is evaporated and converted to steam, the resulting pressure can cause explosive fractures that are sometimes said to be the equivalent of 250 kg of TNT (Golde, 1975, 55).

An example of the explosive effects of a lightning strike to a stone wall and the associated currents in the ground is shown in Fig. 6.7 (see also Idone and Henderson, 1982). Note that the current flowed close to the surface and that the explosive effects of soil heating blew clumps of dirt and sod several meters from the channel. The largest trench was 3.0 m long, 0.8 m wide, and 0.4 m deep (Idone and Henderson, 1982). If the soil density averaged about 2 gm/cm³, then an energy of at least $2 \times$

$10^3$ J-m was required to excavate this amount of material, a value that is consistent with the channel-energy estimates given in "Cloud-to-Ground Lightning" above.

*Damage Caused by Mechanical Effects:* The shock wave produced by the expansion of a return-stroke channel and the magnetic forces created by the lightning currents can cause mechanical damage. As noted above, the shock wave is produced by the rapid heating of the channel by the return stroke (to temperatures on the order of 30,000 K), and the peak overpressures are at least 20 atm. The shock wave heats the air and can cause mechanical damage to distances of a meter or more.

The magnetic forces produced by lightning currents can crush metal tubes and pull wires from walls if they pass around sharp corners (Humphreys, 1964, Chap. 18). If two parallel straight wires share the lightning current, the force between them will be attractive, proportional to the square of the current, and inversely proportional to the distance between the conductors. To minimize these forces in a lightning-protection system, the lightning conductors should not be placed in close proximity to each other (see below, "Basic Principles of Lightning Protection").

### The Sideflash

When a large, rapidly varying current is injected into a lightning conductor (see, for example, Fig. 6.9 below), the inductance of the conductor and the resistance of the ground connection are often large enough to produce a *sideflash,* a discharge from the conductor to a nearby grounded object. A sideflash occurs when the potential of the conductor is raised to a value high enough to initiate a spark and is present long enough for the spark to propagate to the object.

A large variety of sideflash phenomena can occur during strikes to other conducting materials or insulators. One of the greatest hazards in standing near an isolated tree or any other tall object during a thunderstorm is the exposure to a possible sideflash. The damage caused by a sideflash is usually very similar to that of a direct strike.

### Surface Breakdown

When lightning injects a large current into the ground, the resulting voltage gradients usually exceed the breakdown strength of the soil near the strike point, and the current propagates outward in a series of well-defined channels (see Fig. 6.7). These channels are often highly branched and radiate outward for tens of meters or more. Figure 6.8 shows an example of the channels that were burned in the grass of a golfcourse green after the flagpole was struck by lightning (see Krider, 1977, for a more detailed description of this photograph).

Since ground currents are often concentrated on the surface near the strike point and produce large voltage gradients on the surface, the hazards of standing close to an isolated tall object, such as a tree, or of lying stretched out on the ground when exposed to lightning are obvious. A person who is caught in open terrain should stay away from tall objects that are likely to be struck and should also crouch down or kneel so as to minimize both height and the area of the body that is in contact with the ground (Golde, 1975, Chap. 12).

### Nearby Strikes

The electric and magnetic fields produced by nearby lightning can be very large and can induce damage in objects that are not struck directly. These induced effects can broadly be classified into two categories, electrostatic induction and electromagnetic induction.

*Electrostatic Induction:* When a conductor is exposed to an external electric field, a surface charge is induced on the conductor that is proportional to the strength of the field. If the field varies with time, currents flow in the conductor to keep the surface charge in balance with the field. Metal roofs and metal clotheslines should always be grounded to prevent these conductors from reaching harmful potentials in a thunderstorm and to prevent sparking to grounded objects during lightning-field changes.

*Electromagnetic Induction:* During a direct or nearby strike, the amplitudes of the fast-varying

**Figure 6.8.** Lightning damage to a golf-course green (Krider, 1977).

lightning fields are comparable to or may even exceed those produced by a nuclear electromagnetic pulse (Uman et al., 1982). If a closed loop of wire or any other closed conducting path is exposed to a time-varying magnetic field, a current is induced to flow in the circuit. The magnitude of the current is proportional to the time derivative of the magnetic-flux density and inversely proportional to the circuit impedance. This and more complex types of coupling can cause large voltages and currents to flow in conductors, such as power and telephone lines, that are near lightning but are not struck directly by it.

### Basic Principles of Lightning Protection

The protection of a building and its contents against lightning can be achieved by (1) diverting the current produced by a direct strike away from the structure and letting it pass harmlessly to ground and (2) shielding the structure and its contents against any lightning-caused transients. Figure

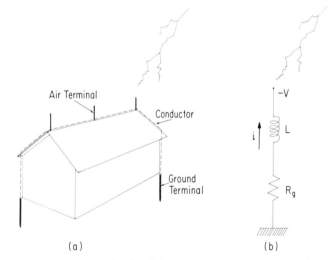

**Figure 6.9.** Sketch of a lightning-protection system that is appropriate for small structures and its equivalent electric circuit.

6.9a shows the classical current-diversion system employed since its invention by Benjamin Franklin, i.e., lightning rods, lightning conductors, and a grounding system. The purpose of a lightning

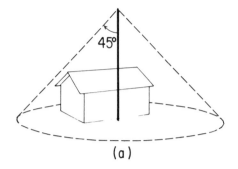

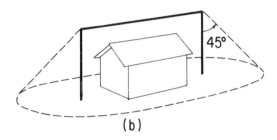

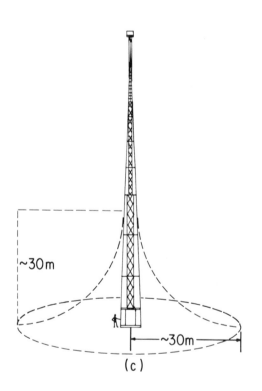

**Figure 6.10.** The zones of protection provided by (a) a vertical mast not exceeding a height of 15 m, (b) an overhead ground wire above a small structure, and (c) a tall tower.

rod, or "air terminal," is to initiate an upward-connecting discharge whenever a stepped leader approaches within the striking distance. During the ensuing return stroke the lightning conductors keep the current outside the structure, and the grounding system keeps the potentials of the entire system low enough to avoid sideflashes and keeps the voltage gradients in the soil below the threshold for surface breakdown. Thunderclouds usually produce high electric fields at the ground, and under these conditions the rods (and any other tall objects or points in the vicinity) may produce point discharges or coronas. The point-discharge currents do *not* neutralize the thundercloud and thereby make the cloud harmless. Again, the function of a rod is simply to create a preferred strike point for any leaders that come within the striking distance. Air terminals do not attract significantly more strikes to the structure than the structure would receive in their absence. A detailed description of the materials and procedures required to protect ordinary buildings from lightning is given in the Lightning Protection Code published by the National Fire Protection Association (NFPA, 1980), and further details are given by Golde (1975, 1977).

The space protected by a grounded air terminal or lightning mast is called the *zone of protection*. According to the U.S. Protection Code, this space can be visualized as a cone that has its apex at the highest point of the rod or mast and a radius at the ground that depends on the height of the mast as shown in Fig. 6.10a. For small structures or masts not exceeding a height of 15 m, the radius of the base equals the height of the mast, and the angle of the cone is 45 degrees. If the building is particularly sensitive to lightning damage, it is best to protect it with an overhead ground wire, as illustrated in Fig. 6.10b.

In general, the zone of protection depends on the striking distance, and the striking distance, in turn, depends on the distribution of charge being lowered by the stepped leader and the geometry of the leader channel. If the leader has a large charge near the ground, the striking distance is large, and vice versa. In most instances the striking distance is thought to exceed 30 m, and if this is true, the U.S. code indicates that a large structure, such as a tall mast, will protect a curved zone as illustrated in Fig. 6.10c.

**Figure 6.11.** A lightning strike to a tall television tower in Tucson, Arizona. The trees in the foreground obscure the channel on the right. Note that the tower was struck below the top and that the channel was nearly horizontal before the strike. Colinear bright points are insulator flashovers on a guy wire (Krider and Alejandro, 1983).

When thinking about the zone of protection, the reader should bear in mind that lightning is an unpredictable phenomenon and that this concept is valid only in a statistical sense. That is, the zone will be protected only *on average,* and individual flashes or upward streamers may occasionally strike within the zone. To illustrate the unpredictable nature of individual flashes, Fig. 6.11 shows lightning striking close to the side of a tall television tower. In this instance the flash struck an insulated guy wire, and the final 70 m of the discharge was nearly horizontal even though the altitude of the channel was only about 80 m above ground. Further details of this photograph have been discussed by Krider and Alejandro (1983).

When lightning strikes a protection system, the effects are often modeled by assuming that the leader channel is a pure current source; that is, the current that flows is assumed to be independent of the impedance of the circuit to ground. The equivalent circuit of the system shown in Fig. 6.9a is given in Fig. 6.9b. Normally the DC resistance of the wires in a protection system is much less than the inductive impedance of the wires or the ground resistance. In this case the magnitude of the voltage, V, at the air terminal is

$$V = iR_g + L\frac{di}{dt},$$

where i is the lightning current (a function of time), $R_g$ is the ground resistance, and L is the total inductance of the lightning conductors. If we assume that the ground resistance is about 30 ohms, that the wire inductance is 15 microhenrys (10 m of wire at 1.5 microhenry per meter), that the lightning current has a peak of 40 kA, and that the average di/dt is about 30 kA/$\mu$s, then V is on the order of 1.6 million volts for about 1 $\mu$s. If there is a grounded object nearby, this voltage and duration can be large enough to cause a sideflash.

All protection systems should be designed so that, as far as is possible, any lightning-caused potentials are the *same* everywhere within the structure and no potential *differences* can develop that will cause sideflashes. This practice, called *bonding,* is implemented by connecting any large metal objects that are close to the conductors in a protection system to that system. Ideally, if we eliminate all harmful potential differences within the

building, there can be no arcing or equipment damage. This could be accomplished by completely enclosing the structure and all of its service wiring, plumbing, etc., within a perfectly conducting shield (a Faraday cage). With this all lightning currents should flow on the low-impedance *outside* surface of the shield rather than inside. In practice such a shield is rarely possible because even an all-metal building has windows, doors, and other apertures and because power lines, telephone lines, pipes, etc., enter the structure and often are poorly shielded or not shielded at all. General topological concepts that can be applied to most lightning-shielding problems are discussed by Tesche (1978).

In practice, protection can usually be obtained by combining what building shielding does exist with proper grounding and bonding. A good grounding system, for example, usually has sufficiently low resistance and inductance that lightning currents cannot produce potential differences large enough to cause a sideflash. Where power lines, communications lines, pipes, or any other conductors enter the structure, they should be equipped with protectors, suppressors, or filters to hold or clamp any lightning-induced transients to a harmless level. Among these devices are such products as lightning arresters, surge arresters, surge suppressors, and transient suppressors. Most of these are *varistors,* which embody a variable resistance that decreases sharply when the applied voltage exceeds some threshold. This electrical behavior can be approximated by the following algebraic expression:

$$i = kV^n,$$

where $k$ is a constant and $n$ provides a measure of the nonlinear relationship between the current, i, and the voltage, V. Silicon carbide has an $n$ in the range from 2 to 7. The zinc-oxide varistor has an $n$ ranging from 20 to 70, and the silicon zener diode has an $n$ that ranges from 100 to 500.

Variable resistors absorb the energy of the transient by transforming it into heat. Zener diodes can absorb up to about 1 J (1 watt-second) of energy, and silicon-carbide and zinc-oxide varistors can absorb 1 to 100 J or more, depending on their size. Since direct lightning strikes produce more energy than can be dissipated by most varistors, other devices, known as *switching protectors,* are

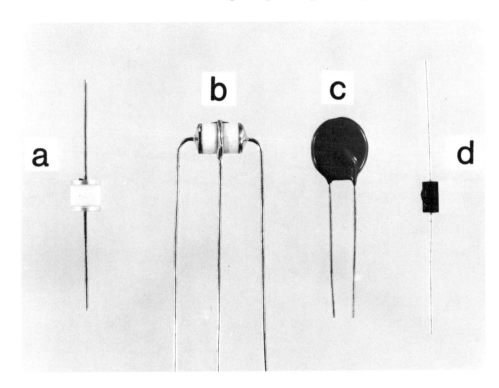

**Figure 6.12.** Examples of typical lightning-protection devices. Devices a and b are sealed spark gaps; c is a metal-oxide varistor, and d is a high-power zener diode. The diameter of the metal-oxide varistor is 1.5 cm.

often used to short-circuit the lightning current and reflect some of the surge energy away from the system before it can reach the varistors. Examples of varistors and switching protectors are shown in Fig. 6.12.

Switching protectors and varistors are frequently used together to provide optimum protection against induced surges. Fig. 6.13 shows a typical protection circuit that might be used on an AC power line. Here a spark gap is used as the switching protector and reflects much of the incoming surge back down the line. The varistor in series with the spark gap prevents a line fault after the spark gap turns on, and the varistor on the right is used to absorb any fast transients that pass the first network during the time it takes the spark to develop in the gap. Surge capacitors and other high-voltage filters can also be used to reflect lightning energy, but these devices must be carefully designed to avoid flashovers.

Fig. 6.14a shows a type of switching protector that is often used on television-antenna wires. This device will not provide adequate protection if there is a direct strike, but it can protect against corona discharges from the antenna in a thunderstorm. The

protector shown in Fig. 6.14b offers very worthwhile protection for most home electrical systems and is available in most electrical-supply stores.

The last matter considered here is the grounding system. Basically, a lightning ground or earth-termination network provides a sink where the light-

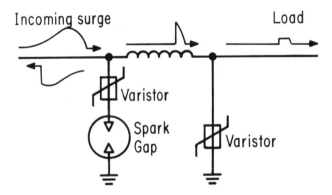

**Figure 6.13.** An example of a circuit that might be used to protect an AC power circuit from a lightning surge. Most of the incoming surge is reflected by the low impedance of the spark gap, and the rest is removed by a second varistor. The delay between the spark gap and the second varistor is necessary because the latter is a faster-acting but lower-power device.

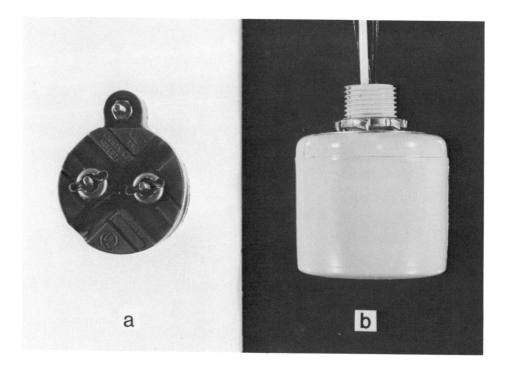

**Figure 6.14.** Surge suppressors often used on homes: (a), a switching protector for a television antenna cable; (b), a varistor for the incoming AC power line. The diameter of each device is approximately 5 cm.

ning current can be discharged harmlessly into the earth. To minimize sideflashes, the ground impedance should be kept as small as possible, and the geometry should be arranged so as to minimize surface breakdown. Many technical articles and books have been written about grounding electric-power systems and associated equipment (see, for example, Sunde [1968] or *Military Handbook*, 1982). Much of this information also applies to a lightning-protection system, though the rapid lightning impulse sometimes poses special problems. For example, if a large current is injected into a short ground rod, the soil surrounding the rod usually breaks down as though it were an insulator. If the current is injected into a long, buried conductor, however, the conductor reacts with its surge impedance, usually about 150 ohms, rather than its steady-state ohmic resistance, and goes into corona. As the initial impulse propagates along the conductor, an increasing fraction of the conductor discharges current into the surrounding soil, and the effective surge impedance decreases with time. The steady-state impedance of the ground is not usually reached until there has been time for several reflections of the current pulse along the buried conductor.[1]

[1] I am grateful to M. W. Maier for providing Fig. 6.1, to V. P. Idone and R. W. Henderson for providing Fig. 6.7, and to M. A. Uman for comments on the manuscript. This effort has been supported in part by the Office of Naval Research, contract N00014-81-K-075.

# 7. Thunderstorms and Aviation

*J. T. Lee and W. B. Beckwith*

## Introduction

Airborne man's confrontation with the forces of thunderstorms was first documented in the days of ballooning, well before the Wright brothers' experiments at Kitty Hawk introduced the era of powered heavier-than-air flight. Early records describe disastrous effects on free balloons of lightning, downdrafts, turbulence, and heavy rains accompanying thunderstorms (Payne, 1977). During the first third of the twentieth century, operation of rigid lighter-than-air craft in thunderstorm environments (Spanner, 1927; Robinson, 1973) was marred by tragedies including the in-flight destruction of British and German zeppelins and the great United States airships *Shenandoah, Akron,* and *Macon.* These losses inhibited further development of the dirigible for air-transportation systems.

Early airplane pilots quickly learned to respect thunderstorms. Since the outward appearance of storms does not reliably indicate hazards within, most pioneering aviators who lived through hazardous weather experiences changed their flight procedure from storm penetration to storm evasion. In the late 1920s and early 1930s, when scheduled flights were introduced to accommodate mail and passenger transport, the need to avoid thunderstorms resulted in delays, flight cancellation, and unscheduled stops. Thunderstorm flight evasion became established airline policy as improved flight safety was sought, and eventually was enforced by government safety bureaus.

Over the years aircraft design and equipment for navigation, storm detection, and communication have been greatly improved, and short-range forecasting and pilot training have become established practices. The United States aviation industry, supported by these improvements, has increased the kilometers flown by private and corporate aircraft from 4.1 billion in 1965 to 7.2 billion in 1976; commercial air carriers flew 2.2 billion km in 1965 and 3.7 billion km in 1976. Between 1965 and 1976, the number of licensed pilots increased from 480,000 to 744,000 (U.S. Bureau of the Census, 1978).

Tables 7.1 to 7.4 show that thunderstorm-related accidents are a continuing problem, though thunderstorm countermeasures have reduced the ratio between storm accidents and level of aircraft activity. Table 7.1, prepared by the U.S. National Transportation Safety Board (NTSB), presents annual aviation-accident statistics for all nonmilitary aircraft. About 43% of all general-aviation fatalities from 1964 to 1981 were weather-related, and about 6% have been related to thunderstorms. Corresponding percentages for the commercial sector are 48% and 13%. The U.S. Air Force and Navy statistics in Table 7.2 suggest that military procedures, which have required strict storm avoidance under noncombat conditions, have been an effective preventive against thunderstorm-related accidents. According to data provided by NTSB, U.S. Air Force thunderstorm-associated damage in flight (37%) has usually been connected with the en route phase as contrasted with takeoffs and landings, and the next most prevalent type of thunderstorm damage has involved parked aircraft (33%). Encounters with storms during prolonged climb account for 5% of the total damage. Similar statistics for air carriers in other parts of the world led O'Hara and Burnham (1968) to state that "thunderstorms are the atmospheric phenomenon which probably causes the greatest single weather hazard to aviation, due to gust, hail and very heavy rain. All parts of the world are affected to some extent,

**Table 7.1.** Annual Summaries of Aircraft Accidents (U.S. Nonmilitary) for 1964-77, Showing Effect of Thunderstorms on Totals (National Transportation Safety Board, Washington, D.C.)

| Year | All accidents | | | Weather-involved accidents | | | Thunderstorm-involved accidents | | |
|------|------|------|------|------|------|------|------|------|------|
| | Total accidents | Total fatal accidents | Total fatalities | Total accidents | Total fatal accidents | Total fatalities | Total accidents | Total fatal accidents | Total fatalities |
| GENERAL AVIATION | | | | | | | | | |
| 1964 | 5,069 | 526 | 1,083 | 798 | 182 | 389 | 56 | 23 | 65 |
| 1965 | 5,196 | 538 | 1,029 | 669 | 215 | 489 | 58 | 47 | 115 |
| 1966 | 5,712 | 573 | 1,149 | 909 | 200 | 463 | 74 | 35 | 96 |
| 1967 | 6,115 | 603 | 1,229 | 1,112 | 202 | 441 | 83 | 38 | 86 |
| 1968 | 4,968* | 692 | 1,399 | 1,067 | 247 | 556 | 69 | 31 | 73 |
| 1969 | 4,767 | 647 | 1,413 | 986 | 237 | 616 | 59 | 31 | 80 |
| 1970 | 4,712 | 641 | 1,310 | 1,014 | 237 | 574 | 68 | 32 | 70 |
| 1971 | 4,648 | 661 | 1,355 | 947 | 246 | 580 | 71 | 39 | 94 |
| 1972 | 4,256 | 695 | 1,421 | 969 | 260 | 606 | 82 | 50 | 119 |
| 1973 | 4,255 | 723 | 1,412 | 976 | 287 | 625 | 74 | 37 | 90 |
| 1974 | 4,425 | 729 | 1,438 | 1,010 | 292 | 701 | 74 | 50 | 140 |
| 1975 | 4,237 | 675 | 1,345 | 990 | 283 | 636 | 67 | 38 | 96 |
| 1976 | 4,193 | 695 | 1,320 | 911 | 266 | 607 | 45 | 26 | 73 |
| 1977 | 4,286 | 702 | 1,436 | 951 | 258 | 608 | 46 | 24 | 61 |
| 1978 | 4,494 | 793 | 1,770 | 946 | 326 | 766 | 54 | 31 | 87 |
| 1979 | 4,023 | 678 | 1,367 | 898 | 284 | 650 | 52 | 32 | 72 |
| 1980 | 3,802 | 674 | 1,393 | 923 | 271 | 661 | 46 | 20 | 49 |
| 1981 | 3,689 | 703 | 1,997 | 1,026 | 292 | 643 | 36 | 14 | 26 |
| Total | 82,847 | 11,948 | 24,866 | 17,101 | 4,585 | 10,611 | 1,114 | 598 | 1,492 |
| AIR CARRIER | | | | | | | | | |
| 1964 | 79 | 13 | 238 | 25 | 6 | 72 | 10 | 3 | 62 |
| 1965 | 83 | 9 | 261 | 33 | 5 | 100 | 17 | 1 | 30 |
| 1966 | 75 | 8 | 272 | 20 | 2 | 125 | 7 | 1 | 42 |
| 1967 | 70 | 12 | 286 | 18 | 2 | 73 | 9 | 0 | 0 |
| 1968 | 71 | 15 | 349 | 33 | 7 | 191 | 11 | 1 | 85 |
| 1969 | 63 | 10 | 158 | 24 | 2 | 52 | 12 | 0 | 0 |
| 1970 | 55 | 8 | 146 | 23 | 2 | 7 | 11 | 0 | 0 |
| 1971 | 48 | 8 | 203 | 22 | 4 | 146 | 8 | 0 | 0 |
| 1972 | 50 | 8 | 160 | 19 | 3 | 68 | 11 | 0 | 0 |
| 1973 | 43 | 9 | 227 | 22 | 4 | 143 | 9 | 2 | 49 |
| 1974 | 47 | 9 | 467 | 24 | 4 | 195 | 13 | 2 | 96 |
| 1975 | 45 | 3 | 124 | 21 | 2 | 122 | 7 | 1 | 112 |
| 1976 | 28 | 4 | 45 | 13 | 4 | 45 | 2 | 0 | 0 |
| 1977 | 26 | 5 | 656† | 13† | 2† | 645† | 2 | 1 | 70 |
| 1978 | 24 | 6 | 163 | 8 | 1 | 3 | 1 | 0 | 0 |
| 1979 | 32 | 6 | 355 | 7 | 3 | 6 | 1 | 0 | 0 |
| 1980 | 19 | 1 | 1 | 6 | 0 | 0 | 3 | 0 | 0 |
| 1981 | 27 | 4 | 4 | 8 | 0 | 0 | 2 | 0 | 0 |
| Total | 885 | 138 | 4,115† | 338† | 53† | 1,993† | 136 | 12 | 546 |

*Decrease in total accidents caused by change in definition of "substantial damage" included in definition of an accident, effective 1 January 1968.
†Includes one accident at Tenerife involving one U.S. and one foreign flag carrier. Investigation was under jurisdiction of Spanish government, which found weather (fog) to be a factor in this accident. Fatalities attributable to Tenerife accident: 575.

but they are a very frequent and particularly troublesome phenomenon in some areas." Turbulence, including thunderstorm turbulence, has been the leading single cause of accidents in U.S. commercial-air-carrier operations (see Table 7.3). Table 7.4 lists some well-known accidents in which thunderstorms figured prominently.

## Thunderstorm Effects on Aviation

Aviation accidents have been caused by various hazards associated with the thunderstorm. An aircraft can quickly fly around a typical single thunderstorm since it affects a relatively small area only 10-20 km across, but storms also form in al-

**Table 7.2.** Number of Thunderstorm-associated Aircraft Accidents in U.S. Military (Excluding Lightning)

| Year | Air Force Total | Air Force Major | Air Force Fatal | Navy Major | Navy Fatal |
|------|------|------|------|------|------|
| 1964 | 13 | 3 | 1 | NA | NA |
| 1965 | 21 | 1 | 0 | NA | NA |
| 1966 | 34 | 5 | 1 | NA | NA |
| 1967 | 7 | 2 | 2 | NA | NA |
| 1968 | 4 | 1 | 0 | 5 | 1 |
| 1969 | 5 | 2 | 1 | 1 | 0 |
| 1970 | 1 | 0 | 0 | 6 | 3 |
| 1971 | 1 | 0 | 0 | 7 | 3 |
| 1972 | 6 | 1 | 1 | 2 | 1 |
| 1973 | 2 | 0 | 0 | 0 | 0 |
| 1974 | 12 | 0 | 0 | 0 | 0 |
| 1975 | 4 | 0 | 0 | 0 | 0 |
| 1976 | 1 | 0 | 0 | 1 | 1 |
| 1977 | 1 | 0 | 0 | 0 | 0 |
| Total | 112 | 15 | 6 | 22 | 9 |

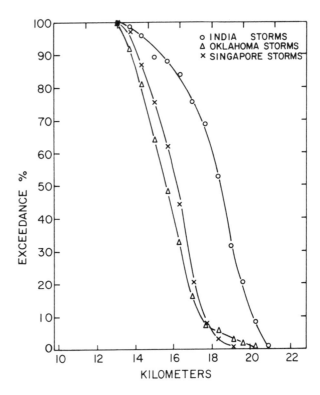

**Figure 7.1.** Cumulative percentage of storm tops exceeding given height.

most continuous lines several hundred kilometers long. In general, thunderstorms do not penetrate far above the tropopause (the top of the troposphere, often near 12- to 15-km altitude), but in some regions sufficient energy is available to carry their tops 5 km or even more above the tropopause. Thus, even jet transports cannot overfly severe thunderstorms. Studies in the midwest United States and in Singapore show tops to 19 km over Oklahoma (6 km above the tropopause) and just short of 18 km (2.5 km above the tropopause) in southeast Asia (Lee and McPherson, 1971). Studies by Spavins (1970) show thunderstorm tops above 20 km in northeast India. Figure 7.1 shows the cumulative distribution of storm tops exceeding given heights in these three locations.

**Table 7.3.** Leading Causes of U.S. Air-Carrier Accidents, 1964-68*

| Accident type | Percent |
|------|------|
| Turbulence | 18.2 |
| Gear collapsed | 10.6 |
| Overshoot or undershoot | 9.2 |
| Engine failure | 7.2 |
| Collision with objects | 7.1 |
| Ground loop | 6.4 |
| Collision with ground | 5.9 |
| Midair near miss | 5.0 |
| Wheel-up landing | 4.9 |

*From Thomas, 1971.

The hazards that led to particular fatal accidents in thunderstorm environments cannot always be identified. In retrospect, all thunderstorm hazards were potentially serious to flight operations during the first quarter of this century. Thanks to improved technology, the number of these hazards has diminished today. The resulting improvement in safety has been remarkable in air-carrier operations, but less so with light aircraft, whose pilots include those with minimal flight experience and skills.

The influence of thunderstorms on aviation safety is considered below in relation to nine specific elements or features.

### Tornado

*Flight Operations:* Pilots have long known about tornadoes and give wide berth to their usually well-recognized funnels. Thus aircraft accidents in tornadoes are very rare. On October 6, 1981, an F-28 airliner apparently traversed a tornado shortly after takeoff from Rotterdam, Netherlands. Flight-recorder data indicated accelerations from +6.9 g

**Table 7.4.** Partial List of Fatal U.S. Air-Carrier Accidents with Thunderstorms as Cause or Major Factor*

| Date | Aircraft type | Location | Attributable cause | Fatalities |
|---|---|---|---|---|
| 1 September 1940 | DC-3 (2-engine prop) | Virginia | Lightning | 25 |
| 29 May 1947 | DC-4 (4-engine prop) | New York | Outflow | 41 |
| 30 August 1948 | Martin 202 (2-engine prop) | Minnesota | Combined effects | 36 |
| 25 June 1950 | DC-4 (4-engine prop) | Lake Michigan | Combined effects | 58 |
| 28 April 1951 | DC-3 (2-engine prop) | Indiana | Outflow | 11 |
| 15 February 1953 | DC-6 (4-engine prop) | Gulf of Mexico | Combined effects | 46 |
| 12 May 1959 | Viscount (4-engine turboprop) | Maryland | Lightning and turbulence | 31 |
| 27 June 1959 | Constellation (4-engine prop) | Italy | Lightning | 68 |
| 19 January 1960 | Viscount (4-engine turboprop) | Virginia | Combined effects | 48 |
| 8 December 1963 | B-707 (4-engine turbojet) | Maryland | Lightning | 81 |
| 7 August 1966 | BAC-111 (2-engine turbojet) | Nebraska | Turbulence | 42 |
| 3 May 1968 | Electra (4-engine turboprop) | Texas | Turbulence | 85 |
| 24 July 1973 | F-27 (2-engine turboprop) | Missouri | Outflow, lightning | 38 |
| 24 June 1975 | B-727 (3-engine turbojet) | New York | Outflow | 112 |
| 7 August 1975 | B-727 (3-engine turbojet) | Colorado | Outflow | 0 |
| 7 November 1975 | B-727 (3-engine turbojet) | North Carolina | Outflow, heavy rain | 0 |
| 4 April 1977 | DC-9 (2-engine turbojet) | Georgia | Heavy rain, hail | 70 |
| 12 June 1980† | SA-226 (2-engine turboprop) | Nebraska | Turbulence, heavy rain | 13 |
| 9 July 1982 | B-727 (3-engine turbojet) | Louisiana | Combined | 153 |

*From Civil Aeronautics Board Accident Reports, National Transportation Safety Board Accident Reports, *New York Times* Index for the published news of 1940-77, and unpublished airline accident reports.

†Commuter airline, not classified as an air carrier.

to −3 g before the aircraft broke up and crashed, with the deaths of all aboard (Wolleswinkel, private communication). Lack of information prevents a firm diagnosis of other possibly similar events. Nighttime tornado encounters and collisions with strong vortices hidden in thunderstorm cloud masses are difficult to confirm (Bates, 1967).

*Ground Operations:* Tornadoes have greatly damaged parked aircraft and aviation ground facilities, but fortunately no large commercial airport has thus far been swept by a major tornado. The most notorious catastrophe of this nature occurred at Tinker Air Force Base near Oklahoma City, Okla., during two successive weeks (20 and 25 March 1948) when tornadoes destroyed military aircraft worth more than $16 million (1948 dollars). In consequence of this event the military established the first tornado-forecasting unit in the world, under Ernest Fawbush and Robert Miller.

### Turbulence

Turbulence was the leading cause of U.S. air-carrier accidents in a study covering the years 1960-69 (Thomas, 1971). Table 7.4 shows the leading causes of air-carrier accidents during 1964-68; tur-

bulence situations are dominant and account for 18%.

Sutton (1955) defines turbulence as "a state of fluid flow in which the instantaneous velocities exhibit irregular and apparently random fluctuations." Thunderstorm turbulence is usually thought of as a sequence of irregular vertical or horizontal motions of air within the storm area. This motion can be divided for convenience into drafts and gusts, though no sharp division exists. The Thunderstorm Project report (U.S. Department of Commerce, 1949) defines these as follows: "Draft—a sustained non-horizontal current of air in a thunderstorm. Drafts are continuous over regions as large as a thunderstorm cell. Gust—an irregular, local, transitory variation in a velocity field."

Gust turbulence can be described in terms of (1) spectral density and (2) discrete gust or derived gust. If the spectral density is known and combined with information on aircraft response in relation to input frequency, the aircraft response can be calculated if response of the aircraft is linearly related to gust spectrum (Houbolt et al., 1964). Spectral-density calculations involve the assumption that the region of turbulence is homogeneous, i.e., statistically uniform.

Thunderstorms are usually not homogeneous, and therefore a discrete or derived gust expression is generally used to define turbulent areas. In studies of aeronautical engineering and thunderstorm turbulence, the discrete-gust method is one in which the basic element is taken to be a single derived gust of prescribed shape and size. A (1-cos) gust shape is generally accepted in which the gust velocity increases from zero to maximum value in 12.5 lengths of the average wing chord, i.e., the average distance across the wing (Fig. 7.2). The derived gust velocity *(U$_{de}$)* is defined (Pratt and Walker, 1954) as follows:

$$U_{de} = \frac{2 \triangle n \, W/S}{\rho_o \, m \, K_g \, V_e}$$

where $\triangle n$ = incremental departure of the vertical component of aircraft acceleration from normal, $W$ = aircraft weight, $\rho_o$ = air density, $m$ = wing lift curve slope, $K_g$ = gust-alleviation factor, $V_e$ = equivalent airspeed, and $S$ = wing area. Categories of turbulence defined in this manner are shown in relation to aircraft response and meteorological phenomena in Tables 7.5 and 7.6.

About two-thirds of the encounters with severe and extreme turbulence are attributable to thunderstorms; the rest are attributable to nonthunderstorm activity including clear-air turbulence (Fig. 7.3 and Table 7.3) (Thomas, 1971). Thunderstorms are the primary source of severe- and extreme-turbulence incidents for light aircraft and for those operating principally at lower flight levels. The chaotic motion and sharp-edged gusts that characterize severe-thunderstorm turbulence can result in a situation in which the pilot loses control and is unable to read his flight instruments, and this can culminate in structural damage to the aircraft. Lesser turbulence, coupled with problems in instrument navigation and other thunderstorm effects, has also resulted in aviation accidents involving inexperienced pilots.

To investigate turbulence and the use of indirect probes to delineate turbulent areas, a series of field experiments was begun in the mid-1960s. Project Rough Rider involved the British Royal Aeronautical Establishment, the National Aeronautical and Space Agency, the U.S. Air Force, the Federal Aviation Administration, and the National Severe Storms Laboratory of the National Oceanic and

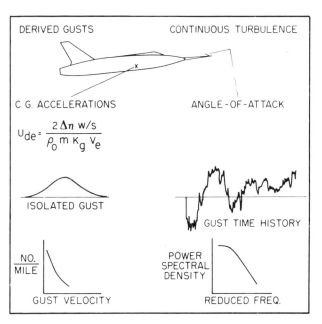

**Figure 7.2.** Measuring and describing atmospheric turbulence (after Steiner and Rhyne, 1962). (Above) Angle of attack is measured at the end of the leading boom, vertical acceleration at the aircraft center of gravity. (Middle and lower left) Isolated gusts are depicted as a harmonic fluctuation and their statistics represented as occurrences per unit distance within defined ranges of intensity. (Middle and lower right) Turbulences are represented by the time history of center-of-gravity accelerations and its power spectrum.

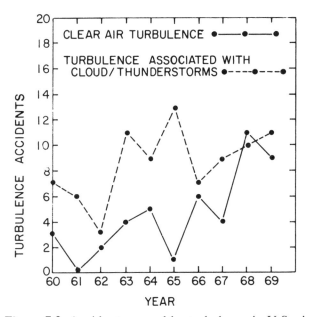

**Figure 7.3.** Accidents caused by turbulence in U.S. air carriers, 1960-69 (after Thomas, 1971).

**Table 7.5.** Forecasting Guide on Turbulence Intensity

| INTENSITY | DERIVED GUST VELOCITY AND TYPICAL RESPONSE OF MOST AIRCRAFT | | | | FREQUENTLY ASSOCIATED METEOROLOGICAL EVENTS | | | |
| | Ude 1/ | Incremental 2/ Vertical Acceleration | | Vertical Wind Shear 3/ | Convective Clouds 4/ | Surface Winds 5/ | Mountain Wave |
| | | Root Mean Square | Peak | | | | |
|---|---|---|---|---|---|---|---|
| Light | 5 to 20 fps | Less than .2 g | Absolute Value > .2 to .5 g | 3-5 kts per 1000 ft | Fair weather cumulus and altocumulus | When surface winds exceed 15 kts and where air is colder than the underlying surface | See Footnote 6/ |
| Moderate | > 20 to 35 fps | .2 to .3 g | Absolute Value > .5 to 1.0 g | 6-9 kts per 1000 ft | Thunderstorms, cumulonimbus, and towering cumulus | When surface winds exceed 25 kts or atmosphere is unstable due to strong insolation or cold air advection | See Footnote 6/ |
| Severe | > 35 to 50 fps | >.3 to .6 g | Absolute Value > 1.0 to 2.0 g | 10 kts or more per 1000 ft | Mature or rapidly growing thunderstorms and occasionally with cumulonimbus or towering cumulus | Not specified | See Footnote 6/ |
| Extreme | More than 50 fps | Over .6 g | Absolute Value >2.0 g | Not specified | Severe thunderstorms | Not specified | See Footnote 6/ |

FOOTNOTES:

1/ **Ude.** The derived gust velocity, Ude, is only a rough approximation of true vertical gust velocity. See Federal Aviation Regulations, Part 23, paragraph 23.341 and Part 25, paragraph 25.341.

2/ **Incremental Vertical Acceleration.** As measured at the center of gravity of an aircraft. For a given intensity of atmospheric turbulence, these accelerations depend on weight, airspeed, and design characteristics of the aircraft. These values are for guidance only and do not indicate precise limits.

3/ **Vertical Wind Shear.** These values (vectors) are statistically typical for a layer 5,000 feet thick as obtained from rawinsonde data encoded for teletypewriter transmissions. Turbulence of these specified intensities is not always present.

4/ **Convective Clouds.** Turbulence associated with convective clouds may be present in the immediate environment of, as well as in, the cloud systems. Severe turbulence may be present in some portion of any thunderstorm. Extreme turbulence may be present in some portion of any mature or rapidly growing thunderstorm. Superadiabatic lapse rates near the surface also may produce moderate turbulence.

5/ **Surface Winds.** Depends on terrain roughness and stability as well as wind speed. Interactions are often present between low-level convective activity and mechanical turbulence.

6/ **Mountain Wave.** Moderate or greater turbulence may be found with strong winds generally normal to the mountain ridge. wind speed increasing with height and relatively stable layers. Turbulence is likely at levels near the ridge height, in relatively stable layers and at the tropopause. Turbulence layers may be up to about 5,000 feet thick and may extend 50 to 100 miles downstream. The presence of troughs and jet streams can enhance wave development. Wind-shear turbulence and mountain wave activity may interact to produce variations in turbulence over a wide range of altitudes. Severe or occasionally extreme turbulence may be found in or near rotor clouds and may extend to the ground. Turbulence may be present in mountain waves even though there is insufficient moisture available for the formation of lenticular or rotor clouds.

**Table 7.6.** Turbulence Reporting Criteria

| INTENSITY | AIRCRAFT REACTION | REACTION INSIDE AIRCRAFT | REPORTING TERM-DEFINITION |
|---|---|---|---|
| Light | Turbulence that momentarily causes slight, erratic changes in altitude and/or attitude (pitch, roll, yaw). Report as Light Turbulence;* or Turbulence that causes slight, rapid and somewhat rhythmic bumpiness without appreciable changes in altitude or attitude. Report as Light Chop. | Occupants may feel a slight strain against seat belts or shoulder straps. Unsecured objects may be displaced slightly. Food service may be conducted and little or no difficulty is encountered in walking. | Occasional – Less than 1/3 of the time. Intermittent – 1/3 to 2/3. Continuous – More than 2/3. |
| Moderate | Turbulence that is similar to Light Turbulence but of greater intensity. Changes in altitude and/or attitude occur but the aircraft remains in positive control at all times. It usually causes variations in indicated airspeed. Report as Moderate Turbulence;* or Turbulence that is similar to Light Chop but of greater intensity. It causes rapid bumps or jolts without appreciable changes in aircraft altitude or attitude. Report as Moderate Chop. | Occupants feel definite strains against seat belts or shoulder straps. Unsecured objects are dislodged. Food service and walking are difficult. | **NOTE** 1. Pilots should report location(s), time (GMT), intensity, whether in or near clouds, altitude, type of aircraft and, when applicable, duration of turbulence. 2. Duration may be based on time between two locations or over a single location. All locations should be readily identifiable. EXAMPLES: a. Over Omaha, 1232Z, Moderate Turbulence, in cloud, Flight Level 310, B707. b. From 50 miles south of Albuquerque to 30 miles north of Phoenix, 1210Z to 1250Z, occasional Moderate Chop, Flight Level 330, DC8. |
| Severe | Turbulence that causes large, abrupt changes in altitude and/or attitude. It usually causes large variations in indicated airspeed. Aircraft may be momentarily out of control. Report as Severe Turbulence. * | Occupants are forced violently against seat belts or shoulder straps. Unsecured objects are tossed about. Food service and walking are impossible. | |
| Extreme | Turbulence in which the aircraft is violently tossed about and is practically impossible to control. It may cause structural damage. Report as Extreme Turbulence.* | | |

\* High level turbulence (normally above 15,000 feet ASL) not associated with cumuliform cloudiness, including thunderstorms, should be reported as CAT (clear air turbulence) preceded by the appropriate intensity, or light or moderate chop.

Atmospheric Administration in a joint effort to explore thunderstorm interiors with instrumented aircraft (Burnham and Lee, 1969). Initial aircraft were the T-33, then the more powerful F-100, British Scimitar, F-102, and F-106, and eventually (in the 1970s) the F-4-C Phantom jet. These aircraft, structurally strong to withstand high-maneuvering load factors, were vectored into thunderstorms under tight radar control to obtain turbulence data while storm radar reflectivity was measured with a weather radar (WSR-57 10-cm radar). More than 1,000 storm penetrations were made. The smoothed cumulative distribution of turbulence encounters stratified according to radar echo intensity is shown in Fig. 7.4. It is apparent that the probability of encountering moderate gusts increases as the radar

reflectivity increases. No area of severe or greater turbulence was found in thunderstorms having less than 40-dBZ maximum radar reflectivity. Turbulence was frequently encountered outside the thunderstorm core, sometimes more than 10 mi from a storm center, and not always in areas of high reflectivities. Reflectivity along the flight path and reflectivity gradient are poorly correlated to turbulence encounters.

The results of two serious encounters with storm turbulence are depicted in Figs. 7.5 and 7.6. Such encounters have become rarer as the altitude at which passenger aircraft typically fly has risen above some storm tops. Careful planning, conservative piloting, and use of modern support facilities, especially ground-based and airborne radar,

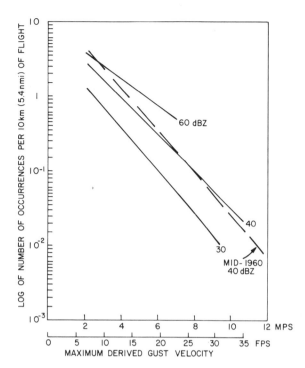

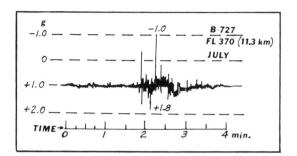

**Figure 7.5.** Severe turbulence in a thunderstorm south of Springfield, Ill., July 1969, illustrated by an accelerometer trace from an onboard flight recorder on a three-engine turbojet transport. The aircraft was detouring an area of heavy thunderstorms at flight level 370 (11.3 km). Turbulence is suspected to have been generated in the wake of two thunderstorm cells with tops of 17 km and 19.5 km.

**Figure 7.4.** Smoothed frequency of derived gust velocities encountered during storm penetrations, normalized to 10 km of flight, categorized by maximum radar reflectivity of storm (1973-77 data, solid line; 1960 data, dashed line).

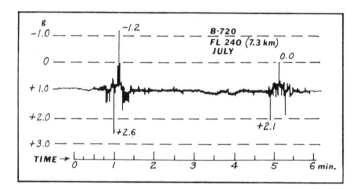

**Figure 7.6.** Severe turbulence in a thunderstorm near Dubuque, Iowa, July 1969, illustrated by accelerometer trace from onboard flight recorder on four-engine turbojet transport. The aircraft was navigating a corridor between two thunderstorms with tops at 11.5 km and 13.5 km. The corridor was narrower than recommended for smooth flight, but the flight was conducted under instructions from the FAA Air Route Traffic Control Center.

reduce exposure to the severe turbulence that injures passengers and cabin crews. The fleet of one major air carrier with routes across the United States thunderstorm belt has lately experienced only one encounter with severe turbulence for every 30 to 40 million airplane miles flown.

Hail

*Flight Operations:* The policy of storm avoidance in the early days of aviation probably resulted in a low rate of aircraft loss from hail. Fabric-covered airplanes were particularly vulnerable to walnut-sized hailstones (30-mm diameter) and larger, which could shred control surfaces and wings. As aircraft became larger, with metal skins, more instrument flying was conducted—much of it closer to the hail-producing cells. Aircraft hail encounters became more numerous but rarely resulted in fatal or serious accidents. Golf-ball-sized hailstones (45-mm diameter) or larger shattered windscreens and

peened skin on leading edges of wings, control surfaces, engine cowls, and nose. Radomes made of nonmetallic material were often perforated and sometimes swept away during such encounters (see Fig. 7.7). During the 1940s, replacement of damaged skin and other components and out-of-service time annually cost the airlines hundreds of thousands of dollars. With the introduction of airborne radar in 1956 (see section "Airborne Radar" below)

**Figure 7.7.** Hail damage to four-engine propeller transport. Aircraft encountered hailstones up to baseball size while flying in clear air beneath anvil of generating thunderstorm near Colorado Springs, Colo. Note shattering and penetrations of pilots' wind screen by hailstones. (Photo courtesy of United Air Lines.)

**Figure 7.8.** Damage to light aircraft with fabric skin suffered from Colorado hailstorm. The aircraft was on a parking ramp when the hailstorm hit. The largest hailstones at this location were golfball size. (Photo courtesy of *Weatherwise*.)

**Figure 7.9.** (Left) The leading edge of turbulent strong winds of the thunderstorm outflow is made visible by dust raised by the wind at Webb Air Force Base, Big Spring, Texas, June 1969. (Photo by Air Weather Service.) (Right) Cool outflow of dissipating thunderstorms near Norman, Okla., on 25 May 1977 is made visible by the low cloud formed in warm air lifted along the system boundary.

and research showing correlation between strong radar reflectivity and hail areas, these costs have dropped dramatically to almost zero.

*Ground Operations:* All aircraft are still subject to varying degrees of hail damage while parked on ramps and in tie-down areas, or otherwise unprotected by hangars. The damage extent is a function of the type and thickness of the skin, the strength of the accompanying wind, and the size of the largest hailstones. Figure 7.8 shows the damage suffered by a fabric-covered airplane from a heavy hailstorm. The metal-clad aircraft of today remain relatively undamaged unless hailstones attain golf-ball size, when severe peening may occur. When hailstones are baseball size (approximately 85-mm diameter), no aircraft of any size or type escapes some damage, including skin penetration. Fortunately, such large hailstones are rare.

### Outflow

The surface wind patterns that result from the inflow and outflow of air in thunderstorm cells are complex and unpredictable in detail (Charba, 1972; Goff, 1975). Depending on the number and intensity of active cells in a thunderstorm, the cold-air downdrafts with horizontal spreading of the air near the ground can produce gusts reaching 100 km/h (54 kn) or more. Two spectacular examples

made visible by cloud and dust are shown in Fig. 7.9. When outflows are from opposing or weak cells, the windshift may be barely perceptible. The gust-front area, marking an outflow leading edge, is one of the most dangerous regions for aircraft during approach and landing configurations and in the takeoff and climb regimes. The greatest vertical and horizontal wind gradients (shear) are found in the outflow region. Horizontal shear results in sudden airspeed changes and in turbulence. A particularly dangerous situation involves horizontal divergence, which necessarily occurs beneath moderate and strong downdrafts; an aircraft landing or taking off can pass quickly from a strong headwind, through a light-wind condition beneath the downdraft core, and even to a strong tailwind on the other side (Fig. 7.10). During takeoffs and landings, loss or gain of airspeed under such variable wind conditions can lead to high sink rates and stalls resulting in landing short of the runway (Fig. 7.11) or excessive airspeeds resulting in over-shooting. Data from a representative gust front are shown in Fig. 7.12. This front was mapped from time-series observations made on a 1,500-ft tower in central Oklahoma on 29 May 1976. Figure 7.12 shows an updraft in the warm air ahead of the front, downdrafts behind the front, and large variability of winds, particularly in the frontal zone.

Although details of gust fronts vary, the statistical character of the flow has marked similarities.

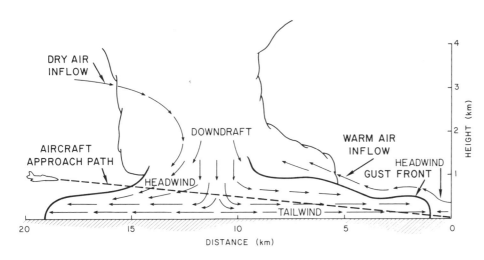

**Figure 7.10.** Schematic of a gust front and associated winds. Note the rapid change from headwind to tailwind along the approach path near the downdraft center. Possibly disastrous effects on the aircraft flight depend on the intensity and scale of the wind-shift phenomenon and details of pilot input and aircraft response.

The Oklahoma observations indicate that surface outflow winds behind the gust front are typically nearly normal to the front. Observations show that the outflow speed in the zone of strongest winds is about 1.5 times faster than the gust-front propagation speed. The strongest horizontal winds in the cold-air outflow are found directly behind the gust-front secondary-outflow boundaries. Measured wind shifts across the gust front have exceeded a vector difference of 25 m/s (50 kn) within a distance of 2 km. Instrumented flights through downdrafts have revealed vector difference in the horizontal wind of 40 m/s in 4 km.

Standard weather radar cannot reliably detect outflow, nor can the usual airport wind-measuring facilities accurately sense the location and intensity of the gust front. Unless accompanied by dust clouds, the outflow is not visible to a pilot on approach or during takeoff, or to control-tower personnel. For larger turbojet aircraft, outflow effects are compounded because inertia is greater and airspeed responds more slowly to added power, compared with propeller-driven aircraft. Wind-shifts along gust fronts may sometimes extend 15 to 20 km or more ahead of the visible or radar-detected edge of the generating thunderstorm. In

**Figure 7.11.** A portion of the wrecked section of a commercial airline multiengine jet aircraft in which 113 passengers and crew died during an attempted landing in a thunderstorm gust-front episode at J. F. Kennedy International Airport on 24 June 1975. (Photo by National Transportation Safety Board.)

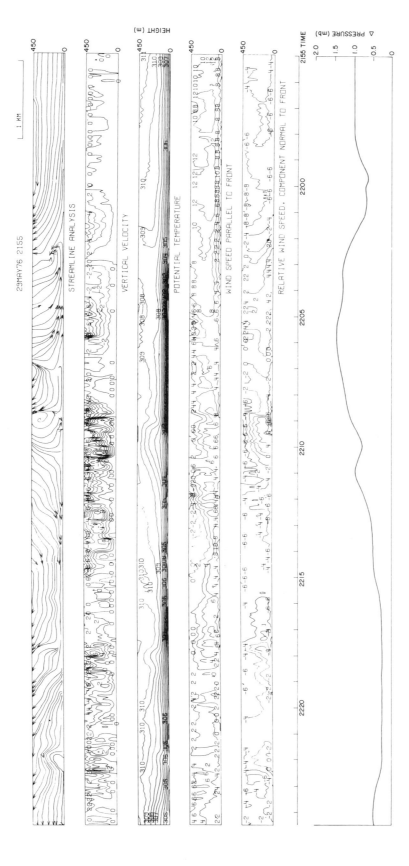

**Figure 7.12.** A thunderstorm outflow, 29 May 1976, determined from a time-height cross section of temperature and wind from a 440-m tower instrumented at seven levels. Isopleths are labeled with windspeed in meters per second and temperature in kelvins. Streamlines are drawn using windspeed $\mu$ relative to the ground and normal to the front, and vertical velocity $w$. A 1-km time-to-space representative length is shown in the upper right. The gust front occurs at 2202 CST. The outflow is moving from left to right. The thunderstorm is on the extreme left.

semiarid regions of the western United States, strong outflow can also be generated from high-base cumuliform clouds that have not reached the thunderstorm stage and that may not appear as significant echoes on weather radars.

Through experience, early aviators became aware of thunderstorm downdrafts and outflow and secured their aircraft to the ground when they were caught in open country. Table 7.4 indicates that these thunderstorm features are still hazardous.

## Lightning

Thunderstorm lightning is the attributable cause or a factor in one-third of the fatal accidents listed in Table 7.4. Electrical discharges also occur as "static discharges" under nonthunderstorm conditions. Air-carrier records indicate that more than half the electrical events are the latter kind, occurring during the following meteorological conditions: (1) rain or snow showers within cumulus clouds, requiring intermittent use of instrument-flight rules, (2) ambient-air temperature in the approximate range −5°C to +5°C, and (3) occasionally Saint Elmo's fire (corona discharge) on the windscreen or nose of the aircraft (Harrison, 1965).

At least two of the five lightning cases in Table 7.4 are suspected to have involved fuel ignition through the fuel-venting system when lightning struck the aircraft. Investigation of the 1940 accident in Table 7.4 suggests that the flight crew may have been incapacitated by lightning, perhaps by concussion, but no such set of circumstances has been found in subsequent aircraft accidents.

Table 7.7 lists the number of thunderstorm-associated lightning and static-discharge accidents reported by the U.S. Air Force. More than 50% of these accidents occurred during flight rather than during landings and takeoffs. In only six of the cases listed in Table 7.7 was there major structural damage.

Because of lightning-caused accidents, the aircraft industry has modified aircraft fuel systems and virtually eliminated the serious fuel-ignition problem (FAA, 1967). Lightning strikes aircraft much less frequently nowadays because pilots usually avoid thunderstorms. Most aircraft now carry static-discharge wicks or sharp-pointed spikes on

**Table 7.7.** Thunderstorm-associated Lightning and Static-Discharge Accidents Reported by U.S. Air Force

| Year | No. of accidents | Year | No. of accidents |
|------|------|------|------|
| 1962 | 26 | 1970 | 67 |
| 1963 | 43 | 1971 | 88 |
| 1964 | 47 | 1972 | 80 |
| 1965 | 63 | 1973 | 106 |
| 1966 | 47 | 1974 | 86 |
| 1967 | 52 | 1975 | 84 |
| 1968 | 64 | 1976 | 63 |
| 1969 | 86 | 1977 | 38 |

the trailing edges of wings to gradually dissipate accumulated electrical charge, but several hundred static-discharge incidents still occur each year in the United States. These and the occasional lightning strikes produce minor structural damage, magnetization of some flight instruments, and damage to integrated-circuit components vulnerable to current surges, but these events are not known to have contributed to recent accidents. Evidence of discharge is not always apparent, though small burned spots are sometimes found on the aircraft skin. In a few cases, the honeycomb nonmetallic radome is ruptured.

We are still concerned with the vulnerability of the aircraft crew to lightning and static discharges, manifested as a temporary blinding of cockpit occupants and an inability of the flight crew to read flight instruments. However, since most turbojet aircraft and more advanced propeller aircraft can be flown with automatic-control systems, the lightning hazard to commercial air carriers of the 1970s is greatly diminished.

## Heavy Rain

Heavy rain in thunderstorms can cause the pilot to lose forward visibility when he is required to maintain ground reference during approach and landing, or on a low-level flight employing visual flight rules. If rain-removal systems for airplane windscreens are inadequate, accumulated rainwater can distort ground reference points through refractive charges—a potential hazard near touchdown. When water has accumulated on the runway, heavy aircraft risk hydroplaning during a high-speed landing. Braking action may be ineffective above certain groundspeeds, and directional control may be lost on the runway (Horne and Dreher, 1963).

Heavy rain may also affect engine operation and result in power loss. Liquid-water concentrations of several tens of grams per cubic meter of air have been measured in heavy thunderstorms in the United States (Roy and Kessler, 1966), and large amounts have also been reported by the Soviet Union. Very heavy rain or slush was reported but not measured at 37,000 ft MSL above the western Pacific Ocean by a DC-8 in 1964. In Georgia in 1977, the heavy rain encountered by a commercial DC-9 may have been a factor in the flameout of its engine (NTSB, 1978).

### Low Ceilings and Poor Visibility

Ceiling and visibility limitations presented serious hazards to pilots and limitations to flight before introduction of modern navigational instrumentation, and still do for those qualified only for visual operations. Many thunderstorms produce rapid changes in ceiling and visibility; scud or roll clouds and heavy rain curtains on the forward edge of the thunderstorm may drop an opaque screen across the flight path. In some arid regions, dense clouds of dust along a gust front sometimes rapidly reduce visibility to low values. Such conditions, especially when coupled with turbulence, increase accident probability by producing pilot disorientations.

### Pressure Change

Rapid atmospheric-pressure changes, which often accompany thunderstorms, can produce altimeter errors of 30 m (100 ft) and occasionally much more. Such changes were not dangerous before instrument approaches were made down to altitudes of 30 m or less. Today, however, rapid pressure changes can be critical during instrument approach and landing below 60-m altitude when the pilot relies on a pressure-actuated altimeter and does not have the current altimeter setting for the airport. Most aircraft that operate at very low minimum altitudes (below 30 m) have automatic guidance systems that rely on radio altimeters not affected by atmospheric-pressure changes.

### Radio Static

Although radio static is seldom a problem today because the radio frequencies are not interrupted by atmospheric static, this feature of thunderstorms was historically very significant. Until higher radio frequencies came into use in the 1940s (VHF—very high frequency, 108-140 MHz; UHF—ultrahigh frequency, 225-330 MHz) air-to-ground voice communications were frequently interrupted, and the early ground-navigation facilities were useless when the broadcast audio signals could not be heard by the pilot.

## Reducing Thunderstorm Hazards to Aviation

Most research into understanding and predicting the thunderstorm has been aimed at reducing deaths and property damage. Government and private projects have also improved aviation safety in severe weather. The thunderstorm phenomenon has defied most attempts at accurate prediction over the broad range of time and space applicable to aviation. The pinpoint accuracy required for avoidance procedures has forced reliance on real-time observations and communications, referred to as nowcasting. Observational tools in use by the late 1970s, management of thunderstorm data, and forecasts and nowcasts all contribute to reduce thunderstorm hazards.

### Airborne Radar

Airborne weather radars were first used on commercial aircraft in 1956, after about 10 years of flight research and hardware development to refine the military radars of World War II. Pilots were enthusiastic, since they could "see" the heart of thunderstorm clouds in plan view (as on a map) and assess the extent of otherwise hidden activity. For planning detours and making evasions needed for safe and comfortable flight, an instrument was required that needed no communication link, even though clearance for changes in heading or altitude still had to be obtained from Air Route Traffic Control Centers (ARTCC) on the ground (Beckwith, 1961).

Even with the refinements of the past two decades, aircraft weather radars are not regularly

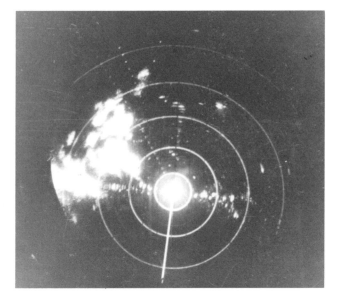

**Figure 7.13.** Scope display of C-band (5-cm wavelength) airborne weather radar during detour of thunderstorm line while the aircraft was climbing northwest from O'Hare International Airport. The aircraft was headed in the direction toward the top of the figure. It was at 8,000 ft (2.4 km) and was clearing the edge of the nearest thunderstorm cell by 18 nmi (33 km). Range circles are 10 nmi apart. (Photo courtesy of United Airlines.)

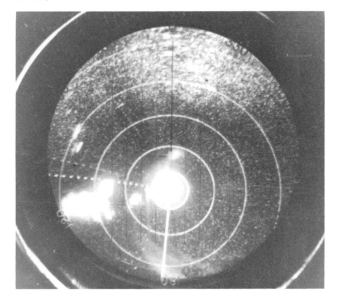

**Figure 7.14.** Scope display from the aircraft of Fig. 7.12, taken 15 min later as the flight was clearing the end of the thunderstorm line near Dubuque, Iowa, at flight level 280 (8.5 km). The nearest cell is left at 16 nmi (30 km), providing more than minimum clearance to avoid hail or turbulence. (Photo courtesy of United Airlines.)

**Figure 7.15.** The thunderstorm cloud mass corresponding to the nearest cell echo in Fig. 7.13. The picture was taken 1 min after that in Fig. 7.13 as the aircraft was turning to take up the route heading. The thunderstorm cloud top was estimated at 45,000 ft (13.7 km). (Photo courtesy of United Airlines.)

used as aids to thunderstorm penetration. Since echo patterns on airborne weather radar scopes are precipitation returns only, they do not directly indicate turbulence and gust fronts or reliably indicate hazards above or below flight altitudes. Flight tracks must be selected to avoid the nearest edge of a thunderstorm radar echo by a prescribed distance, which is a function of the flight altitude and the character and intensity of the echo (see Figs. 7.13-7.15). This elbow room cannot always be maintained in heavy-traffic areas, especially during approaches and departures. Aircraft may occasionally encounter severe turbulence or heavy hail when the ARTCC finds no echo-free corridors in the heavily traveled control zones (see Figs. 7.16 and 7.17). Usually, however, the pilot can avoid cells by monitoring his own weather radar and requesting small changes of heading.

## Ground Radar

Many types of ground-based radars are used today for operational or research purposes. Two systems are employed routinely to help airplanes avoid thunderstorm hazards: the weather radars

**Figure 7.16.** Destruction by hail of the radome on the nose of a three-engine wide-body jet transport (DC-10). The encounter occurred in 1977 at flight level 180 (5.5 km) while the aircraft was climbing through a New Jersey thunderstorm under clearance from Air Route Traffic Center. The static-discharge ground strip remained intact. (Photo courtesy of United Airlines.)

**Figure 7.17.** Hail damage to the aircraft. Note the missing strip of wing skin near the engine pylon caused by erosion of rivet heads by heavy hail. The total cost to repair damage to the airplane was more than $300,000. (Photo courtesy of United Airlines.)

constituting the National Weather Service network and those utilized by the Federal Aviation Administration to supplement air-traffic-control radars. The NWS radar network is the main monitor of severe-weather developments for warning and protection of the general public. The interpreted data from these radar networks are communicated in severe-weather bulletins, advisory messages, and charts. Originating in Kansas City, Missouri, at the National Severe Storms Forecast Center, NOAA, thunderstorm charts and advisories are transmitted to government forecast offices, weather-briefing facilities, airline weather centers, FAA control agencies, and industrial subscribers through high-speed teletypewriter and facsimile circuits and long-line computer links. Each NWS radar site is accessible in nearly real time to government and commercial users through direct phone dial-up facsimile (scope picture) and dedicated teletypewriter channels (coded scope interpretations).

Planning and executing an orderly control and flow of air traffic while avoiding thunderstorm zones require radar displays in each FAA traffic control center. These displays are tied in with NWS weather radars or FAA dual-purpose (traffic and weather) radars. Echo patterns may be superimposed on the traffic radar screens or displayed on adjacent scopes that indicate flight routes and approach-departure corridors intercepting thunderstorm zones.

### Weather Satellites

NOAA geostationary satellites offer a timely and nearly continuous photographic record of developing cloud systems associated with isolated and widespread thunderstorm developments. Although unable to measure the relative intensity of adjacent storms as well as ground radar, the satellites provide blanket coverage of severe-weather cloud patterns and provide remarkable detail on clouds. Satellite pictures are particularly advantageous where radar coverage is not available, for example, over oceans and technologically undeveloped regions.

### Gust-Front Detector Systems

In 1977, the FAA began special wind-sensing installations at major air terminals in the United States. Each installation, known as a low-level wind-shear alert system (LLWSAS), is a mesoscale network (mesonet) of sensors that continuously monitor wind conditions at and around the airport. Wind direction and speed at six instrument sites are transmitted to the control tower through a mini-computer. When a difference in wind vector between any remote site and the standard centerfield site exceeds a preprogrammed threshold value, an alarm is triggered in the control tower, and the winds are indicated on a digital display. The encroachment of a gust front across the mesonet is detected in this manner, and pilots are informed from the tower of the location and intensity of the low-level windshift line with respect to their landing or takeoff patterns (Goff, 1980). From early 1979, seven LLWSAS systems were in operation, and about sixty major airports were so equipped by the summer of 1983.

## Electrical-Discharge Sensor

For light aircraft, an airborne sensor of electrical discharges is available as a low-cost substitute for weather data. This detector system, which does not require a special antenna or radome, includes cockpit display showing the approximate direction from the aircraft to electrical discharges, and on the basis of intensity indicates a theoretical or pseudodistance to the activity centers. Several hundred such devices were in use from 1978.

## Thunderstorm Forecasting

In addition to nowcasting, aviation uses thunderstorm forecasts based on the dynamic properties of weather systems for periods up to a few days and on climatological data for longer periods. Depending on the operational area and season, owners and operators of some light aircraft can decide whether they need to equip their planes with airborne radar. General-aviation VFR pilots use large-scale thunderstorm forecasts of 2 days or longer for planning cross-country flights or local training and pleasure flights without firm schedules. Such pilots may recognize current weather patterns or use satellite displays to update published forecasts of thunderstorm areas. They can improve prelimi-

nary planning of scheduled flight operations by using daily 18-h national-scale forecasts of thunderstorms. These forecasts are issued by the National Severe Storms Forecast Center and are disseminated in plain language by Teletype and as facsimile charts. For specific local areas it is still not possible to predict thunderstorms more than a few hours in advance. The National Weather Service issues short-term severe-weather advisories whenever conditions warrant. Since these forecasts apply to 1- to 6-h periods and define areas of only 20,000 to 30,000 mi$^2$, (50,000 to 80,000 km$^2$), precision and usefulness are greatly enhanced. The advisories are widely distributed to aviation (and the public) by all conventional communications—radio, Teletype, facsimile, and computer links. All segments of aviation use these for current flight planning and changing plans during flight when thunderstorm activity is beyond the maximum range of the aircraft radars.

## Thunderstorms and Aviation Tomorrow

Government and industry are involved in research, hardware development, and advanced communication systems that will help eliminate thunderstorm hazards to aviation (Beckwith, 1975; Crisci, 1978). Some of this activity has reached field testing and prototype manufacture, as discussed below.

## Doppler Radar

Doppler weather radar measures radar-echo intensity and radial motion of reflectors (precipitation, dust) relative to the radar. Since precipitation and other particles respond almost immediately to motion of air through which they fall, Doppler radar in effect measures the wind and allows continuous profiling of horizontal wind at various altitudes. Identifiable features representing wind may be related to turbulent areas and other hazards such as wind shear and vortices. The intensity of the radar return is used to identify heavy-precipitation and hail areas.

Since Doppler radar measures only the wind component toward or away from the radar, two widely spaced units are needed to determine true wind. Such complete detail is not usually required for important operational applications.

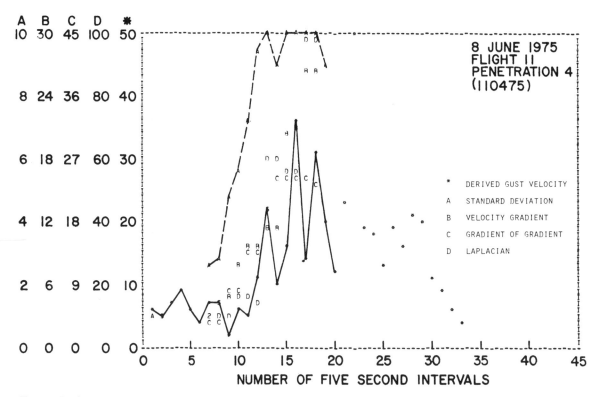

**Figure 7.18.** The record of maximum values of turbulence indicators at 5-s intervals along the track of a storm-penetrating aircraft on 8 June 1975. A: Standard deviation (width) of the Doppler spectrum in m/s determined by radar on the ground. B: Radial gradient of radial Doppler velocity ($s^{-1} \times$ 1000) at the aircraft position. C: Radial gradient of B ($s^{-1} m^{-1} \times$ 1000). D: Laplacian of the Doppler velocity, i.e., C plus the tangential gradient of B; derived gust velocities (m/s) are maximums as determined from instruments on the aircraft.

*In-Flight Use of Ground-based Doppler Radar Data:* In 1973 a series of experiments was begun by federal agencies and universities to investigate use of Doppler weather radar for identifying weather hazards. Radar data were collected with ground-based equipment in conjunction with high-performance aircraft flights wherein in situ wind and turbulence were measured (Lee, 1974).

Data from thunderstorm penetrations were searched for significant correlations. A typical time history of several parameters is shown in Fig. 7.18. Maximum derived gust velocities (turbulence) recorded by the aircraft during each 5 s (approximately 1 km) of flight are shown with Doppler radar observations corresponding in time and space. Note that the turbulence trend matches fairly well the trend in the spectrum-width plot. Altogether 45 penetrations were analyzed, and all evinced a

similar relationship. During these 45 penetrations, 76 turbulence occurrences were found with moderate or greater intensity. Ninety-five percent had spectrum widths of 4.0 m/s or more. In analyses of two cases in which spectrum width was less than 4 m/s and derived gust velocity exceeded 6.1 m/s, the record of aircraft elevator deflection indicates that some component of the vertical acceleration was pilot-induced. The spectrum width may itself at times be biased by wind shear and beam broadening, so in some nonturbulent areas the spectral width may be large. In two tornadic storms studied, however, the cumulative probability for spectrum width 4 m/s or more is only about 30%, and the probability is even less in nonsevere storms. Thus the larger part of echoes could be confidently certified as safe.

The other parameters investigated were not as

promising. When parameters involving shear alone are used, the results depend on viewing angle (tangential shear cannot be determined with a single Doppler radar), thereby reducing the operational utility of the derived data. Measurement of turbulence caused by convective processes is less dependent on viewing angle.

Still under study are locations of large spatial variability of mean Doppler velocity within a storm. Thus, Fig. 7.19, derived from a study of tornadic storms, shows the probable correlation between turbulence and the boundary between updrafts and downdrafts. The maximum reflectivity is north of the updrafts. Areas of large-spectrum broadness probably associated with turbulence appear on the edges of the updraft with a preference for larger widths when a downdraft is close. This association supports the idea that turbulence can be produced by horizontal gradients of the vertical wind.

Federal agencies are developing a plan for procuring advanced radars with Doppler capability and with supporting systems for data processing, communication, and display to replace the current national radar system (NEXRAD, 1980). The new system should become operational by the mid or late 1980s. Some air-carrier companies are already planning to accommodate Doppler radar aboard new jet transports in 1982 and thereafter. Airborne Doppler radar is expected to allow penetration of some thunderstorm cloud systems now avoided, with assurance of safe flight in relatively smooth air. Addition of such detection devices would help save airspace and fuel. Since the maximum range of air-borne Doppler radar for turbulence detection may be only about 50 nmi (80 km), FAA traffic control facilities may still need supplemental airborne-detection information from the flight crew.

*Air-Terminal Use of Doppler Radar:* The ability of Doppler radar to obtain wind data in optically clear air (Hennington et al., 1976) should help improve flight safety in the terminal area. Figure 7.20 represents a vertical cross section of a gust front whose leading edge passed the radar site while rain was still more than 12 km from the station. This front was observed by Doppler radar with the aid of experimental techniques (Lee and Goff, 1976). The cross section is normal to the gust front and

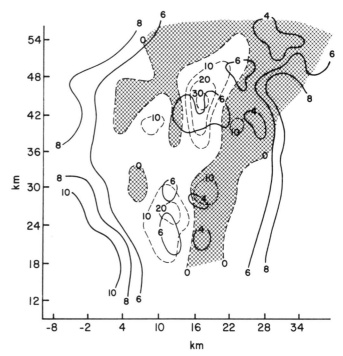

**Figure 7.19.** Plan view of air velocities at 5-km height as defined by dual-Doppler radar scans through a thunderstorm on 8 June 1974. Related to velocity differences are contours of spectrum breadth (m/s) shown as solid lines; vertical motion (m/s) contours are dashed lines; + values are upward; cross-hatched area is downdraft.

illustrates the variable slope of the gust front's upper boundary. Negative windspeeds are in the cold-air outflow from the northwest; positive values are in the overriding warm air from the southeast. Similar wind-shear data can be obtained by using Doppler radar to look up the glide slope of an active runway and can be furnished to pilots during landings and takeoffs. Doppler radar can also identify wind circulations and turbulent regions, further aiding aircraft operations in the terminal area.

## Airborne Multiple-Contour Radar Displays

For more than 20 years commercial airborne weather radars have displayed two levels of echo intensity. A two-level display is useful for locating steep rainfall gradients at the first level for turbulence avoidance but does not reveal the core intensity of severe thunderstorms. Technological advances now provide the advantages of multiple-intensity contours and color-contouring circuits in

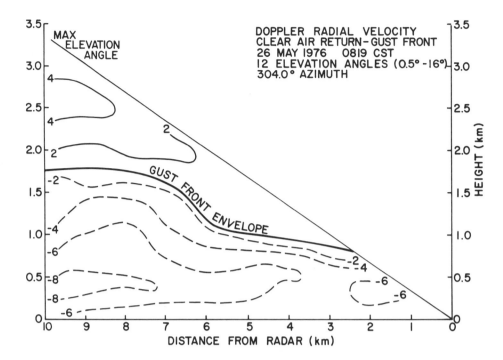

**Figure 7.20.** Contours of radial velocity define the envelope of a gust front in this vertical cross section derived from Doppler radar data acquired at the National Severe Storms Laboratory.

the small reliable package essential for airborne use (see Figs. 7.21 and 7.22). Prototype testing began in the late 1970s, and the airlines ordered this next-generation airborne radar as standard equipment aboard new transport aircraft for delivery in 1982 and later.

## Improved Communications

A weather service is only as useful as the coupling communications. Several ongoing projects are attempting to increase speed and improve selectivity in thunderstorm-data distribution. For example, the AFOS network of NOAA (see Chapter 8) should speed to the users the weather intelligence needed especially by the general-aviation segment (Klein, 1976). Both industry and government are involved in refining meteorological sensors and displays aboard transport aircraft and coupling them to high-speed air-to-ground and air-to-air data links via satellites. The downlink is expected to send several kinds of meteorological data from the aircraft observational platform to centers for traffic control, meteorology, and communications, whereas the uplink will receive real-time data and forecasts for display on cockpit screens.

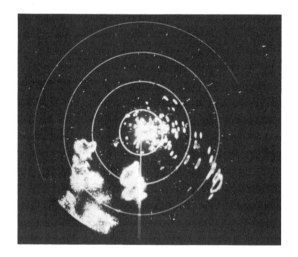

**Figure 7.21.** Scope display of C-band airborne-type weather radar located on the ground. Contouring mode shows dark centers in echoes with heaviest precipitation. These echoes were part of a short squall line that generated a tornado 45 min earlier at the 260°, 17-nmi position. Range circles are at 5-nmi intervals, and north is toward the top. Echoes in the east and southeast sectors are returns from prominent structures, including a cluster of skyscrapers at 120°, 17 nmi. (Photo courtesy of United Airlines.)

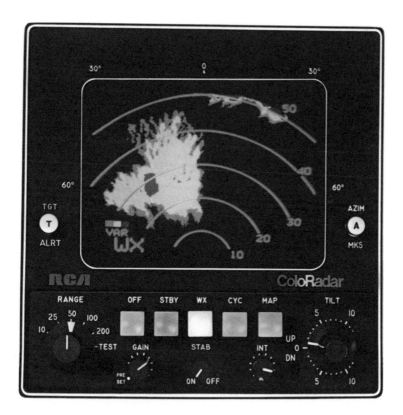

**Figure 7.22.** Prototype of an airborne weather radar-scope display. The scope's three-level contouring feature uses green, yellow, and red to show first, second, and third level of precipitation intensity. This type of indicator is expected to be in general use on late-model transports during the 1980s.

# 8. Severe-Thunderstorm Prediction, Warning, and Disaster Preparedness: Programs of the National Weather Service

*Allen D. Pearson*

## Introduction

Severe local storms (tornadoes and thunderstorms accompanied by large hail, damaging winds, excessive rainfall, and/or lightning) kill several hundred persons and injure many thousands more each year. Property losses in the United States from such storms during the late 1970s exceeded $1 billion annually (Baer, 1979).

By definition, severe local storms usually affect small areas or move in narrow paths. For example, the excessive rainfall that produced the Big Thompson flash flood fell over an area less than 100 mi²; a much larger than average tornado is a quarter

of a mile wide, with a 20-mi long path, and thus affects only 5 mi². Of the roughly 100,000 thunderstorms that bring much-needed rainfall to the United States each year, almost 3,000 meet severe-storm criteria of the U.S. National Weather Service (NWS) by producing tornadoes, flash floods from heavy rainfall, surface winds greater than 58 mi/h (95 km/h), or surface hail larger than three-fourths of an inch (20 mm) in diameter.

In an attempt to reduce damage and casualties from severe local storms, NWS Severe Local Storm Warning, Flash Flood Warning, and Disaster Preparedness programs were developed to inform the public of potentially hazardous weather events and to ensure that the public knows the proper safety actions required should hazardous weather threaten.

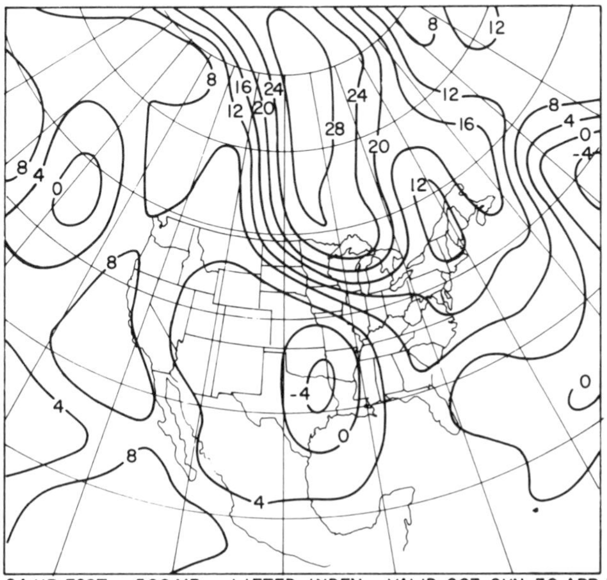

## NWS Organization for Severe-Storm Forecasting and Warning

Although thunderstorms affect relatively small areas over relatively short periods of time, their development is closely related to larger-scale weather patterns. Phenomena associated with long waves in the general circumpolar flows are treated numerically with large computers at the National Meteorological Center (NMC), Camp Springs, Maryland (Brown and Fawcett, 1972; Fawcett, 1977). The forecasts produced there are applicable for periods up to several days and help guide other forecasters in NWS who make specific forecasts. Figure 8.1 is an example of a map produced at NMC and distributed to the National Severe Storms Forecast Center (NSSFC) at Kansas City, Missouri, and to National Weather Service Forecast Offices (WSFOs) across the country.

24 HR FCST    500 MB    LIFTED INDEX    VALID 00Z SUN 30 APR 78

**Figure 8.1.** Sample portion of a northern-hemisphere analysis of forecast Lifted Index, a thunderstorm predictor, at 0000Z (GMT), 30 April 1978.

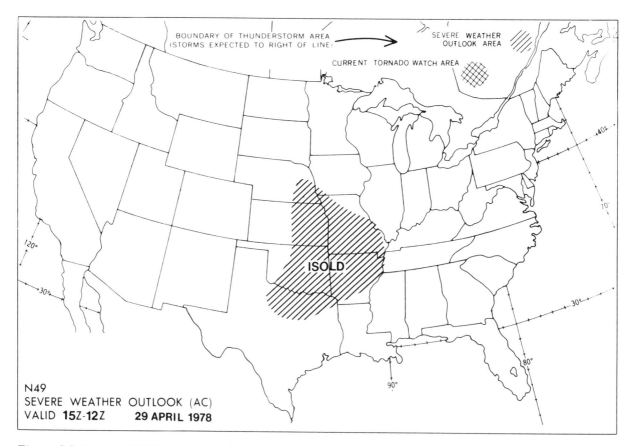

**Figure 8.2.** Sample SELS severe-weather outlook for the period 29 April 1500Z to 30 April 1200Z, 1978. A slight risk of severe thunderstorms is indicated in the shaded area. The format of this outlook map was modified slightly in 1980.

The Severe Local Storms (SELS) Unit of NSSFC has the primary responsibility of providing round-the-clock surveillance and forecasting of severe thunderstorms. NSSFC was established in Washington, D.C., in 1952 and was moved to Kansas City in 1954. Today the SELS staff includes 10 meteorologists whose prime duties are to make outlooks of severe weather for periods up to 30 hours (Fig. 8.2) and specific severe-weather watches valid for 1 to 7 hours (Fig. 8.3). An additional group of five meteorologists and five meteorologist technicians provides forecasts of significant thunderstorms for aviation interests throughout the United States (Fig. 8.4). Advisories prepared in NSSFC are distributed to NWS offices that deliver forecasts and warnings of anticipated weather events to news media and the public.

Different levels in the NWS organization issue different kinds of advisories, reflecting their focus on different time and space. Thus NMC issues forecasts of the general atmospheric flow and of the areas likely to have precipitation well in advance of thunderstorm formation. The medium-range NSSFC severe-weather outlook typically refers to areas of about 100,000 mi$^2$ (260,000 km$^2$). On shorter time scales, NSSFC forecasts define specific areas in which severe thunderstorms and tornadoes are most likely to occur; these *watches* alert the public, reminding them to watch for threatening weather conditions and to listen for further information. The watches cover about 25,000 mi$^2$ (65,000 km$^2$). When thunderstorms are actually formed and identified, the issuances from NSSFC, and more critically from local offices, are called warnings. They commonly project the paths of ongoing storms in considerable detail.

```
BULLETIN
SEVERE THUNDERSTORM WATCH NUMBER 80
NATIONAL WEATHER SERVICE KANSAS CITY MO
6 10 PM CST SAT APR 29 1978

A...THE NATIONAL SEVERE STORMS FORECAST CENTER HAS ISSUED
A SEVERE THUNDERSTORM WATCH FOR

     ...PORTIONS OF NORTH CENTRAL TEXAS
     ...PORTIONS OF SOUTHEASTERN OKLAHOMA

FROM 6 30 PM CST UNTIL 12 MIDNIGHT CST THIS SATURDAY NIGHT.

LARGE HAIL...AND DAMAGING THUNDERSTORM WINDS ARE POSSIBLE
FOR THESE AREAS.

THE SEVERE THUNDERSTORM WATCH AREA IS ALONG AND 60 STATUTE
MILES EITHER SIDE OF A LINE FROM 40 MILES SOUTHEAST OF
TEMPLE TEXAS TO 45 MILES NORTHWEST OF MC ALESTER OKLAHOMA.

REMEMBER..A SEVERE THUNDERSTORM WATCH MEANS CONDITIONS ARE
FAVORABLE FOR SEVERE THUNDERSTORMS IN AND CLOSE TO THE
WATCH AREA...PERSONS IN THESE AREAS SHOULD BE ON THE
LOOKOUT FOR THREATENING WEATHER CONDITIONS AND LISTEN
FOR LATER STATEMENTS AND POSSIBLE WARNINGS.
```

**Figure 8.3.** A Severe Thunderstorm Watch bulletin for 29 April 1978. The watch indicates a specific area of severe-thunderstorm potential, the time at which activity is expected, and a short description of the type of severe activity forecast.

Local forecasts and warning processes are focused in 52 Weather Service Forecast Offices. The WSFOs have a 24-h/day schedule and programs involving agriculture, forestry, aviation, and marine weather, as well as local forecasting and warning. There are also more than 200 Weather Service Offices (WSOs) that provide 24-h/day observations, warnings, and short-range forecasts, but, unlike the responsibilities of WSFOs, their responsibilities to the public do not include generalized forecasts. Finally, there are Weather Service Meteorological Offices (WSMOs), which have no responsibility

```
MKCC WST 212235
CONVECTIVE SIGMET 36C
OK  TX
FROM 1ØS ANY TO 4ØNW TUL TO 2ØS ADM TO 25W SPS
AREA SCT TSTMS MOVG FROM 3225 WITH AN EXTRM LVL6 AND AN INTS LVL5 CELL.
MAX TOPS 52Ø. LTLCG.

AREA SCT TSTMS DFW 338260 DFW 35923Ø DFW 35ØØ8Ø DFW 3ØØ125 MOVG 3225
TOPS 52Ø.
CELL LVL6 DFW 322120 MOVG 3325 TOP 52Ø
CELL LVL5 DFW 3442Ø5 MOVG 3Ø2Ø TOP 4ØØ
```

**Figure 8.4.** A convective SIGMET (*SIG*nificant *MET*eorological information) transmitted over service "A" teletype circuits. The message warns of thunderstorms in progress over Oklahoma and Texas. The location of activity is given with respect to service "A" flight stations ANY, TUL, ADM, and to major navigational references (e.g., azimuth 338°, range 260 mi from Dallas, Tex.).

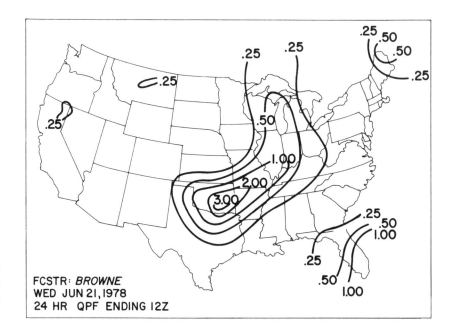

**Figure 8.5.** Computer-derived forecast of anticipated 24-h precipitation totals for the United States beginning at 1200Z on 21 June 1978.

FCSTR: *BROWNE*
WED JUN 21,1978
24 HR QPF ENDING 12Z

for providing forecasts and warnings but whose radars and other equipment provide observational data essential to the preparation of forecasts and warnings in other offices.

The Flash Flood program of NWS does not involve NSSFC. Quantitative precipitation forecasts are prepared at NMC (Fig. 8.5), and the flash-flood watches are prepared by the WSFOs, which use NMC data and their own knowledge of antecedent conditions necessary for flooding (Fig. 8.6). Flash-flood warnings are issued by the same offices responsible for severe-thunderstorm warnings.

### Observation Support

Efforts to provide severe-weather forecasts require some knowledge of three-dimensional atmospheric structure. Such knowledge is provided by networks of stations that make observations in the upper air and at the Earth's surface. The distribution of upper-air stations in the United States is shown in Fig. 8.7. Balloon-borne sensors (rawinsondes) are released twice daily, at approximately 1100 and 2300 GMT; these times are fixed by international agreement. The radio-equipped device typically reaches a height of 30 km in 90 min, while transmitting measurements of temperature

and humidity to the parent station. A pressure-sensing device determines the altitude of the rising sonde, and winds aloft are determined by tracking the instrument from the surface.

Figure 8.8 shows the current network of about 260 stations for surface observations staffed and operated by NWS personnel; about 80% of these provide 24-h coverage. There are also automatic meteorological observation sites (AMOS). AMOS stations are usually located at sites too remote for practical manned operation; they typically provide dry-bulb temperature, dew-point temperature, wind, altimeter setting, and precipitation reports every 20 min. At several manned AMOS locations, an observer adds cloud height, sky condition, visibility, weather, obstruction to vision, and air pressure. The number of automatic sites increased from 16 in 1970 to 51 in early 1981.

Besides the stations discussed above, about 170 stations are operated by the Department of Defense, and about 600 are operated part time by personnel of the Federal Aviation Administration (FAA) and by local operators at their own expense. There also are about 100 contract stations in limited operation with a fee paid to the contract observer for each observation taken. Very few of these provide 24-h reports, and, in several cases, difficulties in data handling lead to delays of up to 2 h before

```
NNNN    A

ZCZC
SWUS RWRC 211605
RIVER STATEMENT
NATIONAL WEATHER SERVICE OKLAHOMA CITY OK
11:05 AM CST WED JUN 21 1978

ONLY MINOR FLOODING ON LOWLANDS IS EXPECTED ON NORTHEASTERN OKLAHOMA
RIVERS.

STATION/RIVER        FS    LATEST STAGE     FORECAST

COPAN OK
LITTLE CANEY RVR    21.0   7AM/6.6          A CREST NEAR 22 FEET THIS
                                              EVENING WILL CAUSE MINOR
                                              AND LOWLAND FLOODING.


BARTLESVILLE OK
CANEY RVR           13.0   7AM/6.6          TO CREST NEAR 3/4 BANKFULL
                                              TOMORROW MORNING


RAMONA OK
CANEY               27.0   7AM/17.2         TO CREST NEAR 3/4 BANKFULL
                                              TOMORROW MORNING


TAHLEQUAH OK
ILLINOIS            11.00  7AM/6.9          TO CREST NEAR 10 FEET AT MID-
                                              DAY, TOMORROW
```

**Figure 8.6.** Flood-guidance message indicating the reporting station and river referred to (column 1), the flood stage in feet (column 2), the time of last report and river height in feet at that time (column 3), and flood-crest forecast information (column 4).

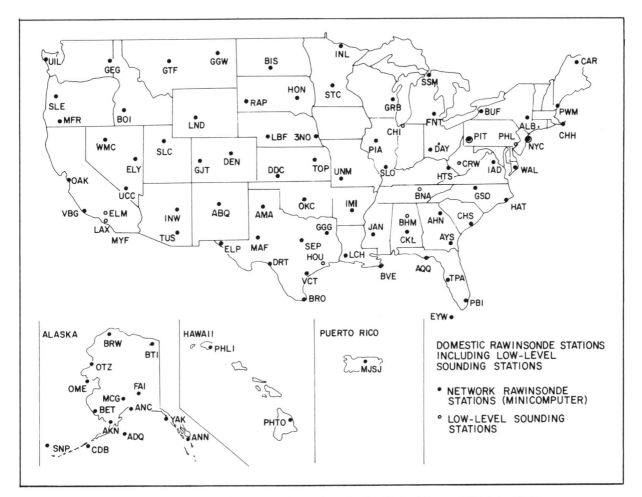

**Figure 8.7.** Network of radiosonde stations in the United States (NOAA, 1979).

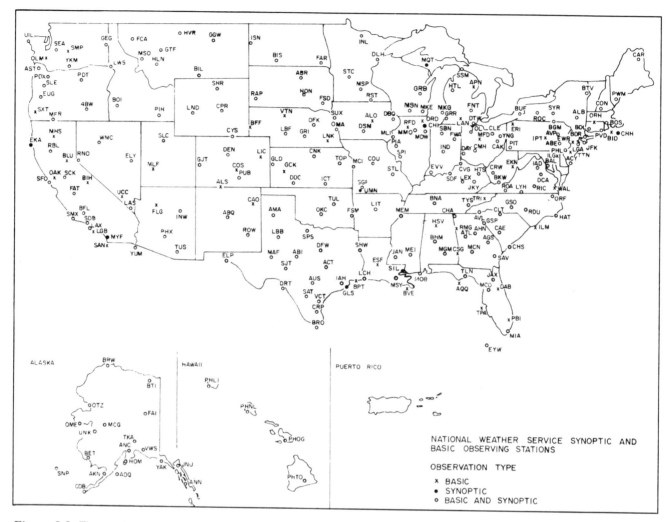

**Figure 8.8.** First-order stations for surface observations (NOAA, 1979). Basic observations made at hourly intervals and observations of significant events during intervening periods are reported in an easy-to-read code. Synoptic observations are made at the world standard synoptic times and transmitted in a numerical code.

data enter the communications system. The contract weather reports often consist of only those meteorological elements required by federal air regulations.

Thus, the surface observations in the United States consist of many different types of reports. About 200 are available 24 h/day; most others do not include all the key meteorological elements.

Although data from the upper-air stations represent an important basis for prediction, i.e., issuance of watches, the spacing of observations limits forecast resolution and accuracy. Thus, the data provided by surface and upper-air networks are

decidedly less valuable for *warning*, since observations are so widely spaced that many existing local storms remain undetected, much less well described. Even relatively large and severe thunderstorm systems are reported only sporadically and almost by chance in the data provided by station networks for surface and upper-air observation.

However, midtwentieth century has brought important new technology to facilitate storm warning. Weather radar presents the spatial distribution of precipitation continuously and with considerable accuracy and is most relied on for up-to-the-minute information on storms in being (Ham-

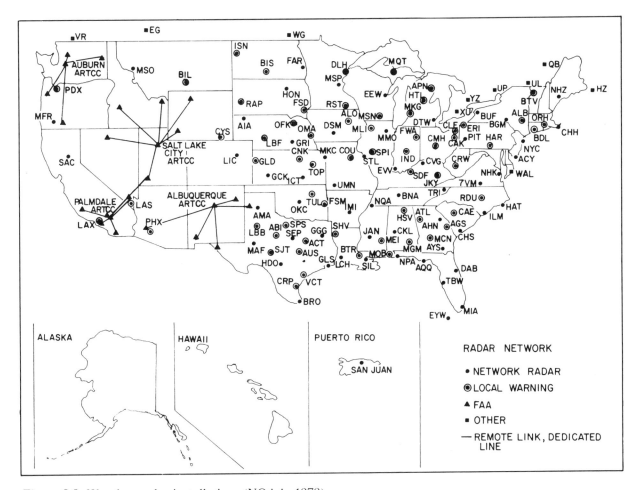

**Figure 8.9.** Weather radar installations (NOAA, 1979).

ilton, 1969). Figure 8.9 is the current radar network operating in the United States. The figure shows several nearby Canadian radar stations and includes some Air Route Traffic Control Center radars operated by FAA in the western United States. The backbone of the National Weather Service radar program is 10-cm-wavelength WSR-57s, shown as network radar in the illustration. The WSR-57s are supplemented by local-warning and military radars. Figure 8.10 shows the visible output, the Plan Position Indicator (PPI), of a WSR-57 radar and illustrates strikingly the immense value of this equipment for storm monitoring and warning.

The radar-observation program, much like the surface-observation program, involves heterogeneous data sources. All data networks were developed over a long period of time in response to the need for observational support to diverse meteor-

ological programs. About half of the warning offices have an on-site radar. Remote readout devices from nearby network radars were used extensively in the past, but in recent years many offices have been given local-use radars solely for monitoring severe weather. These radars also act as backup in case of maintenance problems with nearby network radars.

Views from artificial satellites of the Earth show the distribution of cloudiness and indications of temperature and moisture. Figure 8.11 shows the view from the Synchronous Meteorological Satellite SMS-1 at an altitude of 35,680 km (22,165 mi), geostationary over the Equator. Areal resolution in the picture is about 1 km. The normal picture interval is about 30 min, although photographs covering smaller areas are often collected more frequently during storm outbreaks.

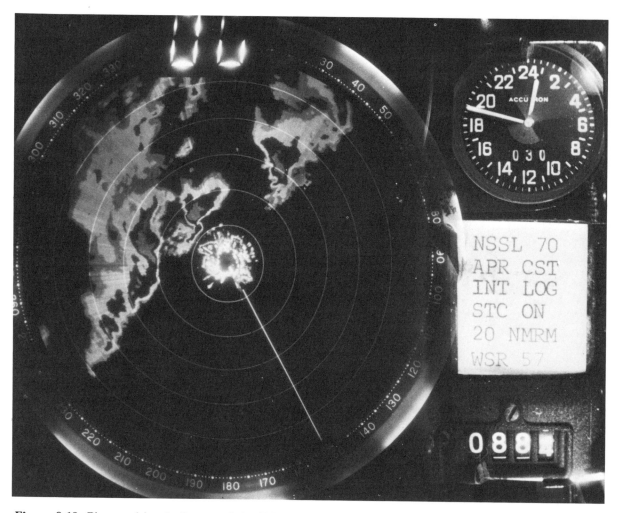

**Figure 8.10.** Plan position indicator of the WSR-57 radar at Norman, Okla., 0048 CST, 30 April 1970. Intensity levels correspond to rainfall rate; the highest intensity is shown as a shade of intermediate brightness surrounded by a dark area and represents about 2 in/h (50 mm/h) rainfall rate. Range is 120 nmi; range marks every 20 nmi. A tornadic storm with notch in reflectivity is located at 330° azimuth and 28-nmi range.

Weather satellites are very useful for monitoring large-scale features and major thunderstorms. An important shortcoming of the present generation of weather satellites is lack of data that can be merged with the existing surface and upper-air observations (i.e., pressure, temperature, humidity, and wind), but this problem is being addressed with radiometric techniques. Both radar and satellite equipment represent vastly improved capabilities for storm detection and warning.

In addition to the technological support described here, there is important input to the storm-warning process from amateur radio groups (NOAA, 1977),

law-enforcement groups, civil-defense personnel, volunteer severe-storm spotters, and reports from the general public. In a few areas, reports of powerline breaks from electric power companies (Schulz and Smith, 1972) may also serve as a basis for issuance of warnings.

### Preparation of Forecasts

Subjective Forecasts

Finley (1881) was the first well-known meteorologist to espouse the plan for a severe-thunderstorm

**Figure 8.11.** Photograph in visible light from Synchronous Meteorological Satellite SMS-1, 6 May 1975, 1407 CST. A major squall line harboring dangerous tornadoes lies across central United States. Lakes Superior, Huron, and Michigan are in upper right.

warning service: "Permit me to suggest that it would be advisable, and without doubt practicable, to station a special observer during the months of May, June and July at Kansas City, who shall receive special reports and instructions from Washington regarding atmospheric disturbances and report the same to various telegraphic stations throughout the Mississippi Valley." There were several significant studies in the 1940s (Lloyd, 1942; Showalter and Fulks, 1943). The main impetus, however, was the work done by a group of U.S. Air Force meteorologists (Fawbush et al., 1951; Fawbush and Miller, 1952, 1953, 1954). Their studies crystallized the subjective methods that became the cornerstone of the early forecasting efforts. The methods have been continually expanded and refined by Miller (1972) and others.

Winston (1956) described the following conditions known to be associated with severe thunderstorm systems and associated phenomena (tornadoes, large hail, damaging surface winds, extreme turbulence):

1. Abundant moisture in the surface layer to a depth of at least 1 km. Moisture and moisture flux are monitored by following surface-dew-point changes and by computing the horizontal convergence of moisture. The presence of a dry air mass at intermediate levels (with base at 1 km to 2.5 km) provides a potential for strong downdrafts through evaporative cooling, and is thus highly favorable though not essential.

2. Ability to sustain deep convection. There are many different methods to assess the stability or

resistance to overturning of the atmosphere. All are highly correlated with each other and are measures of the relative warmth and dampness of lower layers of air, compared with midlayers of air. Assessment methods include the Showalter Index (Showalter, 1953), the Lifted Index (Galway, 1956), the SWEAT Index (Bidner, 1970), and the K Index (George, 1960).

3. The presence of a stable layer or temperature inversion (i.e., a layer with an increase of temperature with height). Such a layer acts to prevent deep convection from occurring until the potential for extremely rapid overturning is established (e.g., Beebe, 1958).

4. A mechanism to remove the stable layer. The most common mechanism is dynamic lifting acting with surface heating and an influx of warm air below the inversion (e.g., Humphreys, 1926). Other possible mechanisms include lifting by terrain and by gravity waves (McNulty, 1977).

5. Significant wind changes with height. Winds that veer (turn clockwise) and increase with height are associated with adjacent cold and warm air masses and zones of temperature change between them where severe thunderstorms most frequently form. Further, such winds can be dynamically related to typical severe-storm structure (e.g., Bates, 1961). Wind direction, windspeed, and temperature changes at levels above 8 km are not as pronounced as in the boundary layer. Considerable attention is focused on upper-level divergence patterns that can promote enhanced processes of storm formation at the surface (Galway and Lee, 1958).

Much about items 1-5 has been detailed in an article by Fulks (1951). Subjective methods currently in use attempt to locate these five antecedent conditions. After completing his diagnosis, the forecaster projects known conditions forward in time. Radar and satellite imagery are used throughout the forecast process to see whether the hour-to-hour changes are consistent with the evolution formulated by the forecaster. When consistency is not indicated, the forecast is amended.

## Objective Forecasts

The parameters measured by surface and upper-air observing stations are used in theoretical atmospheric models for predicting general atmospheric conditions. Although the network data are far too coarse for analysis of some significant details, many severe-thunderstorm systems have been investigated with respect to the general atmospheric (synoptic-scale) conditions, well defined by network data, in which the storms arise. Thus, Williams (1976) objectively determined synoptic-scale surface parameters associated with more than 5,000 tornadoes over a 6-yr period. Figure 8.12 shows the relative frequencies of tornado-related surface temperature, dew point, and sea-level pressure. All three sets of frequencies were determined with the existing surface network, i.e., with an average spacing of about 100 km. David (1976) prepared a similar study of parameters aloft preceding tornadoes for the same time period as Williams's, but with interpolation in time, as well as space, since the actual tropospheric soundings are available only twice daily.

At present there is no operational forecast method based in dynamical models with computer calculations for specific severe-thunderstorm events, though such work has been an intrinsic part of the forecasting of large-scale weather patterns for more than three decades. With thunderstorms the emphasis has been on statistical methods (Miller and David, 1971; David, 1973; Charba, 1975; Reap and Foster, 1979). This emphasis results from the inability of numerical models to provide forecasts down to the thunderstorm scale in the absence of observations on that scale.

The NWS Techniques Development Laboratory has developed and put into routine operation objective systems that produce probabilistic forecasts of severe local storms (Reap and Foster, 1979; Charba, 1975), using model output statistics (Glahn and Lowry, 1972) from the current numerical models produced at the National Meteorological Center. Multiple screening regression is used to derive predictive equations for local storms whose scale is too small to be predicted numerically.

Special procedures have been developed to enhance the predictive value of meteorological quantities used as predictors. One of these procedures correlates predictor pattern with severe weather. Another procedure involves transforming each predictor to a variable that is linearly related to the predictand's relative frequency of occurrence. A third technique uses interactive predictors. Such

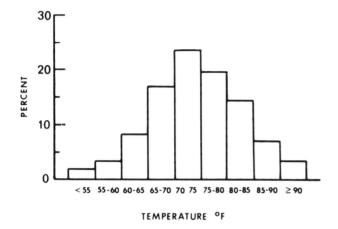

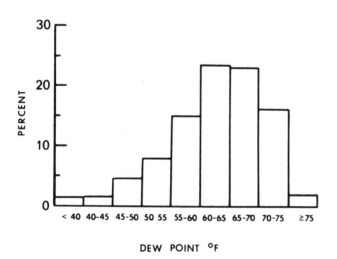

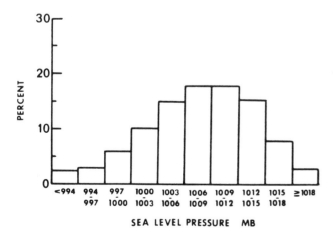

**Figure 8.12.** Statistical distribution of temperature, dew point, and pressure at the Earth's surface, 0 to 3 h before tornado occurrences (from Williams, 1976).

predictors are a combination of observed parameters. For instance, the climatological-thunderstorm frequency is multiplied by a stability index. This results in modulating the historical record by the synoptic situation.

### Forecasts and Warnings

When the forecaster has decided that thunderstorms will form, he then must decide just how severe the thunderstorms might become and how they will evolve. Miller (1972) has listed 14 key parameters with threshold values which characterize a weather system as having weak, moderate, or strong convective potential. But even after this has been done, he notes, "one of the most difficult problems faced by the severe weather forecaster is whether to forecast severe thunderstorms, or severe thunderstorms *accompanied* by tornadoes. For the most part, the same parameters will probably be present, in varying degrees of intensity for either phenomenon." The major tornado-producing weather systems occur with stronger upper tropospheric wind flows, with a greater degree of instability, and ahead of intense mesoscale wind perturbations. Before thunderstorm development, the first two features are generally easier to detect with the present observing system than is the last.

NSSFC issues all severe-thunderstorm watches for the contiguous United States. Watches may be issued up to several hours before the watch period begins. When weather developments are very rapid, it is quite common to amend existing watches on the basis of incoming reports.

As noted in the section "NWS Organization for Severe-Storm Forecasting and Warning" above, warnings on storms in being are issued by 217 WSFOs and WSOs. A typical warning is valid for an hour and applies to three or four counties. Radar indications are the most common basis for all warnings, but tornado warnings are more dependent on visual sightings.

The weakest link in the watch-warning process is dissemination. Radio and television stations are the major channels for communicating weather information to most United States residents. Warnings are usually distributed to the radio and television stations by one of the wire services or by the NOAA Weather Wire, a Teletype system controlled by and partly funded by NWS. Less than 25% of TV and radio stations currently subscribe to the NOAA Weather Wire.

NWS operates its own VHF-FM radio broadcasting stations throughout the country. Warnings are given the highest priority for dissemination. The broadcasts blanket areas that include more than 90% of the United States population.

## The Disaster Preparedness Program

NWS gives much attention to disaster preparedness because improved forecasts and warnings of severe local storms and other hazardous-weather events may prove useless unless community preparedness plans are developed and people react promptly and positively to weather watches and warnings. A program was authorized by Congress in 1971 to provide information to the public on storm preparedness and on how to respond to storm advisories, and to improve the accuracy of advisories and their timeliness in delivery. Primary initial emphasis was on hurricane warnings, but the program has since been expanded to include severe local storms, winter storms, and floods. Nevertheless, most of the nearly 20,000 urban and rural communities in this country remain unprepared to cope with natural disasters.

At the present time, 19 Weather Service Forecast Offices (WSFOs) have been assigned a meteorologist whose sole function is to develop the disaster preparedness program locally (Fig. 8.13). NWS plans additional positions at other WSFOs if resources become available. These meteorologists provide the link between hazardous-weather watches-warnings, and an effective citizen response to them in several ways:

1. They hold preparedness meetings with state, county, and local officials, law-enforcement agencies, school officials, amateur radio groups, and others to establish and maintain local warning communication systems, storm-spotter networks, and other aspects of an active preparedness program.

2. They work with groups at the national, state, county, and local levels and with engineers, scientists, and others to formulate weather-safety information. Recently attention has focused on weath-

er safety in schools and on structural-safety design for homes and mobile homes (DCPA, 1974, 1975a, 1975b, 1976; Eagleman et al., 1975; Abernethy, 1976).

3. They work with state officials to encourage tornado drills in schools. Many state, county, and local school districts require tornado drills.

4. They work with the mass media to ensure that weather watches and warnings and storm-safety information are rapidly and reliably disseminated.

5. They distribute publications, slides, films, and news releases to inform the public about hazardous weather and to provide an improved response to warnings.

NWS is also examining the sociological impact of its warning program (McLuckie, 1973). The National Science Foundation has supported a comprehensive research assessment of the severe-local-storm hazard and the natural-hazard warning systems in the United States (Brinkmann, 1975; Mileti, 1975).

Where there have been good preparedness plans and an educated citizenry, deaths and injuries from severe thunderstorms have been minimized. During the record widespread tornado outbreak of 3-4 April 1974, preparation of tornado warnings, broadcast of these warnings by the news media, and protective actions taken by community officials and the public were credited with saving thousands of lives. Yet many communities were unprepared, and so there still was significant loss of life.

There are many instances when timely warnings, coupled with an educated and responsive citizenry, have worked to save lives. For example, on 12 May 1980 a tornado destroyed 62 units of a 64-unit mobile-home park in Sedalia, Mo., but there were no deaths because nearly 100 park residents had gone to safe refuge in a nearby basement (Ostby and Pearson, 1981). The Omaha tornado of 6 May 1975, the most expensive tornado in history (Ostby and Pearson, 1976) and the Topeka tornado of 8 June 1966 (Galway, 1966) provide additional testimony to the value of preparedness.[1]

[1]Appreciation is expressed for contributions by Joseph T. Schaefer and by Frederick P. Ostby, who succeeded Mr. Pearson as Director of the National Severe Storms Forecast Center.

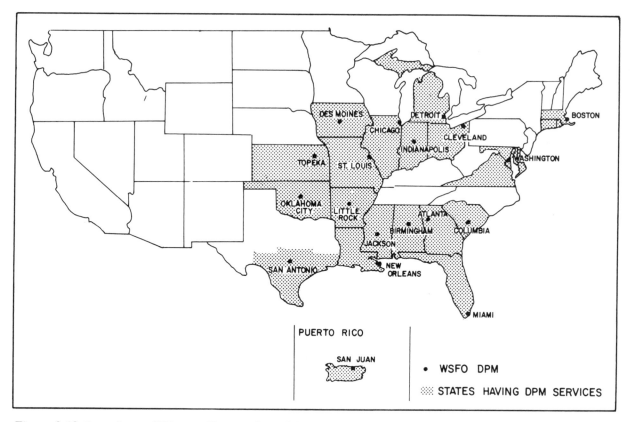

**Figure 8.13.** Locations of Disaster Preparedness Meteorologists, late 1977 (NOAA, 1979).

# 9. Storm Research in the United States: Organizations and Major Facilities

*Ronald L. Lavoie*

## Introduction

It is difficult to set logical boundaries around research to advance knowledge of thunderstorms. In meteorological terms, the thunderstorm is part of a continuum of atmospheric processes from the molecular to global scales: it cannot be studied in isolation. Furthermore, studies aimed at one aspect of the thunderstorm bear fruit in other unexpected areas. Instrument development, creation of numerical models, novel laboratory experiments, and refinement of analytical techniques can be sources of advancement in thunderstorm research.

Most severe-storm research in the United States is supported or conducted by the federal government. The National Science Foundation is the main source of financial support to storm research in academic institutions, and the National Oceanic and Atmospheric Administration, in the Department of Commerce, conducts the nation's principal operational activities in weather and climate, as well as many-faceted research on thunderstorms. Severe local storms affect flight services regulated by the Department of Transportation and many activities in the Department of Defense; these departments have a long history of active involvement in thunderstorm research. The Departments of Agriculture and Interior, the Energy Research and Development Administration (in the Department of Energy since 1979), and the Nuclear Regulatory Commission are concerned with specialized aspects of storms and have supported occasional studies on thunderstorms. Table 9.1 gives estimates of fiscal year 1977 funds expended by federal agencies to support research directly related to thunderstorms. Since there is no federal cross-cut analysis of work or funding in this field, the funds

were estimated by consulting appropriate program managers. The funding identified with thunderstorm research was about 8% of the total federal research budget for meteorology in FY 1977.

Although funding patterns vary from year to year and organizational structures also change, areas of research emphasis shift more slowly. The following description of United States agency activity in FY 1977 is representative of agency relationships in thunderstorm-research programs as they have subsequently evolved.

## Agencies in Storm Research and Their Programs

The Department of Agriculture is interested in thunderstorms because of their importance to for-

**Table 9.1.** Funding for Thunderstorm Research by Agency, FY 1977

| Agency | Funding (thousands of dollars) |
|---|---|
| Department of Agriculture | $ 125 |
| Department of Commerce (NOAA) | 4,600 |
| Department of Defense | |
| Air Force | 900 |
| Army | 1,900 |
| Navy | 300 |
| Department of the Interior | 1,950 |
| Department of Transportation (FAA) | 375 |
| Energy Research and Development Administration | 175 |
| National Aeronautics and Space Administration | 900 |
| National Science Foundation | 5,700 |
| Nuclear Regulatory Commission | 500 |
| | Total $17,400 |

ests and crops. The department's Forest Service is responsible for preventing and controlling lightning-generated forest fires. From 1960 to 1973 the Forest Service sponsored Project Skyfire near Missoula, Montana, to determine whether seeding clouds with silver iodide could reduce the frequency of incendiary lightning strokes. Results were promising but inconclusive, and the program was terminated because of other research priorities. Research continues on the characteristics of lightning in Montana thunderstorms, especially cloud-to-ground strokes. With the University of Arizona and the Bureau of Land Management, of the Department of the Interior, the Forest Service is developing a network of lightning detectors to monitor and locate strokes with high potential to ignite forest fires.[1] The Department of Agriculture has also conducted studies of wind and hail damage to crops from thunderstorms, but no funding is available for such studies at present.

Major NOAA components that participate in thunderstorm research include the National Weather Service, the National Environmental Satellite Service, the Environmental Data Information Service, and the Environmental Research Laboratories. All conduct research aimed at improving prediction of severe storms.

The National Weather Service (NWS) conducts fine-mesh modeling studies at the National Meteorological Center in Camp Springs, Maryland. The model development program plans to use numerical prediction to define the subsynoptic-scale (~200 km) features that accompany developing severe local storms. The Techniques Development Laboratory (TDL) studies statistical methods for predicting severe weather. A third NWS group, located in the National Severe Storm Forecast Center in Kansas City, Missouri, uses data from surface and upper-air stations and weather satellites to refine procedures for identifying areas in which outbreaks of severe thunderstorms are likely. In addition, the NWS Hydrology Research Laboratory is investigating optimum mixes of data from rain-gage networks, digitized radar systems, and

satellites to describe the distribution and intensity of rainfall from thunderstorms.

Five units of NOAA's Environmental Research Laboratories (ERL), with headquarters in Boulder, Colorado, contribute to thunderstorm research. ERL's National Severe Storms Laboratory (NSSL) in Norman, Oklahoma (Fig. 9.1), is dedicated entirely to this research and conducts observational, experimental, and theoretical studies (Kessler, 1976). NSSL pioneered in applying Doppler radar to thunderstorm investigations and tornado detection. It makes specialized use of surface and upper-air networks, a 444-m instrumented tower, and radar systems to observe the characteristics of Oklahoma thunderstorms. Conceptual, mathematical, and laboratory models are developed and tested in relation to observations. NSSL has recently begun study of the electrical characteristics of severe storms. The laboratory accounts for about 40% of NOAA's research budget for severe local storms.

ERL's Wave Propagation Laboratory (WPL) in Boulder, Colorado, has applied several remote-sensing techniques to thunderstorm studies. These techniques include using multiple Doppler radar systems to observe three-dimensional motions within rain systems. During 1977 a major WPL research study tested a passive space-time mapping technique that tracks lightning discharges in three dimensions as a function of time to allow study of the relationships between lightning and precipitation patterns. WPL has developed techniques that employ acoustic-echo sounders and networks of pressure sensors to study surface gust fronts emanating from thunderstorms.

The ERL National Hurricane and Experimental Meteorology Laboratory (NHEML) in Miami, Florida, has conducted intensive studies of convective clouds with emphasis on their modification by cloud seeding. The Florida Area Cumulus Experiment (FACE) has used massive seeding with silver iodide to attempt to transform cumulus congestus clouds into cumulonimbus clouds. One of FACE's major objectives is to test the hypothesis that cumulonimbus clouds can be merged into small mesoscale systems by systematic application of dynamic seeding techniques and rainfall thus increased over a considerable area. Summer field programs in southern Florida have used Doppler radars, re-

---

[1] This network was virtually complete in the western United States in 1981, and the lightning data are now available at the National Severe Storms Forecast Center [Ed.].

**Figure 9.1.** Headquarters of NOAA's National Severe Storms Laboratory on the North Campus of the University of Oklahoma, Norman. The building is leased by NOAA from the university. Behind the building is the radome that houses the antenna of a WSR-57 10-cm radar.

search aircraft, and mesoscale observing networks. The FACE scientists have pioneered a technique for estimating thunderstorm rainfall by analyzing the imagery provided at 30-min intervals by geostationary satellites. NHEML also directed Project Stormfury, in which the dynamic seeding technique is used on the convective clouds of hurricanes to study the possibility of mitigating their extreme winds. The data gathered by research aircraft in hurricanes have been used to clarify the role of thunderstorms in these tropical disturbances.

Another component of ERL, the Atmospheric Physics and Chemistry Laboratory (APCL), has been engaged in a program to develop mesoscale numerical models that simulate interactions between severe convective storms and their environment. This program includes parameterization of the convective component of precipitation. Parameterization implies the description of results of many intricate and detailed processes. Data from

the program should help in predicting heavy thunderstorm rains associated with flash floods. Staff of APCL conduct detailed analyses of flash flood events and categorize these events according to atmospheric characteristics. APCL has also studied thunderstorm electricity and pioneered seeding with metalized fibers (chaff) in an attempt to suppress lightning.

ERL's Geophysical Fluid Dynamics Laboratory (GFDL) in Princeton, New Jersey, pursues theoretical and numerical modeling studies on a wide range of meteorological scales, including three-dimensional models of the cloud scale.

NOAA's National Environmental Satellite Service (NESS) uses satellite sensors to recognize precursors of severe storms and to monitor their development, severity, and track. Severe-storm research in NESS during FY 1977 centered on the structure of anvil-shaped cloud tops and its relationship to storm severity. From this work in collaboration with the University of Chicago, NESS has developed the hypothesis that thunderstorms with strong surface effects are characterized by the rapid collapse of domes in the anvil. It is proposed that storms with strong surface effects can often be recognized in advance by unique signatures in the thermal maps of the anvil tops, derived from infrared satellite data.

Finally, NOAA's Environmental Data and Information Service (NEDIS)[2] conducts research in several centers, in addition to managing data. The Center for Experiment Design and Data Analysis (in 1980 the Center for Environmental Assessment Services) processed and interpreted observations on the cloud scale, including thunderstorm data, collected during the GARP (Global Atmospheric Research Program) Atlantic Tropical Experiment (GATE) in 1974.

Severe local storms are of great concern to the military units of the Department of Defense, both in peace and in war. All branches of the service are affected, and each has a history of involvement in, and frequently leadership of, thunderstorm research.

In the Air Force most thunderstorm research is conducted through the Air Force Geophysics Laboratory (AFGL), in Bedford, Massachusetts. Most of AFGL's severe-storm research during the late 1970s and early 1980s involved the use of Doppler radar and was aimed at refining techniques for identifying severe storms and improving prediction of their motion. The Air Force also cooperates with NOAA's National Severe Storms Laboratory in radar research during the peak tornado season in Oklahoma and in a project to demonstrate the qualities of Doppler radar in operational environments.

The Army's research on severe storms is concentrated in the Atmospheric Sciences Laboratory of the Electronics Command, at the White Sands Missile Range in New Mexico. This research centers on the use of cloud imagery from the geostationary satellites to identify and predict the characteristics of severe local storms. Specialized techniques for processing and analyzing data have

been developed in cooperation with NASA and university investigators.

The Navy's Office of Naval Research supports several university research projects relating to thunderstorms, including study of the mechanisms of charge generation in cumulus convection and the effect of electric fields on precipitation formation. Research on the characteristics of lightning includes observational and modeling studies and development of techniques for warning of lightning and protecting against it. The Naval Research Laboratory also used its instrumented aircraft for cloud-electrification studies in the Thunderstorm Research International Project (TRIP) at the Kennedy Space Center in 1977.

In the Department of the Interior (DOI), thunderstorm research is conducted mainly by the Bureau of Reclamation. The bureau's cooperative High Plains Experiment (HIPLEX) is attempting to remove critical uncertainties about modifying summer cumulus clouds to increase rainfall. The program, started in 1973, has progressed to background field studies at experimental sites in Montana, Kansas, and Texas. Although thunderstorms are not a specific subject of the project, they are critical to the summer rainfall around the sites. The program uses numerical modeling of thunderstorms and individual cloud processes. Radar and satellite studies have also been supported under HIPLEX. Half of the FY 1977 budget for HIPLEX included the DOI funding (Table 9.1), or $1.9 million, is directly relevant to thunderstorm research.

The Geological Survey in DOI is studying the frequency of lightning strikes on various rock formations and the possibility of using this information to date rocks. The survey is also interested in rainfall runoff and flash flooding and conducts detailed case studies of thunderstorm-rain events. However, total funding for these specialized activities in the survey is less than $50,000 a year.

The Federal Aviation Administration (FAA), of the Department of Transportation, is interested in studying thunderstorms, particularly as they affect flight safety. Recent work, much of it in collaboration with the National Weather Service and the Environmental Research Laboratories, has concentrated on short-term prediction techniques for use in air traffic control. Low-level wind shear near thunderstorms, especially in the outflow re-

---

[2] In 1982, NESS and NEDIS were merged to form NESDIS, the National Environmental Satellite and Data Information Service.

gions known as gust fronts, is especially important to aircraft landing and takeoff. Funds from FAA have supported studies of data from NSSL's instrumented tower and installation of pressure sensors around Dulles and O'Hare airports to explore their utility as detectors of gust-front conditions.

During 1977 the Energy Research and Development Administration (more recently the Department of Energy) spent about $175,000 on three projects involving thunderstorms. One project concerned the potential effects of trace concentrations of krypton 85 on thunderstorm frequency. Krypton 85 is produced during generation of nuclear power, and even small amounts of artificially produced radioactive gas can significantly affect the production of ions and thereby influence local electric fields. Another project investigated the possibility that heat generated at large power plants might initiate severe local storms under certain atmospheric conditions. In FY 1977, Project METER (Meteorological Effects of Thermal Energy Releases) concentrated on developing or using numerical models of cooling-tower plumes and strong local heat sources. Another ERDA program dealt with the characteristics of thunderstorms and tornadoes as they pertain to the design and construction of energy installations.

The National Aeronautics and Space Administration (NASA) has used aircraft and satellites to study thunderstorms. It has emphasized development of very-high-resolution sensors designed to detect incipient storms and measure the atmospheric conditions under which the storms develop. An array of such sensors, the Visible and Infrared Spin Scan Radiometer Atmospheric Sounder (VAS), is planned for installation on a geostationary satellite scheduled for launch in the 1980s.[3] This research tool should provide temperature and moisture soundings of the atmosphere with sufficient spatial resolution to be useful in characterizing the environment of large thunderstorm complexes. NASA also conducts or supports several analytical and modeling studies of thunderstorms that use satellite and aircraft data. Major storm-research programs are conducted from NASA's Goddard Laboratory for Atmospheric Sciences, Suitland,

Maryland, and the Marshall Space Flight Center, Huntsville, Alabama.

The National Science Foundation (NSF) is the major source of research support for academic scientists. NSF also provides funds to the National Center for Atmospheric Research (NCAR), which conducts major research projects in cooperation with universities and other organizations.

The largest NSF thunderstorm research project in recent years has been the National Hail Research Experiment (NHRE) managed by NCAR (Fig. 9.2). NHRE began in 1970 with twin objectives: to investigate the processes involved in hail production in severe thunderstorms and to perform a randomized test of a hail-suppression technique adapted from the reportedly successful operational program in the Soviet Union. Results of a 3-yr seeding program, which ended in 1974, were inconclusive and unpromising regarding the efficacy of that seeding technique for ameliorating northeast Colorado storms. An additional field project in 1976 was directed toward elucidating the physics of growth of natural hail. Facilities included a dual-wavelength radar, two C-band and two X-band Doppler radars, and six instrumented aircraft including a jet, a sailplane, and a T-28 plated with armor to withstand hail assaults. Data were collected with cloud photography and from 3 rawinsonde sites, 46 automatic weather stations, 727 precipitation-measurement stations, and 4 mobile sampling vehicles.

The massive quantities of NHRE data were analyzed during 1977-78. Funding for NHRE in FY 1977 totaled about $3.9 million. NCAR supplied nearly 40% in the form of personnel and facilities funded through its regular budget from the Atmospheric Sciences Division of NSF. The remainder was funded by the Weather Modification Program in the Research Applied to National Needs (RANN) directorate within NSF. The funding provided support to 13 university groups as participants in NHRE.

NSF/RANN, in its final stage of support of METROMEX, the Metropolitan Meteorological Experiment, was completing analysis of data from 5 years of summer field measurements in Saint Louis in FY 1977, to determine the effects of city activities on weather. A major conclusion was that severe thunderstorms were more frequent just downwind of the city.

---

[3] The VAS satellite was actually placed in geosynchronous orbit in 1981.

**Figure 9.2.** Aerial view of the headquarters site and operations control center of the National Hail Research Experiment, on the High Plains at Grover, Colorado, 135 km NNE of Denver.

In FY 1977, the Atmospheric Research Section (ARS) in NSF awarded 24 grants totaling $1,715,000 to research groups in 15 universities to investigate the thunderstorm and associated severe storms. The largest among these devoted to field measurements was the South Park Area Cumulus Experiment (SPACE), conducted by Colorado State University to study thunderstorm genesis near the Continental Divide in Colorado. The observation program in SPACE was closely tied to three-dimensional model development aimed at understanding the interactions of cumulus clouds with their mesoscale environments.

NSF awarded a number of grants to investigators proposing to use the data stores of NOAA's National Severe Storms Laboratory. The NSSL Doppler radars and mesoscale vertical-sounding network are favorite data sources for a variety of analyses conducted to test severe-storm hypothe-

ses. In addition, several grants enabled researchers to participate in the Thunderstorm Research International Project at the Kennedy Space Center during the summer of 1977.

Six ARS grants, totaling $450,000, were devoted to studies of lightning and thunderstorm electricity, and eight, for $582,000, dealt with numerical modeling of thunderstorms and their mesoscale forcing. Computer time for these studies was frequently provided by NCAR, usually by time-sharing terminals installed at the principal investigator's university. NCAR's cost-free provision of such facilities to university researchers has not been included in the NSF funding estimate in Table 9.1.

The Nuclear Regulatory Commission (NRC) supports tornado research in collaboration with NOAA and several universities. The primary program objective is to provide design engineers with the quantitative tornado parameters they need to assure that nuclear facilities can survive these storms. NRC supports climatological studies of tornado frequency, structure, and regional distribution. It funds Doppler radar and Doppler lidar studies of tornado-vortex characteristics. Direct aircraft probing of waterspouts in the Florida Keys was made possible by NRC support to a Colorado State University program during FY 1977. NRC-supported studies also include theoretical analyses and numerical modeling of tornado structure.

## Coordination and Management of Storm Research

The policy of the federal government is to allow its agencies to justify and pursue severe-storm research to the extent required by their individual missions. Although no lead agency has been formally designated, mechanisms exist within the executive branch to coordinate activities. For more than 20 years, until the late 1970s, basic research programs in meteorology were reviewed and coordinated through the Interdepartmental Committee for Atmospheric Sciences (ICAS), established by the Federal Council for Science and Technology in 1959 (e.g., ICAS, 1976). Thunderstorm research was on the agenda during many ICAS monthly meetings. Severe storms were an active topic in the early 1960s, and in 1963 ICAS formally recommended a National Mesometeorological Research Program. ICAS had neither management nor budget authority, however, and such a program never materialized. During the late 1960s, ICAS recommended the national effort to study hailstorms and test Soviet techniques of hail suppression by cloud seeding. ICAS reviewed the experiment periodically and encouraged collaboration by other agencies in the ambitious field program.

In a reorganization in 1980, ICAS was replaced by the Subcommittee on Atmospheric Research of the Committee of Atmospheres and Oceans, under the Federal Coordinating Council for Science, Engineering, and Technology. FCCSET is part of the Office of Science and Technology Policy in the Executive Office of the President.

The Federal Committee for Meteorological Services and Supporting Research (FCMSSR) was formed in response to Public Law 87-843. FCMSSR has contributed to the systematic development of forecast and warning services, radar and satellite applications, and other programs related to severe storms. Its annual publication (FCMSSR, 1977) provides a valuable summary of agency programs and plans for the succeeding fiscal year. Among the specialized publications of the FCMSSR is an annually revised National Severe Local Storm Operations Plan. In addition to coordination of agency programs by such committees, a number of bilateral arrangements exist, like those between NASA and NOAA and between NOAA and DOD, to deal with specific problem areas.

The National Academy of Sciences (NAS) acts as scientific adviser and reviewer to federal agencies. With broad-based agency support NAS maintains panels and committees with special expertise in the environmental sciences. The standing Committee on Atmospheric Sciences, in particular, has frequently examined the federal effort in severe-storm research, and its reports are rich with recommendations for new policies and programs (e.g., NAS, 1977).

Professional scientific societies also contribute to the vitality of severe-storm research. The American Meteorological Society has standing committees on severe local storms, atmospheric electricity, radar meteorology, and cloud physics that issue periodic statements assessing progress in their disciplines and arrange national conferences to speed the exchange of information and research results. The American Geophysical Union also has been very active in advancing the study of thunderstorms through special symposia at its semiannual meetings and the effort of its meteorology section.

## Outlook

With increasing complexity and centralization of industries and services, society seems destined to become more rather than less vulnerable to the effects of severe local storms. For example, two well-placed lightning strikes initiated collapse of electrical service to New York City in July 1977. Partly in recognition of increasing vulnerability, the intensity of research on thunderstorms has increased modestly in recent years. Scientists have recognized that the application of new technologies to thunderstorm research increases the likelihood of more timely and accurate warnings and forecasts. Thus major new research programs in severe storms are being proposed with increased frequency; nevertheless, prospects for major funding increases are dim in 1980.

A draft program-development plan for Project SESAME (Severe Environmental Storms and Mesoscale Experiment) was first issued in June 1974. With NSF collaboration NOAA conceived the program to (1) enlarge the scientific understanding of how convective storms evolve from their mesoscale environment; (2) test the ability of new direct and remote sensing systems, including those on satellites, to produce reliable and timely measurements of mesoscale and convective storm potential and evolution; and (3) support the development and testing of regional and smaller scale numerical simulation models, which will contribute to the understanding and the prediction of severe storms.

The design of Project SESAME reflects the fact that the multiplicity of processes at work in thunderstorms requires that a diversity of sensors and talents be used for simultaneous measurements and subsequent analysis. SESAME was designed to investigate storms occurring in "family" outbreaks and thus focused on thunderstorms in their larger-scale context rather than on individual cumulonimbus clouds. SESAME was not funded by a federal agency, but a scaled-down effort relying on allocation by interested parties from existing budgets took place in Oklahoma during spring 1979. A more recent plan (NOAA, 1976) and the accompanying planning-documentation volume (Lilly, 1977) proposed a 4-yr research program costing $21 million.

Various approaches have been taken to organize separate research teams in the same field program while retaining individual initiative. For instance, in the Thunderstorm Research International Project of 1976, a confederation of more than a dozen research teams was loosely coordinated by a two-man "secretariat" (Pierce, 1976). NASA provided basic facilities at the Kennedy Space Center, and each principal investigator furnished his own funding and equipment. Types of measurement and timing were left up to each participant. On

the other hand, NHRE's observational program was carefully forged in advance, and each investigator received funding specifically to participate as part of a team. Decisions on when and where to deploy were made by the NHRE director or his delegate. The management of METROMEX combined the approaches of TRIP and NHRE. That is, funding was from several agencies, and the planning, conduct, and reporting of the program were carefully coordinated by a committee of representatives of the research teams (Changnon et al., 1971), but little attempt was made to develop central control.

Research on thunderstorm systems is sufficiently demanding of talents and resources to suggest multinational effort. Although the multinational GARP Atlantic Tropical Experiment of 1974 included study of cumulonimbus cloud systems, the focus was on larger-scale global weather patterns. Nevertheless, GATE demonstrated the feasibility of marshaling the international community to work together in an intensive and highly interactive field project.

The desire for weather modification will probably be an important stimulus for international research on the mesoscale. The possibility of human intervention to ameliorate damaging local storms or to augment large-area rainfall is appealing. However, scientific uncertainties associated with weather modification research may give rise to social, political, and legal problems. For instance, it might be difficult to persuade a neighboring country that an experiment is not deleterious to areas beyond the limits of the experiment.

Active international collaboration in thunderstorm research has begun. Switzerland, France, and Italy have recently cooperated in a hail suppression experiment called Grossversuch IV (Federer et al., 1977). The World Meteorological Organization, an agency of the United Nations, has begun in Spain the Precipitation Enhancement Project (PEP), the first international weather modification experiment. In June 1977 the Executive Committee of WMO asked that plans be drawn up for an international hail-suppression experiment.

# References

## Chapter 1

Barrows, J. S., 1966. Weather modification and the prevention of lightning-caused forest fires. In *Human Dimensions of Weather Modification*, W. R. Sewell (ed.), Univ. of Chicago Press, Chicago, pp. 159-82.

Boffey, P. M., 1978. Investigations agree N.Y. blackout of 1977 could have been avoided. *Science* 201:994-98.

Changnon, S. A., Jr.; B. C. Farhar; and E. R. Swanson, 1978. Hail suppression and society. *Science* 200:387.

Farhar, B. C. (ed.), 1977. Hail suppression: society and environment, selected contributions to the technology assessment of hail suppression. Program on Technology, Environment and Man, Monograph No. 24, Institute of Behavioral Science, Univ. of Colorado, Boulder. 293 pp.

Foote, G. B., and Knight, C. A. (eds.), 1977. *Hail: Review of Hail Science and Hail Suppression.* Meteorological Monographs, Vol. 16, No. 38. 277 pp.

Francaviglia, R. V., 1978. Xenia rebuilds: effects of predisaster conditioning on postdisaster redevelopment. *J. Am. Inst. Plann.* 44(1):13-24.

Glass, R. I., R. B. Craven, D. J. Bergman, B. J. Stoll, N. Horowitz, P. Kerndt, and J. Winkle, 1980. Injuries from the Wichita Falls tornado: implications for prevention. *Science* 207:734.

Golde, R. H., 1973. *Lightning Protection.* Edward Arnold Publishers, London. 220 pp.

Hartman, L. M., D. Hollard, and M. Giddings, 1969. Effects of hurricane storms on agriculture. *Water Resour. Res.* 5:555-62.

Independent Protection Company, 1965. Lightning protection—improved lightning rods. Pamphlet, Independent Company, Goshen, Ind.

———, 1970. How to meet today's lightning protection requirements. Pamphlet, Independent Protection Company, Goshen, Ind.

Jackson, P., 1977. An investigation of the spatial aspects of tornado hazard and mobile housing policy in Kansas. Ph.D. dissertation, Univ. of Kansas. 110 pp.

Kessler, E., and J. T. Lee, 1978. Distribution of the tornado threat in the United States. *Bull. Am. Meteorol. Soc.* 59(1):61-62.

Langston, T. O., 1977. Tornadic wind effects and mobile homes: the human response to damage mitigation equipment and storm shelters. Master's thesis, Southern Illinois University. 57 pp.

Logan, B., 1978. Human response to the tornado hazard in Clay Center, Kansas. *Kansas Geographer,* No. 13, 1978.

Meinzer, O. E. (ed.), 1939. *Hydrology.* McGraw-Hill, republished, 1942, by Dover Publications. 712 pp.

Mogil, M. H., M. Rush, and M. Kutka, 1977. Lightning—an update. Preprints, Tenth Conference on Severe Local Storms, American Meteorological Society, Boston, pp. 226-30.

National Academy of Sciences, 1973. *Weather and Climate Modification, Problems and Progress.* Washington, D.C. 258 pp.

National Science Foundation, 1980. *A Report on Flood Hazard Mitigation.* Washington, D.C., 253 pp.

Oparin, A. I., 1953. *The Origin of Life.* Dover Publications, New York, 270 pp. (trans. by S. Morgulis; republication of the translation first published in 1938).

Pautz, M. E. (ed.), 1969. Severe local storm occurrences 1955-1967. ESSA Technical Memorandum WBTM FCST 12, Silver Spring, Md. 77 pp.

Rasmussen, E. M., 1971. Diurnal variation of summertime thunderstorm activity over the United States. Technical Note 71-4, U.S. Air Force Environmental Technical Applications Center. 15 pp.

Rydant, A. L., 1979. Adjustments to natural hazards: factors affecting the adoption of crop-hail insurance. *Prof. Geogr.* 31(3):312-20.

Sims, J. H., and D. D. Baumann, 1972. The tornado threat: coping styles of the North and South. *Science* 176:1386-92. See also correspondence in *Science* 180: 545-47.

Taylor, A. R., 1969. Lightning effects on the forest complex. Proc., Annual Tall Timbers Fire Ecology Conference, Forest Service, U.S. Dept of Agriculture., pp. 127-50.

U.S. Department of Commerce, 1976. *Statistical Abstract of the United States.* Washington, D.C. 1025 pp.

———, 1980. Red River Valley tornadoes of April 10, 1979. A report to the Administrator of the National Oceanic and Atmospheric Administration. Natural Disaster Survey Report, NOAA-NDSR 80-1. 62 pp.

U.S. Forest Service, 1972. Fire in the environment. Symposium proceedings, May 1-5, 1972, Denver, Colo. December 1972. 151 pp.

Urey, H. C., 1952. *The Planets: Their Origin and Development.* Yale Univ. Press, New Haven, Conn. 245 pp.

Vigansky, H. N., 1979. General summary of lightning. U.S. Dept of Commerce, NOAA, *Climatological Data National Summary,* 3(13). 8 pp.

Weekly Compilation of Presidential Documents, 1978. Vol. 14, No. 23, June 12. Office of the Federal Register, National Archives and Records Service, General Services Administration, Washington, D.C., pp. 1044-51.

White, G. F., 1975. Flood hazard in the United States: a research assessment. Program on Technology, Environment and Man, Monograph No. 6, Institute of Behavioral Science, Univ. of Colorado, Boulder. 141 pp.

Zalikhanov, M. C., and F. F. Davitaya, 1980. Natural calamities in mountain regions. Unpublished paper presented at the International Geographical Congress, Tokyo, Japan.

Zegel, F. H., 1967. Lightning deaths in the United States: a seven-year survey from 1959 to 1965. *Weatherwise* 20(4):168-73, 179.

## Chapter 2

AMS (American Meteorological Society), 1978. A statement of concern . . . . Flash floods—a national problem. *Bulletin Am. Meteorol. Soc.* 59(5):585-86.

Baily, J. F., J. L. Patterson, and J. L. H. Paulhus, 1975. Hurricane Agnes rainfall and floods, June-July 1972. Geological Survey Professional Paper 924. 403 pp.

Dennis, A. S., R. A. Schleusener, J. H. Hirsch, and A. Koscielski, 1973. Meteorology of the Black Hills Flood of 1972. Institute of Atmos. Sci. Report 73-74, South Dakota School of Mines and Technology, Rapid City. 41 pp.

Drabek, T. E., 1969. Social processes in disaster: family evacuation. *Social Problems* 16(3):336-49.

———, and K. Boggs, 1968. Families in disaster: reactions and relatives. *J. of Marriage and the Family* 30: 443-51.

———, and J. S. Stephenson, III, 1971. When disaster strikes. *J. of Applied Social Psychology* 1(2):187-203.

Grozier, R. U., J. F. McCain, L. F. Lang, and D. C. Merriman, 1976. The Big Thompson River Flood of 31 July-1 August 1976, Larimer County, Colorado. U.S.G.S. and Colorado Water Conservation Board Flood Information Report, Denver. 78 pp.

Grunfest, E. C., 1977. Behavior during the Big Thompson flood. Institute of Behavioral Science, University of Colorado, Boulder.

Hales, J. F., Jr., 1978. The Kansas City flash flood of 12 September 1977. *Bull. Am. Meteorol. Soc.* 59:706-10.

Hoxit, L. R., R. A. Maddox, C. F. Chappell, F. L. Zuckerberg, H. M. Mogil, and I. Jones, 1978. Meteorological analysis of the Johnstown, Pennsylvania, flash flood, 19-30 July 1977 (appendices by D. R. Greene, R. E. Saffle, and R. A. Scofield). NOAA Technical Report ERL 401-APCL 43, NOAA Environmental Research Laboratories, Boulder, Colo. 83 pp.

Hutton, J. R., 1976. The differential distribution of death in disaster: a test of theoretical propositions. Paper presented at the Joint Meeting of the Society for the Study of Social Problems and the American Sociological Association, New York (unpublished MS).

Land, L. F., 1978. Analysis of flood resulting from the Toccoa Falls, Georgia, dam break. Preprints, Conference on Flash Floods: Hydro-Meteorological Aspects, Los Angeles. American Meteorological Society, Boston, 127-30.

Mack, R. W., and G. W. Baker, 1961. The occasion instant. National Research Council Disaster Study 15, National Academy of Sciences, Washington, D.C.

Maddox, R. A., F. Caracena, L. R. Hoxit, and C. F. Chappell, 1977. Meteorological aspects of the Big Thompson flash flood of 31 July 1976. NOAA Tech. Rep. ERL 388-APCL 41, NOAA Environmental Research Laboratories, Boulder, Colo. 87 pp.

———, C. F. Chappell, and L. R. Hoxit, 1979. Synoptic and meso-α scale aspects of flash flood events. *Bull. Am. Meteorol. Soc.* 60(2):115-23.

Mileti, D. S., 1974. A normative causal model analysis of disaster warning response. Unpublished dissertation. Department of Sociology, University of Colorado, Boulder.

———, 1975. Natural hazards warning systems in the United States: A research assessment. Institute of Behavioral Science, University of Colorado, Boulder.

Mogil, H. M., and H. S. Groper, 1976. On the short range prediction of localized excessive convective rainfall. Preprints, Conf. on Hydrometeorology, Ft. Worth. American Meteorological Society, Boston, pp. 9-12.

———, J. C. Monro, and H. S. Groper, 1978. The National Weather Service flash flood warning and disaster preparedness program. *Bull. Am. Meteorol. Soc.* 59:690-99.

NOAA (National Oceanic and Atmospheric Administration), 1971. Arizona floods of September 5 and 6, 1970: a report to the administrator. Natural Disaster Survey Report 70-2, NOAA, Rockville, Md. 39 pp.

———, 1973. Final report of the disaster survey team on the events of Agnes: a report to the administrator. Natural Disaster Survey Report 73-1, NOAA, Rockville, Md.

———, 1976. Big Thompson Canyon flash flood of 31 July-1 August, 1976. Natural Disaster Survey Report 76-1, NOAA, Rockville, Md. 41 pp.

NWS (National Weather Service), 1978a. The Appalachian floods and flash floods of April 2-5, 1977. NWS, Silver Spring, Md. 82 pp. (unpublished report).

———, 1978b. Southern California floods, flash floods and mudslides of February 8-10, 1978. NWS Western Region, Salt Lake City, Utah. 73 pp.

Quarantelli, E. L., 1960. Images of withdrawal behavior in disasters: some basic misconceptions. *Social Problems* 8:68-79.

Sowers, G. F., 1978. Reconnaissance report on the failure of Kelly Barnes Lake Dam, Toccoa Falls, Georgia. Committee on Natural Disasters, National Academy of Sciences, Washington, D.C. 19 pp.

White, G. F., 1975. Flood hazard in the United States: a research assessment. Institute of Behavioral Science, University of Colorado, Boulder.

———, and J. E. Haas, 1975. Assessment of research on natural hazards. MIT Press, Cambridge, Mass. 487 pp.

## Chapter 3

Abbey, R. F., 1976. Risk probabilities associated with tornado windspeeds. Proc., Symposium on Tornadoes: Assessment of Knowledge and Implications for Man, Lubbock, Tex., June 24-26, Texas Tech. Univ., Lubbock, pp. 177-236.

———, and T. T. Fujita, 1975. Use of tornado path lengths and gradations of damage to assess tornado intensity probabilities. Preprints, Ninth Conference on Severe Local Storms, Norman, Okla., American Meteorological Society, Boston, pp. 286-93.

———, and ———, 1979. The DAPPLE method for computing tornado hazard probabilities; refinements and theoretical considerations. Preprints, 11th Conference on Severe Local Storms, Kansas City, Mo., American Meteorological Society, Boston, pp. 241-48.

Agee, E. M., J. T. Snow, and P. R. Clare, 1976. Multiple vortex features in the tornado cyclone and the occurrence of tornado families. *Mon. Weather Rev.* 104(5):552-63.

———, et al., 1975. Some synoptic aspects and dynamic features of vortices associated with the tornado outbreak of 3 April 1974. *Mon. Weather Rev.* 103(4): 318-33.

Darkow, G. L., and R. L. Livingston, 1975. The evolution of the surface static energy fields on 3 April 1974. Preprints, Ninth Conference on Severe Local Storms, Norman, Okla., American Meteorological Society, Boston, pp. 264-69.

Forbes, G. S., 1975. Relationship between tornadoes and hook echoes on April 3, 1974. Preprints, Ninth Conference on Severe Local Storms, Norman, Okla., American Meteorological Society, Boston, pp. 280-85.

———, 1976. Photogrammetric characteristics of the Parker tornado of April 3, 1974. Proc., Symposium on Tornadoes: Assessment of Knowledge and Implications for Man, Lubbock, Texas, June 24-26, Texas Tech. Univ., Lubbock, pp. 58-77.

———, 1978. Three Scales of Motion Associated with Tornadoes. NUREG/CR-0363, U.S. Nuclear Regulatory Commission, Washington, D.C. 359 pp.

Fujita, T. T., 1971. Proposed characterization of tornadoes and hurricanes by area and intensity. SMRP Res. Paper No. 91, Univ. of Chicago, Chicago.

———, 1974. Jumbo tornado outbreak of 3 April 1974. *Weatherwise* 27(3):116-26.

———, 1975. Superoutbreak tornadoes of April 3-4, 1974. Final-edition map, University of Chicago, Chicago.

———, 1976. Graphic examples of tornadoes. *Bull. Am. Meteorol. Soc.* 57(4):401-12.

———, 1978. Workbook of Tornadoes and High Winds for Engineering Applications. SMRP Res. Paper No. 165, Univ. of Chicago, Chicago.

———, and A. D. Pearson, 1973. Results of FPP classification of 1971 and 1972 tornadoes. Preprints, Eighth Conference on Severe Local Storms, Oct. 15-17, American Meteorological Society, Boston, pp. 142-45.

———, and G. S. Forbes, 1974. Superoutbreak tornadoes of April 3, 1974, as seen in ATS pictures. Preprints, Sixth Conference on Aerospace and Aeronautical Meteorology, El Paso, Texas, American Meteorological Society, Boston, pp. 165-72.

———, A. Pearson, G. S. Forbes, T. A. Umemhofer, E. W. Pearson, and J. J. Tecson, 1976. Photogrammetric analysis of tornadoes. Proc., Symposium on Tornadoes: Assessment of Knowledge and Implications for Man, Lubbock, Texas, June 24-26, Texas

Tech. Univ., Lubbock, pp. 43-88.

Golden, J., 1976. An assessment of wind speeds in tornadoes. Proc., Symposium on Tornadoes: Assessment of Knowledge and Implications for Man, Lubbock, Texas, June 24-26, Texas Tech. Univ., Lubbock, pp. 5-42.

Hoxit, L. R., and C. F. Chappell, 1975. Tornado Outbreak of April 3-4, 1974: Synoptic Analysis. NOAA Technical Report ERL 338-APCL 37. 48 pp.

NOAA (National Oceanic and Atmospheric Administration), 1974. The widespread tornado outbreak of April 3-4, 1974: A report to the administrator. Natural Disaster Survey Rep. 74-1. 42 pp.

Purdom, J. F. W., 1974. The April 1974 tornado outbreak. *Weatherwise* 27(3):120-21.

Ward, N. B., 1972. The exploration of certain features of tornado dynamics using a laboratory model. *J. Atmos. Sci.* 29(6):1194-1204.

White, G. F., and J. E. Haas, 1975. *Assessment of Research on Natural Hazards.* MIT Press, Cambridge, Mass. 487 pp.


## Chapter 4

Ahmad, N., and A. J. Roblin, 1971. Crusting of river estate soil, Trinidad, and its effect on gaseous diffusion, percolation, and seedling emergence. *J. Soil Science* 22(1):23-31.

Allison, F. E., 1973. *Soil Organic Matter and Its Role in Crop Production.* Elsevier, Amsterdam. 639 pp.

Baker, C. H., and R. D. Horrocks, 1975. CORNMOD: a dynamic simulator of corn production. *Agr. Systems* 1:57-77.

Chameides, W. L., 1975. Tropospheric odd nitrogen and the atmospheric water vapor cycle. *J. Geophys. Res.* 80:4989-96.

———, D. H. Stedman, R. R. Dickerson, D. W. Rusch, and R. J. Cicerone, 1977. $NO_x$ production in lightning. *J. Atmos. Sci.* 34:143-49.

Changnon, S. A., 1957. Thunderstorm-precipitation relations in Illinois. Report of Investigation 34, Illinois State Water Survey, Urbana, Ill. 24 pp.

Chow, V. T., 1964. *Handbook of Applied Hydrology.* McGraw-Hill, New York, (various pagings).

Curry, R. B., and L. H. Chen, 1971. Dynamic simulation of plant growth. Part II. Incorporation of actual daily weather and partitioning of net photosynthate. *Trans. Am. Soc. Agr. Eng.* 14(6):1170-74.

———, C. H. Baker, and J. G. Streeter, 1975. SOYMOD I: a dynamic simulator of soybean growth and development. *Trans. Am. Soc. Agr. Eng.* 18(5):963-68.

Cutler, M. R., 1977. New directions in century three: a USDA view. *J. Soil and Water Conserv.* 32(5):196-98.

Dendy, F. E., and G. C. Bolton, 1976. Sediment yield-runoff-drainage area relationships in the United States. *J. Soil and Water Conserv.* 31(6):264-66.

———, W. A. Champion, and R. B. Wilson, 1973. Reservoir sedimentation surveys in the United States. Geophysical Monograph Series, Am. Geophys. Union, Washington, D.C., 17:349-57.

Donigian, A. S., and N. H. Crawford, 1976. Modeling pesticides and nutrients on agricultural lands. EPA-600/2-76-043, Athens, Ga. 318 pp.

Dow Chemical Co., 1972. An economic analysis of erosion and sediment control. Methods for watersheds undergoing urbanization. Natl. Tech. Inf. Service, Springfield, Va. (PB 208 212). 181 pp.

Evans, D. D., and S. W. Boul, 1968. Micromorphological study of soil crusts. *Soil Sci. Soc. Am. Proc.* 32: 19-22.

Fred, D., and E. Kessler, 1980. Pesticide accidents in relation to weather conditions. *Environmental Cons.* 7:219-22.

Frere, M. H., 1976. Nutrient aspects of pollution from cropland. In *Control of Water Pollution from Cropland,* Vol. 2, B. A. Stewart, D. A. Woolhiser, W. H. Wischmeier, J. H. Caro, and M. H. Frere (eds.), USDA Rep. No. ARS-H-5-2, pp. 59-90.

———, C. A. Onstad, and H. N. Holtan, 1975. ACTMO: An agricultural chemical transport model. USDA Rep. No. ARS-H-3. 54 pp.

Glymph, L. M., and H. C. Storey, 1967. Sediment—its consequences and control. Proc. Symposium on Agriculture and the Quality of Our Environment. Publ. 95, Am. Assoc. Advance. Sci., Washington, D.C., pp. 205-20.

Griffing, G. W., 1977. Ozone and oxides of nitrogen production during thunderstorms. *J. Geophys. Res.* 82:943-50.

Holeman, J. N., 1968. The sediment yield of major rivers of the world. *Water Resour. Res.* 4(4):737-47.

Hudson, N., 1971. The physics of rainfall. In *Soil Conservation.* Cornell Univ. Press, Ithaca, N.Y. 320 pp.

Hutchinson, G. E., 1954. The biogeochemistry of the terrestrial atmosphere. In *The Earth as a Planet,* G. P. Kuiper (ed.). Univ. of Chicago Press, Chicago. 754 pp.

Jones, J. W., J. D. Hesketh, R. F. Colwick, H. C. Lane, J. M. McKinion, and A. C. Thompson, 1975. Predicting square, flower and boll production in a stand of cotton at different stages of organogenesis. Proc. Conference on Beltwide Cotton Products Research, Nat. Cotton Council, New Orleans, La., pp. 108-13.

Knisel, W. G. (ed.), 1980. CREAMS: A field scale model

for chemicals, runoff, and erosion from agricultural management systems. U.S. Department of Agriculture, Conserv. Res. Report No. 26. 640 pp.

Kowalczyk, M., and E. Bauer, 1981. Lightning as a source of $NO_x$ in the troposphere. Report to Dept. of Transportation on Contract DT-FA01-81C-10011. 84 pp. (available from NTIS, Springfield, Va. 22151).

Laws, J. O., and D. A. Parsons, 1943. The relation of raindrop size to intensity. *Trans. Am. Geophys. Union* 24:452-59.

Leonard, W. H., and J. H. Martin, 1963. *Cereal Crops.* Macmillan, New York. 824 pp.

Leopold, L. B., M. G. Wolman, and J. P. Miller, 1964. *Fluvial Processes in Geomorphology.* Freeman, San Francisco. 522 pp.

List, R. J., 1958. *Smithsonian Meteorological Tables.* Smithsonian Institution, Washington, D.C. 527 pp.

Lyles, L., 1977. Soil detachment and aggregate disintegration by wind-driven rain. *Soil Erosion: Prediction and Control,* Soil Conserv. Soc. Am., Special Publ. No. 21, Ankeny, Iowa, pp. 158-59.

McDowell, L. L., and E. H. Grissinger, 1976. Erosion and water quality. Proc. Twenty-third Natl. Watershed Congr., Biloxi, Miss., pp. 40-56.

McGregor, K. C., and C. K. Mutchler, 1977. Status of the R factor in northern Mississippi. *Soil Erosion: Prediction and Control,* Soil Conserv. Soc. Am., Special Publ. No. 21, Ankeny, Iowa, pp. 135-42.

McIntyre, D. S., 1958. Permeability measurements of soil crusts formed by raindrop impact. *Soil Sci.* 85: 85-189.

McKinion, J. M., J. W. Jones, and J. D. Hesketh, 1975a. A system of growth equations for the continuous simulation of plant growth. *Trans. Am. Soc. Agr. Eng.* 18 (5):954-79.

———, D. N. Baker, J. D. Hesketh, and J. W. Jones, 1975b. SIMCOT II. A simulation of cotton growth and yield. In *Computer Simulation of a Cotton Production System: User's Manual,* Agr. Res. Ser., U.S. Dept. of Agriculture, Washington, D.C., ARS-S-52, pp. 27-82.

Mannering, J. V., and D. Wiersma, 1970. The effect of rainfall energy on water infiltration into soils. *Indiana Acad. Sci. Proc.* 79:407-12.

Marshall, J. S., and W. McK. Palmer, 1948. The distribution of raindrops with size. *J. Meteorol.* 5:165-66.

Merkle, M. G., and R. W. Bovey, 1974. Movement of pesticides in surface water. In *Pesticides in Soil and Water,* Soil Sci. Soc. Am., Madison, Wis., pp. 99-106.

Meyer, L. D., 1971. Soil erosion by water on upland areas. In *River Mechanics,* H. W. Shen (ed. and publisher), Fort Collins, Colo., Vol. 2, 27.1-27.5.

———, D. G. DeCoursey, and M. J. M. Römkens, 1976.

Soil erosion concepts and misconceptions. Proc. Third Federal Inter-Agency Sedimentation Conf., Sedimentation Committee Water Resources Council, Denver, Colo., pp. 2-1-2-21.

Miles, G. E., R. J. Bula, D. A. Holt, M. M. Schreiber, and R. M. Peart, 1973. Simulation of alfalfa growth. Paper No. 73-4547, Am. Soc. Agr. Eng., Saint Joseph, Mo. 18 pp.

Mutchler, C. K., and R. A. Young, 1975. Soil detachment by raindrops. In *Present and Prospective Technology for Predicting Sediment Yields and Sources,* Agr. Res. Ser., U.S. Dept. of Agriculture, Washington, D.C., ARS-S-40, pp. 113-16.

Myers, L. E., 1975. Water harvesting 2000 B.C. to 1974 A.D. Proc. Water Harvesting Symp., Phoenix, Ariz., 26-28 March 1974, U.S. Dept. of Agriculture Rep. No. ARS-W-22, pp. 1-7.

Noxon, J. F., 1976. Atmospheric nitrogen fixation by lightning. *Geophys. Res. Lett.* 3:463-65.

Osborn, H., and R. Hickock, 1968. Variability of rainfall affecting runoff from a semiarid rangeland watershed. *Water Resour. Res.* 4(1):199-203.

Pendleton, J. W., 1965. Increasing water use efficiency by crop management. In *Plant Environment and Efficient Water Use,* W. H. Pierre, D. Kirkham, J. Pesek, and R. Shaw (eds.), Am. Soc. Agron., Madison, Wis., pp. 236-58.

Piest, R. F., 1963. The role of the large storm as a sediment contributor. Proc. Federal Inter-Agency Sedimentation Conf., U.S. Dept of Agriculture, ARS Misc. Publ. No. 970, pp. 98-108.

———, and A. J. Bowie, 1974. Gully and streambank erosion. Proc. Twenty-Ninth Annual Meeting, Soil Conserv. Soc. Am., Ankeny, Iowa, pp. 188-96.

Shaw, R. H., and D. R. Laing, 1965. Moisture stress and plant response. In *Plant Environment and Efficient Water Use,* W. H. Pierre, D. Kirkham, J. Pesek, and R. Shaw (eds.), Am. Soc. Agron., Madison, Wis., pp. 73-94.

Soil Conservation Service, 1960. *National Engineering Handbook.* Sec. 15, Irrigation. 83 pp.

Stewart, B. A., D. A. Woolhiser, W. H. Sichmeier, J. H. Caro, and M. H. Frere, 1975. Control of water pollution from cropland, Vol. 1—A manual for guideline development. USDA-ARS and EPA. 112 pp.

Taylor, A. R., 1969. Lightning effects on the forest complex. Proc. Annual Tall Timbers Fire Ecology Conf., 10-11 April, pp. 127-50 (reprint available from U.S. Forest Service, Northern Forest Fire Laboratory, Missoula, Mont.).

von Liebig, J., 1827. Une note sur la nitrification. *Ann. Chem. Phys.* 35:329-33.

Wadleigh, C. H., 1968. Wastes in relation to agriculture

and forestry. U.S. Dept. of Agriculture, Misc. Publ. No. 1065. 112 pp.

Williams, J. R., 1982. EPIC: a model for assessing the effects of erosion on soil productivity. Third Int. Conf. on State-of-the-Art in Ecological Modeling. Colorado State University, Fort Collins, May 24-28.

Wischmeier, W. H., 1962. Storms and soil conservation. *J. Soil and Water Conserv.* 17(2):55-59.

————, and D. D. Smith, 1965. Rainfall-erosion losses from cropland east of the Rocky Mountains. Agr. Handbook No. 282, U.S. Dept. of Agriculture, Washington, D.C. 47 pp.

Zel'dovitch, V. B., and V. P. Raizer, 1966. *Physics of Shock Waves and High-Temperature Hydrodynamic Phenomena,* Academic Press, New York. 445 pp.

Zipf, E. C., and M. Dubin, 1976. Laboratory studies on the formation of $NO_x$ compounds and ozone by lightning. *Trans. Am. Geophys. Union* 57:965.

## Chapter 5

ANSI (American National Standards Institute), 1972. American national standard building code requirements for minimum design loads in buildings and other structures. Standard A58.1-1972, ANSI, New York. 60 pp.

ASCE Task Committee on Wind Forces, 1961. Wind forces on structures. *Trans. Am. Soc. Civ. Eng.* 125 (2):1124-98.

Booker, C. A., 1954. On transmission towers destroyed by the Worcester, Massachusetts, tornado of June 9, 1953. *Bull. Am. Meteorol. Soc.* 35(6):225-29.

Brinkman, W. A. R., 1975. Severe local storms hazard in the United States: A research assessment. NSF-RA-E-75-011, Institute of Behavioral Science, Univ. of Colorado, Boulder. 154 pp.

Davenport, A. G., 1960. Wind loads on structures. Technical Paper No. 88, Div. of Building Research, National Research Council of Canada, Ottawa. 38 pp.

————, 1961. The application of statistical concepts to the wind loading of structures. *Proc. Inst. Civ. Eng.* 19:449-72.

DCPA (Defense Civil Preparedness Agency), 1975a. Wind-resistant design concepts for residences. TR-83, DCPA, U.S. Dept. of Defense, Washington, D.C. 52 pp.

————, 1975b. Interim guidelines for building occupant protection from tornadoes and extreme winds. TR-83A, DCPA, U.S. Dept. of Defense, Washington, D.C. 24 pp.

Eagleman, J. R., V. U. Muirhead and N. Willems, 1975. *Thunderstorms, Tornadoes, and Damage to Build-ings.* Lexington Books, Lexington, Mass. 317 pp.

Handa, K. N., 1971. Dynamic response of tall structures to atmospheric turbulence. Proc., Wind Effects on Buildings and Structures, Tokyo, Sept. 6-9, 1971. Saikon Co., Tokyo, pp. 409-20.

Kessler, E., 1976. Recent developments in tornado research. Proc., Symposium on Tornadoes: Assessment of Knowledge and Implications for Man, Lubbock, Tex., June 24-26, R. E. Peterson (ed.), Texas Tech Univ., Lubbock, pp. 431-35.

Kiesling, E. W., and D. E. Goolsby, 1974. In-home shelters from extreme winds. *Civ. Eng.* 44(9):105-107.

Langston, T. O., 1977. Tornadic wind effects and mobile homes. M.A. thesis, Department of Geography Graduate School, Southern Illinois Univ., Carbondale. 65 pp.

McDonald, J. R., 1975. Development of windspeed risk models for the Savannah River plant site. Institute for Disaster Research, Texas Tech Univ., Lubbock. 71 pp.

MBMA (Metal Building Manufacturers Association), 1976. 1976 Metal Building Systems Fact Book. MBMA, Cleveland, Ohio. 8 pp.

Mehta, K. C., 1976. Windspeed estimates: Engineering analyses. Proc., Symposium on Tornadoes: Assessment of Knowledge and Implications for Man, Lubbock, Tex., June 24-26, R. E. Peterson (ed.), Texas Tech Univ., Lubbock, pp. 89-103.

————, J. E. Minor, and J. R. McDonald, 1976. Windspeed analyses of April 3-4, 1974, tornadoes. *J. Struct. Div., Am. Soc. Civ. Eng.* 102(ST9):1709-24.

————, ————, ————, B. R. Manning, J. J. Abernethy, and U. F. Koehler, 1975. Engineering aspects of the tornadoes of April 3-4, 1974. Report to the National Academy of Engineering, National Academy of Sciences, Washington, D.C. 110 pp.

Minor, J. E., J. R. McDonald, and K. C. Mehta, 1977. The tornado: An engineering-oriented perspective. Tech. Memo. ERL-NSSL-82, NOAA Environmental Research Laboratories, Boulder, Colo. 192 pp.

OEP (Office of Emergency Preparedness), 1972. Report to the Congress: disaster preparedness. OEP, Executive Office of the President. 3 vols., 184 pp., 26 pp., and 143 pp.

Rouse, H., 1938. *Fluid Mechanics for Hydraulic Engineers.* McGraw Hill, New York. 422 pp.

Segner, E. P., 1960. Estimates of minimum wind forces causing structural damage in the tornadoes at Dallas, Texas, April 2, 1957. The tornadoes at Dallas, Texas . . . , U.S. Weather Bureau Research Paper No. 41, pp. 169-75.

Smart, H. R., L. K. Stevens, and P. N. Joubert, 1967. Dynamic structural response to natural wind. Proc.,

Wind Effects on Buildings and Structures, Vol. 1, Univ. of Toronto Press, pp. 595-630.

Thom, H. C. S., 1968. New distributions of extreme winds in the United States. *J. Struct. Div., Am. Soc. Civ. Eng.* 94(ST7):1787-1801.

Vann, W. P., and J. R. McDonald, 1978. An engineering analysis: mobile homes in windstorms. Institute for Disaster Research, Texas Tech Univ., Lubbock. 144 pp.

Walker, G. R., 1976. The rational design of low rise housing in tropical cyclone prone areas. Proc., 1976 Annual Engineering Conference, Institution of Engineers, Australia, pp. 248-53.

Wiggins, J. H., 1974. Toward a coherent natural hazards policy. *Civ. Eng.* 44(4):74-76.

## Chapter 6

Berger, K., R. B. Anderson, and H. Kroninger, 1975. Parameters of lightning flashes. *Electra* 80:23-37.

Brook, M., M. Nakano, P. Krehbiel, and T. Takeuti, 1982. The electrical structure of the Hokuriku winter thunderstorms. *J. Geophys. Res.* 87:1207-15.

Few, A. A., 1982. Acoustic radiations from lightning. In *CRC Handbook of Atmospherics,* Vol. 2, H. Volland (ed.). CRC Press, Boca Rotan, Fla., 257-90.

Golde, R. H. (ed.), 1977. *Lightning.* Vol. 2, *Lightning Protection.* Academic Press, New York.

Hill, R. D., 1979. A survey of lightning energy estimates. *Rev. Geophys. Space Phys.* 17:155-64.

Humphreys, W. J., 1964. *Physics of the Air,* Dover, New York.

Idone, V. P., and R. W. Henderson, 1982. An unusual lightning ground strike. *Weatherwise* 35:223-24.

Krider, E. P., 1977. On lightning damage to a golf course green. *Weatherwise* 30:111.

———, and S. B. Alejandro, 1983. Lightning: an unusual case study. *Weatherwise* 36:71-75.

———, and C. Guo, 1983. The peak electromagnetic power radiated by lightning return strokes. *J. Geophys. Res.* (forthcoming).

———, and C. G. Ladd, 1975. Upward streamers in lightning discharges to mountainous terrain. *Weather* 30:77-81.

Lee, W. R., 1977. Lightning injuries and death. Chap. 16 in *Lightning.* Vol. 2, *Lightning Protection,* R. H. Golde (ed.). Academic Press, New York.

Livingston, J. M., and E. P. Krider, 1978. Electric fields produced by Florida thunderstorms. *J. Geophys. Res.* 83:385-401.

McEachron, K. B., 1939. Lightning to the Empire State Building. *J. Franklin Inst.* 227:149-217.

McIntosh, D. H., 1973. Lightning damage. *Weather* 28: 160-61.

Maier, M. W., 1983. Private communication.

*Military Handbook,* 1982. *Grounding, Bonding, and Shielding for Electronic Equipments and Facilities,* Vols. 1, 2. MIL-HDBK-419. U.S. Government Printing Office, Washington, D.C.

NFPA, 1980. Lightning Protection Code, NFPA-78. National Fire Protection Association, Inc.

Salanave, L. E., 1980. *Lightning and Its Spectrum.* University of Arizona Press, Tucson.

Schonland, B. F. J., 1956. The lightning discharge. *Handbuch der Physik,* 22:576-628. Springer-Verlag, Berlin.

———, 1964. *The Flight of Thunderbolts.* Clarendon Press, Oxford.

Sunde, E. D., 1908. *Earth Conduction Effects in Transmission Systems.* Dover, New York.

Tesche, F. M., 1978. Topological concepts for internal EMP interaction. *IEEE Trans. on EMC.* EMC-20, 60-64.

Uman, M. A., 1969. *Lightning.* McGraw Hill, New York.

———, 1971. *Understanding Lightning.* Bek Technical Publications, Inc., Carnegie, Pa.

———, and E. P. Krider, 1982. A review of natural lightning: experimental data and modeling. *IEEE Trans. on EMC.* EMC-24, 79-112.

———, M. J. Master, and E. P. Krider, 1982. A comparison of lightning electromagnetic fields with the nuclear electromagnetic pulse in the frequency range $10^4$-$10^7$ Hz. *IEEE Trans. on EMC.* EMC-24, 410-16.

Viemeister, P. E., 1961. *The Lightning Book.* Doubleday, New York.

Wiedman, C. D., and E. P. Krider, 1980. Submicrosecond risetimes in lightning return-stroke fields. *Geophys. Res. Letters* 7 (2):955-58. See also C. D. Weidman and E. P. Krider, 1982. Correction. *J. Geophys. Res.* 87:7351.

Winn, W. P., T. V. Aldridge, and C. B. Moore, 1973. Video-tape recordings of lightning flashes. *J. Geophys. Res.* 78:4515-19.

## Chapter 7

Bates, F. C., 1967. A major hazard to aviation near severe thunderstorms. Aviation Safety Monogr. No. 1, Saint Louis Univ., Mo. 57 pp.

Beckwith, W. B., 1961. The use of weather radar in turbojet operations. United Air Lines Meteorol. Circ. No. 53, Denver, Colo. 67 pp.

———, 1975. Aircraft operational requirements for weather service, now and in the future. Proc., 1975 Annual Assembly Meeting Radio Tech. Commission

For Aeron., Washington, D.C., pp. B21–B29.

Burnham, J., and J. T. Lee, 1969. Thunderstorm turbulence and its relationship to weather radar echoes. *J. Aircr.* 6(5):438–55.

Charba, J., 1972. Gravity current model applied to analysis of squall-line gust front. NOAA Technical Memorandum ERL NSSL-61, Environmental Research Laboratories, Boulder, Colo. 58 pp.

Crisci, R. L., 1978. A plan for improved short-range aviation weather forecasts. Final Report of NWS for FAA, FAA-RD-78-73, Washington, D.C. 34 pp.

FAA (Federal Aviation Administration), 1967. Federal Aviation Regulations Section 25.954, Amendment 25-14, published August 11. 1 p.

———, 1972. Flight service: Phase V; the preflight position. Vol. 1, 4th ed. (National Air Traffic Training Program), FAA Aeronautical Center, Oklahoma City. 364 pp.

Goff, R. C., 1975. Thunderstorm-outflow kinematics and dynamics. NOAA Technical Memorandum ERL NSSL-75, Environmental Research Laboratories, Boulder, Colo. 63 pp.

———, 1980. Low Level Wind Shear Alert System (LLWSAS). Report FAA-RD-80-45, National Aviation Facilities Experimental Center, Atlantic City, N.J. 120 pp.

Harrision, H. T., 1956. The display of weather echoes on the 5.5 cm airborne radar. United Air Lines Meteorol. Circ. No. 39, Denver, Colo. 96 pp.

———, 1965. UAL turbojet experience with electrical discharges. United Air Lines Meteorol. Circ. No. 57, Chicago. 97 pp.

Hennington, L., R. J. Doviak, D. Sirmans, D. Zrnic, and R. Strauch, 1976. Measurements of winds in optically clear air with microwave pulse-Doppler radar. Preprints, 17th Radar Conference, American Meteorological Society, Boston, pp. 342–48.

Horne, W., and R. Dreher, 1963. Phenomenon of pneumatic tire hydroplaning. NASA Tech. Note D2056, Langley Research Center, Va. 54 pp.

Houbolt, J. C., R. Steiner, and K. Pratt, 1964. Dynamic response of airplanes to atmospheric turbulence including flight data on input and response. NASA Tech. Rep. TR R-199, NASA, Washington, D.C. 115 pp.

Klein, W. H., 1976. AFOS Forecast Applications. Proc., 6th Conference on Weather Forecasting and Analysis, May 10-13, 1976, Albany, N.Y., pp. 36–43.

Lee, J. T., 1974. Thunderstorm turbulence—Concurrent Doppler radar and aircraft observations 1973. Preprints, 6th Conference on Aerospace and Aeronautical Meteorology, November 1974, American Meteorological Society, Boston, pp. 295–98.

———, and A. McPherson, 1971. Comparison of thunderstorms over Oklahoma and Malaysia based on aircraft measurements. Proc. International Conference on Atmospheric Turbulence, London, May 1971, Royal Aeronautical Society. 13 pp.

———, and R. C. Goff, 1976. Gust front wind shear and turbulence—Concurrent aircraft and surface based observations. Preprints, 7th Conference on Aerospace and Aeronautical Meteorology, American Meteorological Society, Boston, pp. 48-55.

NEXRAD, 1980. Next generation weather radar (NEXRAD): Joint Program Development Plan. Prepared by the NEXRAD Joint System Program Office assisted by the MITRE Corporation. Washington, D.C. 7 sections with appendices and tables.

NOAA (National Oceanographic and Atmospheric Administration), 1976. Project development plan. Severe Environmental Storms and Mesoscale Experiment, Environmental Research Laboratories, Boulder, Colo. 60 pp.

NTSB (National Transportation Safety Board), 1974. Special study of fatal, weather-involved, general aviation accidents. NTSB-AAS-74-2, Washington, D.C. 21 pp.

———, 1978. Aircraft accident report Southern Airways, Inc.: DC-9-31 N335V, New Hope, Ga., April 4, 1977. NTSB-AAR-78-3, Washington, D.C. 106 pp.

O'Hara, F., and J. Burnham, 1968. The atmospheric environment and aircraft—now and the future. *R. Aeronaut. Soc. J.* 72(690):467–80.

Payne, L., 1977. Lighter than air—an illustrated history of the airship. A. S. Barnes, South Brunswick and New York. 250 pp.

Pratt, K. G., and W. G. Walker, 1954. A revised gust load formula and reevaluation of V-G data taken on civil transport airplanes from 1933–1950. NACA Report-1206. 10 pp.

Robinson, D. H., 1973. *Giants in the Sky.* Univ. of Washington Press, Seattle. 275 pp.

Roys, G. P., and E. Kessler, 1966. Measurements by aircraft of condensed water in Great Plains thunderstorms. Technical Note 49-NSSP-19, U.S. Weather Bureau. 17 pp.

Spanner, E. F., 1927. *This Airship Business.* William and Norgate, London. 435 pp.

Spavins, C. S., 1970. Pre-monsoon storms over northeast India—an airborne radar and photogrammetric study. RAE Tech. Rep. 70245. 17 pp.

Steiner, R., and R. H. Rhyne, 1962. Some measured characteristics of severe storm turbulence. National Severe Storms Project Report No. 10, U.S. Weather Bureau. 17 pp.

Sutton, O. G., 1955. *Atmospheric Turbulence.* 2d ed. Methuen, London. 107 pp.

Thomas, D. D., 1971. Turbulence related accidents, worldwide synopsis. Final Report FAA Symposium on Turbulence, March 1971. 16 pp.

U.S. Bureau of the Census, 1978. *Statistical Abstract of the United States.* Washington, D.C.

U.S. Department of Commerce, 1949. The thunderstorm: report of the Thunderstorm Project. Washington, D.C. 287 pp.

Wolleswinkel, H. N. (International Inspection Directorate, Ministry of Transport and Public Works, Netherlands). Personal communication.

**Chapter 8**

Abernethy, 1976. Protection of people and essential facilities. Proc. Symposium on Tornadoes, Texas Tech Univ., Lubbock, R. E. Peterson (Ed.), pp. 107-417.

Baer, D. H., 1979. Building Losses from Natural Hazards Yesterday, Today and Tomorrow. National Science Foundation, Washington, D.C. 20 pp.

Bates, F. C., 1961. The Great Plains squalline thunderstorm: a model. Ph.D. Dissertation, Saint Louis University, 164 pp. (available from University Microfilms, Ann Arbor, Mich.).

Beebe, R. G., 1958. Tornado proximity soundings. *Bull. Am. Meteorol. Soc.* 39:195-201.

Bidner, A., 1970. The AFGWC severe weather threat index: a preliminary report. Aerospace Sciences Review-AWS RP-105-2, No. 70-3, pp. 2-5.

Brinkmann, W. A. R., 1975. Severe local storm hazard in the United States: a research assessment. NSF-RA-E-75-011, Institute of Behavioral Science, Univ. of Colorado, Boulder, 171 pp. (PB-262 025/(0GA).

Brown, H. E., and E. B. Fawcett, 1972. Use of numerical guidance at the National Weather Service's National Meteorological Center. *J. App. Meteorol.* 11:1175-82

Charba, J. P., 1975. Operational scheme for short range forecasts. Preprints, Ninth Conference on Severe Local Storms, Norman, Okla. American Meteorological Society, Boston, pp. 51-57.

David, C. L., 1973. An objective method for estimating the possibility of severe thunderstorms using predictions from the NMC (PE) numerical prediction model and from observed surface data. Preprints, Eighth Conference on Severe Local Storms, Denver, Colo. American Meteorological Society, Boston, pp. 223-25.

——, 1976. A study of upper air parameters at the time of tornadoes. *Mon. Weather Rev.* 104:546-51.

DCPA (Defense Civil Preparedness Agency), 1974. Protecting mobile homes from high winds. DCPA TR-75, Washington, D.C. 16 pp.

——, 1975a. Wind-resistant design concepts for residences. DCPA TR-83, Washington, D.C. 52 pp.

——, 1975b. Interim guidelines for building occupant protection from tornadoes and extreme winds. DCPA TR-83A, Washington, D.C. 24 pp.

——, 1976. Tornado protection: selecting and designing safe areas in buildings. DCPA TR-83B, Washington, D.C. 29 pp.

Eagleman, J. R., V. U. Muirhead, and N. Willems, 1975. *Thunderstorms, Tornadoes, and Building Damage.* Heath, Lexington, Mass. 317 pp.

Fawbush, E. J., and R. C. Miller, 1952. A mean sounding representative of the tornado air mass. *Bull. Am. Meteorol. Soc.* 33:303-307.

——, and ——, 1953. A method of forecasting hailstone size at the earth's surface. *Bull. Am. Meteorol. Soc.* 34:235-44.

——, and ——, 1954. The types of air masses in which tornadoes form. *Bull. Am. Meteorol. Soc.* 35: 154-65.

——, ——, and L. G. Starrett, 1951. An empirical method of forecasting tornado development. *Bull. Am. Meteorol. Soc.* 53:143-49.

Fawcett, E. G., 1977. Current capabilities in prediction at the National Weather Service's National Meteorological Center. *Bull. Am. Meteorol. Soc.* 53:143-49.

Finley, J. P., 1881. Tornadoes of May 29 and 30, 1879, in Kansas, Nebraska, Missouri and Iowa. U.S. Signal Service Professional Paper No. 4. 116 pp.

Fulks, J. R., 1951. The instability line. In *Compendium of Meteorology,* American Meteorological Society, Boston, pp. 647-54.

Galway, J. G., 1956. The lifted index as a predictor of latent instability. *Bull. Am. Meteorol. Soc.* 37:528-29.

——, 1966. The Topeka tornado of 8 June 1966. *Weatherwise* 19: 140-44.

——, and J. T. Lee, 1958. The jet chart. *Bull. Am. Meteorol. Soc.* 39:217-23.

George, J. J., 1960. *Weather Forecasting for Aeronautics.* Academic Press, New York. 673 pp.

Glahn, H. R., and D. A. Lowry, 1972. The use of Model Output Statistics (MOS) in objective weather forecasting. *J. Appl. Meteorol.* 11:1203-11.

Golden, J., 1973. Some statistical aspects of waterspout formation. *Weatherwise* 26(3):109-17.

Hamilton, R. E., 1969. A review of use of radar in detection of tornadoes and hail. ESSA Technical Memorandum WBTM-ER-34. 64 pp.

Humphreys, W. J., 1926. The tornado. *Mon. Weather Rev.* 54(12):501-503.

Lloyd, J. R., 1942. The development and trajectories of tornadoes. *Mon. Weather Rev.* 70:65-75.

McLuckie, B. F., 1973. The warning system: a social

science perspective. NOAA National Weather Service, Fort Worth, Texas. 66 pp.

McNulty, R. P., 1977. On the use of gravity waves in operational convective forecasting. Eleventh Annual Congress, Canadian Meteorological Society, 1–3 June 1977, Winnipeg, Canada (unpublished manuscript).

Mileti, D. S., 1975. Natural hazard warning systems in the United States: a research assessment. NSF-RA-E-75-013, Institute of Behavioral Science, Univ. of Colorado, Boulder. 97 pp. (PB-261 547/4GA).

Miller, R. C., 1972. Notes on analysis and severe weather forecasting procedures of the Air Force Global Weather Central. AWS Technical Report 200 (Revised), U.S. Air Force, Belleville, Ill. 190 pp.

Miller, S. R., and C. L. David, 1971. A statistically generated aid for forecasting severe thunderstorms and tornadoes. Preprints, Seventh Conference on Severe Local Storms, Kansas City, Missouri. American Meteorological Society, Boston, pp. 42–44.

NOAA (National Oceanic and Atmospheric Administration), 1974. The widespread tornado outbreak of April 3-4, 1974: A report to the administrator. Natural Disaster Survey Report 74-1. 42 pp.

———, 1977. Appalachian flood April 2-5, 1977: a disaster report. NOAA National Weather Service, Garden City, N.Y. 314 pp.

———, 1979. Operations of the National Weather Service. U.S. Superintendent of Documents, Washington, D.C. 251 pp.

Ostby, F. P., Jr., and A. D. Pearson, 1976. The tornado season of 1975. *Weatherwise* 29:17–23.

———, and A. D. Pearson, 1981. Tornado. *Weatherwise* 33:26–32.

Reap, R. M., and D. S. Foster, 1979. Automated 12-36 hour probability forecasts of thunderstorms and severe local storms. *J. Appl. Meteorol.* 18:1304–15.

Schulz, W. A., and D. L. Smith, 1972. Powerline breaks: Potential aid in tornado identification and tracking. *Mon. Weather Rev.* 100:307–308.

Showalter, A. K., 1953. A stability index for thunderstorm forecasting. *Bull. Am. Meteorol. Soc.* 34:250–52.

———, and J. R. Fulks, 1943. Preliminary report on tornadoes. U. S. Weather Bureau, Washington, D.C. 162 pp.

Williams, R. J., 1976. Surface parameters associated with tornadoes. *Mon. Weather Rev.* 104:540–45.

Winston, J. S., 1956. Forecasting tornadoes and severe thunderstorms. U.S. Weather Bureau Forecasting Guide No. 1, Kansas City, Mo. 34 pp.

## Chapter 9

Changnon, S. A., F. A. Huff and R. G. Semonin, 1971. METROMEX: an investigation of inadvertent weather modification. *Bull. Am. Meteorol. Soc.* 52:958–67.

FCMSSR (Federal Coordinator for Meteorological Services and Supporting Research), 1977. The Federal Plan for Meteorological Services and Supporting Research, Fiscal Year 1978. U.S. Superintendent of Documents, Washington, D.C., Stock No. 003-017-00403-1. 42 pp.

Federer, B., A. Waldvogel, W. Schmid, F. Hampel, E. Rosini, D. Vento, P. Admirat and J. P. Rouet, 1977. Grossversuch IV: Design of a Randomized Hail Suppression Experiment Using the Soviet Method. Atmospheric Physics Dept., ETH, 8093 Zurich, Switzerland. 35 pp.

ICAS (Interdepartmental Committee for Atmospheric Sciences), 1976. National Atmospheric Sciences Program, Fiscal Year 1977. Federal Council for Science and Technology, Executive Office of the President, Washington, D.C. 103 pp.

Kessler, E., 1977. History and 1976 program of the National Severe Storms Laboratory. NSSL Special Report, June 1977; revised December 1977. NOAA Environmental Research Laboratories, Boulder, Colo. 66 pp.

Lilly, D. K. (ed.), 1977. Project SESAME Planning Documentation Volume. NOAA Environmental Research Laboratories, Boulder, Colo. 308 pp.

NAS (National Academy of Sciences), 1977. Severe Storms: Prediction, Detection, and Warning. Report of the Panel on Short Range Prediction and the Panel on Severe Storms to the Committee on Atmospheric Science, Assembly of Mathematical and Physical Sciences, Washington, D.C. 78 pp.

NOAA (National Oceanic and Atmospheric Administration), 1976. Project SESAME, Project Development Plan. NOAA Environmental Research Laboratories, Boulder, Colo. 60 pp.

Pierce, E. T., 1976. The thunderstorm research international program (TRIP)—1976. *Bull. Am. Meteorol. Soc.* 57:1214–19.

# The Authors

**Robert Fred Abbey, Jr.,** is Director of the Meteorological-Hydrological Research Program in the Nuclear Regulatory Commission, Washington, D.C. Since 1972 he has held similar positions in the Atomic Energy Commission and the Energy Research and Development Administration. He studied history and physics as an undergraduate at the University of Oregon and received an M.A. degree in history from the same university. He also has an M.S. degree in atmospheric science from Colorado State University and M.A. and Ph.D. degrees in public administration from the University of Southern California. He has been Chairman of the American Meteorological Society's Committee on Severe Local Storms, Member of the ANSI Committee for Developing Standards and Guidelines for Extreme Wind and Tornado Criteria, and Member of the Committee for Wind Effects of the Structural Division, American Society of Civil Engineers.

**W. Boynton Beckwith** is a meteorological consultant. He holds an S.B. degree in general engineering from the Massachusetts Institute of Technology, where he also studied synoptic meteorology. For forty years with United Air Lines he held various supervisory positions involving weather support to operations, and he was UAL's Manager of Meteorology when he retired in 1976. He is widely recognized for his service to the aviation community through his participation in the work of various committees and through his publications.

**William L. Chameides** is Associate Professor in the School of Geophysical Sciences, Georgia Institute of Technology, Atlanta. From 1976 to 1980 he was an Assistant Professor in the Physics Department in the University of Florida, Gainesville. He obtained a B.A. degree in physics from the State University of New York at Binghamton and M.Ph. and Ph.D. degrees from Yale University in geology and geophysics. His research interests include the physical and chemical processes that control the trace-gas composition of planetary atmospheres. His studies in tropospheric and stratospheric composition have included numerical simulations of

global and urban photochemistry and high-temperature chemistry of atmospheric lightning. In collaboration with the National Aeronautics and Space Administration, he has developed a program to measure air pollution from space platforms.

**Charles F. Chappell** is a Senior Scientist in the NOAA/ERL Weather Research Program, Boulder, Colorado, having previously directed the ERL Office of Weather Research and Modification. He holds a B.S. degree in electrical engineering from Washington University (Saint Louis) and M.S. and Ph.D. degrees in atmospheric science from Colorado State University. His specialties include severe-local-storm prediction, thunderstorm-environment interaction, and weather modification. He has served on the Committees on Weather Modification and Hydrometeorology of the American Meteorological Society.

**Donn G. DeCoursey** studied agricultural engineering at Purdue University and received his doctorate in civil engineering from the Georgia Institute of Technology in 1970. He was a hydraulic engineer with the Indiana Flood Control and Water Resources Commission during the late 1950s and was hydraulic engineer and location leader at the Southern Great Plains Watershed Research Center, Chickasha, Oklahoma, from 1961 to 1974. From 1974 to 1981 he was Director of the U.S. Department of Agriculture's Sedimentation Laboratory at Oxford, Mississippi. In 1981 he became Research Leader of the Hydro-Ecosystem Research Unit and National Technical Adviser for Hydrology at Fort Collins, Colorado. His specialties include hydrologic analysis and hydrologic-model development.

**Maurice H. Frere** is Assistant Regional Administrator for the U.S. Department of Agriculture, Science and Education Administration, in New Orleans, Louisiana, and former research leader for the Southern Great Plains Watershed Research Center, Chickasha, Oklahoma. He holds B.S. and M.S. degrees from the University of Wyoming and a Ph.D. degree in soil science from the

University of Maryland. His research contributions have been primarily in development of mathematical models to describe pollution in water runoff from agricultural land.

**T. Theodore Fujita** is Professor in the Department of Geophysical Sciences and Director of the Satellite and Mesometeorology Research Project in the University of Chicago. He graduated from Meiji College of Engineering in Japan and received the Sc.D. degree from Tokyo University. He has made pioneering contributions to data analysis and presentation and to the representation of airflow in thunderstorms. His work has recently focused on air circulation in severe storms and tornadoes and assessment of damage in terms of the windspeed that produces it. He has received awards from both American and Japanese meteorological societies, the Flight Safety Foundation, and the National Weather Association.

**L. Ray Hoxit** is Acting Director of the National Climatic Data Center, Asheville, North Carolina. From 1974 until 1981 he was a research meteorologist in the NOAA/ERL Office of Weather Research and Modification, Boulder, Colorado, where he studied and published on extreme-precipitation events. He holds B.A. and M.S. degrees from Florida State University and a Ph.D. degree in atmospheric science from Colorado State University. From 1967 through 1974 he was employed at the National Climatic Center in Asheville, where he studied tropical-cyclone development and movement and analyzed diurnal variations in stratospheric temperatures. He was also a part-time instructor in the University of North Carolina at Asheville.

**Edwin Kessler** has been Director of NOAA/ERL's National Severe Storms Laboratory, Norman, Oklahoma, since 1964 and is an Adjunct Professor of Meteorology in the University of Oklahoma. He graduated from Columbia College, New York City, and in 1957 received the doctorate in meteorology from the Massachusetts Institute of Technology. Before joining NOAA, he worked at the Weather Radar Branch, Air Force Cambridge Research Laboratories and at the Travelers Research Center, Hartford, Connecticut. His meteorological papers have dealt mainly with applications of radar and with relationships between distributions of water substance in the atmosphere and the coevolving wind field. He has been a Councilor of the American Meteorological Society.

**E. Philip Krider** received the B.A. degree in physics from Carleton College in 1962 and the M.S. and Ph.D.

degrees in physics from the University of Arizona in 1965 and 1969. From 1969 to 1971 he held a National Academy of Sciences postdoctoral appointment in space physics at the NASA Manned Spacecraft Center, Houston, Texas. Since 1971 he has been Professor in the Institute of Atmospheric Physics and the Department of Atmospheric Sciences in the University of Arizona, where he teaches and directs a research program in lightning and atmospheric electricity. His research publications treat elementary-particle physics, cosmic-ray physics, and, most recently, the physics of lightning and thunderstorm electricity. He is a former Associate Editor of the *Journal of Geophysical Research.*

**Ronald L. Lavoie** is Chief, Program Requirements and Planning Division, in the National Weather Service, Silver Spring, Maryland. He moved there in 1982 after serving as Director of the Science and Academic Affairs Office in NOAA's research-and-development component. He holds an A.B. degree in mathematics from the University of New Hampshire and M.S. and Ph.D. degrees in meteorology from Florida State University and Pennsylvania State University, respectively. He was for 13 years on the faculties of the University of Hawaii and Pennsylvania State University, where his research interests were tropical meteorology, numerical modeling, and cloud physics. In his 10 years with NOAA he has played a key role in coordinating federal programs in weather modification, climate, and storm-scale research.

**Jean T. Lee** has been in charge of the project on aviation meteorology at the National Severe Storms Laboratory, Norman, Oklahoma, since its founding in 1964. He received B.S. and M.S. degrees from the University of Chicago. Before joining NSSL, he served in the U.S. Weather Bureau in various research and forecasting capacities, and during World War II he was a station weather officer with a tour of duty in the South Pacific. His contributions to tornado forecasting and thunderstorm aviation earned him Silver Medals from the U.S. Department of Commerce in 1958 and 1977 and the Losey Award from the American Institute of Aeronautics and Astronautics in 1981.

**Herbert S. Lieb** was Chief of the Disaster Preparedness Office of the National Weather Service in Washington, D.C., from August 1, 1974, when that office was established, until his retirement in 1978. The Disaster Preparedness Office provides technical assistance to community-preparedness planners throughout the United States. He was graduated from the University of Missouri in 1949. He entered the U.S. Weather Bureau in 1950 at the Analysis Center in Washington, D.C., and served in various public-information posts in the Environmental Science Services Administration, NOAA's predecessor, and in NOAA. In 1974 he received the Silver Medal from the Department of Commerce for his work in community-preparedness and educational-awareness efforts.

**James D. McQuigg** is a consulting meteorologist in Columbia, Missouri. He received his early training in meteorology at the University of Chicago during World War II, and he holds an M.S. degree in agricultural economics and a Ph.D. degree in atmospheric science from the University of Missouri. He was Director of the NOAA Center for Climatic and Environmental Assessment, where weather-yield models were developed to monitor the impact of weather and climate in a number of major crop-production regions around the world. His specialties are applied climatology and applied statistics with emphasis on agriculture.

**Joseph E. Minor** is Professor of Civil Engineering and Director of the Institute for Disaster Research and of the History of Engineering Program in Texas Tech University, Lubbock, Texas. He received B.S. and M.Eng. degrees from Texas A&M University and the Ph.D. in civil engineering from Texas Tech University. His professional work ranges widely over effects of wind on structures, window-glass technology, and the economics and technology of wind-resistant construction. As a member of a team responding to an invitation of the Australian government, he inspected damage at Darwin caused by cyclone Tracy in 1974 and contributed to that government's decisions concerning postdisaster reconstruction. He returned to Australia with a Fulbright Senior Scholarship. He serves on many professional boards and committees.

**H. Michael Mogil** is a consulting meteorologist in Fort Worth, Texas. From 1966 until 1983 he was employed in the National Weather Service. He was a Lead Forecaster and Disaster Preparedness Meteorologist at San Francisco and Acting Chief of the Fort Worth Forecast Office. Earlier he held assignments with the National Meteorological Center, the National Severe Storms Forecast Center, the Techniques Development Laboratory, and other units involving weather forecasting and disaster preparedness. He received B.S. and M.S. degrees from Florida State University in 1967 and 1969. He holds the AMS TV Seal of Approval, is an Able Toastmaster,

and is widely known for his articles, courses, and lectures on severe storms.

**Arlin D. Nicks** received the B.S. and M.S. degrees in agricultural engineering from Oklahoma State University and the Ph.D. degree in civil engineering from the University of Oklahoma. From 1961 to 1982 he was employed at the Southern Great Plains Watershed Research Center, U.S. Department of Agriculture, Chickasha, Oklahoma. In 1982 he became Research Leader for Water Resources Research of Durant, Oklahoma. His principal investigations have dealt with the temporal and spatial variations of rainfall and runoff in an 1,100-square-mile watershed, as recorded by more than 200 recording rain gages with complementary stream gages.

**Allen D. Pearson** was Director of the National Weather Service Central Region from August 1979 until his retirement in June 1981. Previously, from August 1965, he was Director of the National Severe Storms Forecast Center, where responsibility is centered for predicting tornadoes and severe thunderstorms nationwide. A native of Mankato, Minnesota, he attended the Universities of Minnesota, California (UCLA), and Hawaii. He received the B.A. from UCLA and the M.S. from Hawaii. His Navy service during World War II included a tour of duty on Wake Island. His Weather Service career began in Honolulu, Hawaii, following employment with Pan American Airways. He was the recipient of the Department of Commerce Silver Medal in 1968 and the Gold Medal in 1974.

**Gilbert F. White** is President of the Scientific Committee on Problems of the Environment, International Council of Scientific Unions. He received undergraduate and graduate degrees from the University of Chicago. He was Vice-Chairman of the President's Water Resources Policy Commission, 1950; Chairman of the Bureau of Budget Task Force on Federal Flood Policy, 1965-1966; and Professor of Geography and Director of the Institute of Behavioral Science in the University of Colorado, Boulder, from 1970 to 1978. He is a member of the National Academy of Sciences and was Chairman of the Commission on Natural Resources of the National Research Council. He has received several awards for teaching and service and for studies in the fields of water resources management and natural-hazard assessment.

# Index